[handwritten inscription]
Neil D. Kelly
August 12, 2015
Seaside FL

Benchwarmer

Benchwarmer

A Sports-Obsessed
Memoir *of* Fatherhood

JOSH WILKER

PublicAffairs
New York

PublicAffairs books are available at special discounts for bulk purchases in
the U.S. by corporations, institutions, and other organizations. For more
information, please contact the Special Markets Department at the Perseus
Books Group, 2300 Chestnut Street, Suite 200, Philadelphia, PA 19103, call
(800) 810-4145, ext. 5000, or e-mail special.markets@perseusbooks.com.

Book Design by Jack Lenzo

The Library of Congress has cataloged the printed edition as follows:
Wilker, Josh.
   Benchwarmer : A Sports-Obsessed Memoir of Fatherhood / Josh Wilker. --
First Edition.
      pages cm
      ISBN 978-1-61039-401-7 (hardcover) -- ISBN 978-1-61039-402-4 (e-book)
   1. Sports--Miscellanea. 2. Sports--Anecdotes. 3. Wilker, Josh. 4. Sportswrit-
ers--United States. 5. Fatherhood--Anecdotes. I. Title.
   GV707.W24 2016
   796--dc23

                              2014041273

First Edition
10 9 8 7 6 5 4 3 2 1

Dedication
See **Zidane, Zinedine**

Author's Note

See **Tainted.**

Volume 1:

0–3 Months

A

Aardsma, David

Who could ever come before Aaron, Hank? That's what I used to think. Because of his name, he started all encyclopedias, at least the ones I cared about, and because he'd pummeled major league pitching with metronomic constancy for over two decades, he also reigned over the most revered of sports lists: career home runs. From an early age I looked for order and wonder and calm in such lists, especially that list, so his alphabetic primacy felt majestic, a manifestation of divine right. After Aaron, Hank, the progression of players from A through Z was shapeless, good giving way to bad and bad to obscure and back to good or inane or nondescript or anything or nothing. Yet this otherwise indecipherable sprawl of names began, beautifully, with the All-Time Home Run King, Aaron, Hank, and so the world made sense.

Over the years this evidence of a guiding intelligence in the universe survived the disintegration of childhood, the combination-lock loneliness of high school, the panicking digression of college, the flailing and torpor of unemployment, underemployment, employment, the years behind a cash register, the years as a cubicled temp, the years waiting for buses and untangling the wires of headphone buds and memorizing reruns and on hold with the help desk, the graying, the receding, the unstoppable ear hair. Through it all, no matter what, Aaron, Hank, came first. Then, at some point when I wasn't paying attention, David Aardsma slouched toward a major league mound for the first time.

What can you make of David Aardsma? He's never led the league in anything, never lasted anywhere. Not long after his name started appearing at the bottom of box scores like equivocating textual marginalia—an inning of relief work here, a third of an inning there—the unambiguous order-centering legend he supplanted at the head of the alphabet also had his home run record surpassed, acrimoniously, ingloriously (*see asterisk*). I was almost forty. I'd never led the league in anything, never lasted anywhere. My wife was a little younger. We'd been married for a while, and the years were starting to lurch by like ghostly freight cars. We talked sometimes about having a kid. I wanted to get everything sorted first. But the world just kept getting more unsortable. I no longer even knew where to begin.

Addition by Subtraction

Nonetheless, eventually we started trying. Nothing happened for a long time. I assumed there was something wrong with me. This is my default explanation for everything: I'm lacking. *Wherever I am / I am what is missing*—so goes a piece of a Mark Strand poem I learned in college and have clung to ever since. I even clung to it one morning when it seemed like something might be happening. Abby set up an appointment with her doctor to find out for sure. I rose before she did on the morning of the appointment and wandered to the window, a hollow of hope and dread in my stomach, and those lines of poetry pulsed in my head.

I was in Chicago, had been in Chicago for years, had no clear answer for why I was in Chicago. I noticed a man across the street with his hands on his knees, his face aimed toward the sidewalk. I thought he'd dropped his keys. He began puking. He puked for a few seconds, hunched and convulsing, splattering the sidewalk, and then he straightened and began walking away. The morning trickle of pedestrians up and down the block generally doesn't involve people vomiting, and for a moment I figured he was homeless. Night, day, inside, outside—who gives a shit? But he crossed the street, got into a newish car, and drove off. I had no clear answer for anything. I stared at the empty space where the car had been.

Abby got up and headed off to the doctor. Neither one of us was in the habit of believing good news, but even so, I had intended to spend the morning in a frenzy of unprecedented productivity. I wanted to get my entire life in order, catalog everything A to Z. But I kept standing there by the window, gazing out at the parking space. Finding a parking space can be difficult. Whenever I see one I feel the urge to get the car and park it in the new spot, simply to take advantage of the opportunity. A key element of this urge is that it's hypothetical, leaving out my lifelong struggle with parallel parking. I imagine filling these empty spaces flawlessly. But if I ever successfully executed this urge, I'd be creating an even fresher emptiness where the car had been parked, and in my experience urges give way to more urges, so I'd then be trapped in an endless perpetual filling of emptiness, moving from one open space to another.

"I move," the Mark Strand poem concludes, "to keep things whole."

Teams that are *losing* will sometimes resort to transactions considered to be cases of "addition by subtraction." A member of the team is identified as an entity worse than neutral. Removing such a player even when getting nothing in return will, the thinking goes, improve the fortunes of the team. But taking away one or more of the team's primary examples of disappointment will not put an end to the general disappointment, which is unstoppable, and it could be argued that the term "addition by subtraction" is not one used as part of a blueprint for improvement but rather as a way to level a complicated insult at one who has so stingingly disappointed, a way to say to that person: you're worse than *zero*.

I tell myself such things all the time, always have. Piece of shit. Useless. But where am I going to go? You can't trade yourself out of your life. The only way to addition is addition. More life, more love. I pretend to understand this. I want to understand.

When Abby returned from the doctor I was at my desk pretending to write. I could feel her in the office doorway behind me like the sun coming free from clouds. I swiveled from all my pointless transactions to her. She was smiling.

Adrift

I rose from the chair. Was risen? Think of unbuckling into the weightlessness of a space station, gravity subtracted. Think of wanting something to hold onto. Think of a base runner adrift, daydreaming while an infielder sneaks in behind him. Think of a journeyman adrift, scudding without impact year after year from team to team, or of an entire team adrift, playing out the string in the haze of mathematical elimination. Then think of the most beautiful thing you've ever seen. That was me, adrift, looking down at my beaming wife.

"So?" I said.

"It's official," Abby said.

Think of a guy adrift from any solidity. Even the seemingly inviolable notion of time slips away. Suddenly we were looking for a new place to live. Suddenly a doctor was moving a jelly-covered wand over my wife's little belly bump, the white noise ushering out of the monitor forming into a rushing rhythm, a heartbeat. I thought of this tiny pumping heart and tried to cry but couldn't. A few weeks after that we sank most of our savings into a down payment on a condo where things immediately began to break. People started giving us clothing. I would hold these miniature garments in my hands and be convinced that the whole idea was impossible. The due date careened toward us. My wife's belly grew into a wrecking ball. I braced myself.

A few days beyond the due date Abby and I took two canvas folding chairs to the edge of Lake Michigan and sat with our feet in the water. We sipped beer from blue plastic tumblers and passed a canister of original-style Pringles back and forth. Amplified chanting from a large Hare Krishna rally nearby wafted toward us on the breeze. A wiry man in a scuba mask and snorkel waded past us out to a waist-high depth and shoved his head under the surface briefly before straightening and lurching back toward shore. To his right a young girl bobbed in the water, clinging to a bright orange life preserver and barking orders at an amused, sunburned oaf.

"No smiling, Daddy!" the girl said. "You don't smile!"

The wiry scuba guy stalked past us back toward the city, his breath whistling angrily out his snorkel. I looked from him to my wife's huge belly, then to her face, those pale blue eyes, a few faint freckles, each one beloved. The chanting persisted, swirling, spiraling, melancholy, endless. The cool water was lapping over our bare ankles. My wife's dazzling face, the whole dumb world aglow. Again I tried to cry but couldn't. I've never been able to cry about my life but only over aging sports heroes getting their numbers retired.

Adversity

Abby writhed on a hospital bed. I stood beside her. A large monitor was beeping. My feet seemed to not exactly be connected to anything.

"I can't do this!" she said. "You don't understand."

"You can do it," I said, but it came out like a question.

She was suffering the relentless knifing pain of pharmaceutically induced labor and looked past me to search the faces of hospital staff for help. She knew I could tell her nothing. This had been going on all day, all night.

"You can do it," I continued to recite.

In the first few hours she had been able to hobble to the adjoining bathroom and vomit. When she became immobilized she used a wastebasket. At some point I carried it to the bathroom to rinse. I caught a glimpse of a grizzled figure in the mirror. Calvin Schiraldi, Game Six of the 1986 World Series, the moment too much.

"Hey," Schiraldi murmured as I was leaving.

"No, you don't understand, I can't do this," my wife was saying.

Nurses and specialists huddled around her. I got up near her head with the puke bucket.

"You can do it," I mumbled.

Eventually I was subtracted from the room so Abby could receive an epidural. She'd hoped to avoid this back when we imagined that together we could visualize away the rumored pain of contractions. We'd simply ride rising and falling waves.

During the administration of the shot into Abby's spine I sat in a little waiting room alone. It was two or three in the morning, somewhere in there. I stared at the dim institutional carpeting, hoping and praying, two activities of limited if not altogether invisible impact. I waited.

What kind of asshole, his wife in agony, naps? I fought it, but it kept pulling at me. I'd drift off in my chair for a second before wrenching awake. Then sleep would pull me down again, some brief, shallow version teeming with visions. Figures in motion, senseless, sprinting, hurdling, vaulting. Then I was in motion, drowsing on a bus, a grizzled figure seated beside me, Calvin Schiraldi again. *The moment too much.* When my head grazed his shoulder, the gray away-uniform sleeve, I snapped awake. I glared at the waiting room carpet.

"Please, please, *please,*" I said, punching and punching my thigh.

I wanted Abby to be all right but couldn't do anything about it. I was scared that the epidural would lead to some kind of complication. I was also scared it simply wouldn't work, that we'd have to go on as before, one of us in spasms on a hospital bed like a fish suffocating at the bottom of a boat, the other standing alongside, powerless, hoping and praying. I was scared that the moment would be too much, that I'd be faced for the first time in my life with true adversity and that it'd go down for me like it had for Calvin Schiraldi.

Calvin Schiraldi had been a rookie in 1986, brought up from the minors in midseason. The Red Sox had jumped off to a fast start that year but had a distinct flaw, a hole at the end of their bullpen. The rookie filled this hole instantly and flew through the regular season virtually untouched, relying on a blazing fastball to rack up strikeouts and saves and a stunning 1.41 ERA. He didn't face any adversity until the playoffs, and then he seemed to handle the first tremor of misfortune well, following up a blown save and loss in Game Four of the American League Championship Series with two scoreless appearances in Games Five and Seven. He extended this scoreless streak into Game One of the World Series, in which he earned a save. He didn't pitch again for a week, when he was brought in to close out Game Six, which would have given the Red Sox their first World Series Championship in sixty-eight years. He gave up one hit, then another, then another. Schiraldi took the loss in that game and in the decisive Game Seven two nights later. The look on his face in those two games as the adversity mounted, as it proved too much for him, has haunted me ever since.

I drifted off to sleep again. The bus was crowded. We were headed somewhere where we wouldn't be bothered, somewhere painless. We were being subtracted. The passenger at my side leaned so close I felt his unshaven cheek on my own.

"Hey," Schiraldi murmured, and the bus began to speed. I snapped awake. The careening of the bus carried over into this world for a moment, the empty waiting room seeming so much to be racing down a sharp incline toward impact that I grabbed the armrests of my chair.

Agony of Defeat, the

In a famous video clip a ski jumper hurtling out of control down the steep ramp tries to stop himself, almost appearing as if he wants to gently sit down. Who hasn't had this hope? The one that goes, *Just stop, please. I changed my mind. Can't we just stop?* But it's too late. Gravity has taken over, history has taken over. He flails off the ramp sideways, flipping and whirling into the air before smashing down onto the slope. When first aired during the opening montage of the weekly show *ABC's Wide World of Sports*, the clip elicited gasps and grave concern. As the years went on, the footage evolved into a warm constant. The catastrophic fall punctuated the voiceover phrase "the agony of defeat," which was preceded by the phrase "the thrill of victory"; victory was illustrated over the years by a rotating roster of images of winning, but the clip for defeat never changed. It was always a Yugoslavian ski jumper losing control of one of his efforts during a competition in Oberstdorf, West Germany, in 1970.

Yugoslavian? West Germany? Thrills come and go, winners come and go, even borders and nations come and go. But the agony of defeat guy abides. Beloved was this guy, who happened to be named Vinko Bogotaj. At a star-studded thirtieth anniversary gathering for *ABC's Wide World of Sports* in 1991, Bogotaj received the loudest ovation of any of the internationally famous athletes assembled. Muhammad Ali asked him for an autograph. But if you stay with anything long enough, you see that nothing abides. The footage of Vinko Bogotaj is fading from the world. *ABC's Wide World of Sports* was canceled long ago. The concept of a weekly show is itself disintegrating. You can still find grainy clips of the show's opening sequence on the Internet. I watched it recently and was surprised by how quickly Bogotaj came and went. In my memory—watching on Saturdays, a morning of cartoons behind me, a bowl of SpaghettiOs with meatballs in my lap—his fall went on and on. But it's over, naturally, in the time it takes Jim McKay to say seven syllables. The footage cuts off as Bogotaj bounces up from his initial impact. He is rising. He rises into the mind to fall and rise and fall and rise. In my mind he tumbles, rising and falling, rising and falling, down a mountain forever.

The epidural worked for a while, then gave way to more agony, even worse than before. I can catalog the bullshit miscellany of life but can't find words for what my wife endured nor for the way it finally ended: a blood-slick newborn tumbling out into the world face-up, a boy, tumbling then rising up wailing, choking, wailing, to me.

Armstrong, Lance
See Asterisk.

Asterisk
The world once made some sense to me, based on all my childhood sorting, based on the encyclopedias that enabled this sorting, gleaming as they were with pure facts, or so it seemed. I loved those facts, loved every game that made them, loved baseball, football, basketball, boxing, tennis, golf, hockey, soccer, auto racing, bike racing, horse racing, boat racing, sprinting, swimming, skating, slaloming, diving, hurdling, flinging, vaulting, tumbling, lifting, leaping, anything and everything that bred winning and losing, greats and nobodies, grace from chaos. I loved it all, and it gave back to me a beautiful undulating order, a way to understand the world. Over the years that way of holding the world dissolved. Life goes on, doubts increase. I'd

never been someone prone to thrusting myself into the middle of the action—from the beginning my encyclopedic approach to the world was a way to hold it at arm's length, to be a spectator, a fan—and as I grew older my tendency toward the sidelines only increased, as if I were seeking a still point from which I could gaze safely out at the baffling blur. But where is there a still point? Where is there an encyclopedia with facts beyond question? There's no moral order to any alphabetical listing, just as there's no Home Run King anymore. Here's what reigns: *

It's always lingering, that stick-figure star, waiting to attach itself to any name, any win, any moment of bliss, to twist itself into the skin of certainty and connect it to equivocating textual marginalia. It has most commonly happened after the fact, such as in the case when one of the most accomplished athletes ever, Lance Armstrong, was found to have been illegally doping his blood and had all seven of his Tour de France titles retroactively stripped, necessitating the affixing of asterisks to any encyclopedia's mention of victories attached to his storybook name. But it can happen before the fact too, as in the case of the current holder of the record for career home runs, Barry Bonds. Because he was generally assumed to have used banned substances to enhance his already prodigious skills (and perhaps also because of the widespread perception that he was a surly asshole), Bonds, in the court of public opinion, had his name branded with an asterisk even before he dethroned Hank Aaron. This preemptive affixing of asterisks is becoming the norm, as if soon all transcendence will be suspect, all facts leaky, unsound, all pinnacles shadowed with doubt.

Pushing against this blooming of asterisks is my compulsion to put words to the very first minutes of my son's life. But I can't find words except to say that in the very first minutes of his life I was seized with the belief that my love for him would burn all the shittiness of me clean away, leaving something pure. And it did—it does—but only for a moment. And then my failings return. It's as if some part of me doesn't want the life I've known to be wholly erased and replaced by something else altogether.

I need an encyclopedia for all my failings, my memories and fantasies, my desires and repulsions, my appetites and revulsions, my incremental invisible diminishment. I need an encyclopedia to explain the moment when all my failings dissolved, leaving me defenseless. The baby in my arms jerked and reached and squalled. He was the only fact in the whole wide world. I was surprised by the life in him, the strength. I could barely hold him. We had a name picked out, but he was too new for it. In those first few minutes is what I will believe forever, despite myself. There were no words. There was nothing to which an asterisk could attach.

B

Benchwarmer

We spent a couple of days in a recovery room. Abby had the bed, I had a chair, and the baby was in her arms or my arms or in a metal thing with wheels on it. Nobody slept much. There was a window, but it faced a brick wall, and we kept the blinds down most of the time anyway, so it was never really clear whether it was the middle of the night or noon or somewhere in between. At one point I wandered into the adjoining bathroom. The baby had fallen asleep in my arms. My plan was to hold him with one arm for a few seconds so I could take a leak, but I only got the one arm about an inch away from the baby before wrapping it back around him and pulling him tighter to my chest. I wasn't ready for any fancy one-armed stuff.

I stared down at the object of my two-armed hold. There were moments in those first couple of days when I believed I'd just marvel at him unblinkingly for the rest of my life, but there were other moments when it all seemed too much and I had to look away. In this particular instance I looked from the baby to the big mirror behind the sink. I'd avoided looking in that mirror to that point, as I'd wanted to steer clear of any additional visitations from the overwhelmed unshaven reliever at the center of the Red Sox's 1986 World Series collapse. But it turned out that by this time, a day or so into my son's life, these visions of Schiraldi were in remission. The mirror contained only its usual occupant.

Caucasian, early forties, unruly receding hair, thick glasses, fairly tall. Not so tall as to suggest the high probability of a history as a college basketball player but tall enough nonetheless to have served as a backup to the backup forwards on the 1987–88 Johnson State College Badgers. Still generally as weakling-thin as during that season and all preceding losing seasons, but now with a minor yet irreducible thickness around the midsection. Gray-flecked Vandyke goatee grown in an attempt to cover the age-related disintegration of the jawline and to balance severe eyebrows and bulging eyes. In those bulging eyes: worry.

Worry had been with me for a long time but now had sprung into full bloom, due to the other face visible in the reflection: pink, tiny, crinkled, so new that flecks of his mother's blood still clung to the folds of his ears. The feeling of lightness in my arms was the source of the worry. Jack was his name. *Jack.* He weighed less than a shoebox of baseball cards. He weighed so little as to be almost weightless, filled with helium, the worry that a single instance of carelessness in what has been a careless, mistake-riddled life would lead to this being slipping from my grasp, lifting up and out the window, and disappearing into the sky. How do you even hold something so fragile, light, loved?

In the mirror, finally, was a reluctant adult, still clinging, even in his mid-forties, to an identity as a boy: I was wearing a T-shirt of the team I'd loved since childhood, the Boston Red Sox. I deliberately chose to pack the shirt in an overnight bag for the trip to the hospital. I wanted to have it on during the biggest moment of my life. The T-shirt celebrates a victorious season, 2004, the year I believed Calvin Schiraldi and everything was finally redeemed: *World Champions!*

But the face above this T-shirt and above the sleeping baby was not of one redeemed or of a champion of any kind or even of one who vied for a championship and lost. It was the face of a benchwarmer, and not just of any benchwarmer but of the all-time single-season record holder for benchwarming. This distinction isn't supported in the usual manner of sports records—by numerical data—but instead by the extent to which the record holder was able to extend himself into some ineffable qualitative remove from meaningful action. He was the last player off the bench on a pale, diminutive northern Vermont college team that started a melancholy six-foot-four Grateful Dead fan at center and lost unceasingly.

This record-setting remove can be illustrated in terms of a Russian nesting doll of athletic inconsequentiality. Consider first the three divisions of descending levels of collegiate competition in the NCAA, soaring, balletic world-class athletes clashing in thronged arenas at the top of this ladder and earthbound chest-passing eighteenth-century French Lit majors toiling in half-empty rustic gymnasiums at the bottom; consider below that hierarchy altogether the NAIA, the indistinct off-brand national athletic association for college squads unequal to the mild, plodding rigors of life on the lowest rung of the NCAA's three divisions; consider the shortest, weakest, whitest subcell in the NAIA, the Mayflower Conference, tucked away in the gentle, rolling mountains and pastures of northern New England; consider that in 1987–88, a few years before the conference ceased to exist altogether, disbanding, the worst team by far in the Mayflower Conference was the Johnson State College Badgers; consider, finally, the figure sitting at the very end of this team's bench.

For a moment, in the recovery room toilet area, this benchwarmer took possession of the mirror, glimmering into view in his entirety, the goatee gone, the thick glasses replaced by eye-reddening contact lenses, the World Champions T-shirt giving way to a sleeveless V-neck uniform top and shorts, white with green piping, and "JOHNSON" arcing in green block lettering above a partially obscured number.

I was nineteen again, maybe twenty. I was on my feet as if my name had finally been called.

Then it was over. It seemed briefly that the uniform number below the college's name was obscured by a basketball, but that vision dissolved before it had fully formed, and I was once again holding my son. My glasses, my goatee, my World Champions T-shirt returned. The lines in my face returned. My expression was for the most part the same as it'd always been, but the presence of the baby had added something. It was the expression of a benchwarmer called into a game, the game he'd been avoiding and dreading all his life. There was something else too, contrasting and accentuating the apprehension. This capitulating marginal journeyman face, exhausted, dreadful, was also now inarguably alight.

Beautiful, terrible hope and joy. You may one day be handed these things like you're being handed a ball. Like you've been called into a game.

The tiny boy in my arms was beginning to stir. In a moment he'd be awake. What had I been called into? What was I doing here? I wasn't ready, didn't know the plays, didn't have any moves. There was nothing between me and this beautiful boy.

Bene, Bill

"I fooled them for a while," Bill Bene said.

This was in the spring of 1988, just before the major league draft. Bene, a flame-throwing college pitching prospect at the center of a tornado of predraft hype, was admitting to a reporter from the *Los Angeles Times* that his high school career, spent exclusively as an outfielder, had been iffy. He'd known the best he could ever do was bluff and hope.

"I was never a very good hitter," he said. "I guess I was meant to pitch."

I guess. Who knows what we are meant for? When I was a kid I used to fantasize about being discovered, delivered in an instant to what I was meant for. The fantasy started modestly, when my older brother was in little league. As I watched his games I imagined that a foul ball would bound my way, and I'd scoop it up and fire it back onto the field, wowing everyone with the strength and accuracy of my arm. As the years went on, the fantasy drifted ever farther from any reasonable version of reality, until eventually it involved a limousine pulling up at the edge of our driveway as I was throwing a tennis ball at the duct tape strike zone on the garage door. The backseat window would come down, revealing Carl Yastrzemski's somber features creased into a smile.

"Quite an arm, son," he would say. He'd produce a major league contract, holding it out the window toward me. "It's just what we need."

This is a deep American dream: to be discovered. To be told with certainty, beyond any guesswork, that at our core we are aglow, gifted, meant for great things.

This is what happened to Bill Bene.

See **Bust**.

Blame

The day we were allowed to leave the hospital with the baby I ran and got the car from the lot and pulled it to the front entrance, then I ran back up to the room and grabbed everything but the baby and my wife and lugged it down to the car, the weight of it and my own ability to do something I knew how to do—carry things—offering a brief, comforting respite of familiarity and competence. Then I ran up to the room again, empty-handed. I was sweating profusely, like a panicking reliever, the guy in the middle of a team's unraveling. Schiraldi was one of these perspiration-glazed hurlers. They always seem lonely out there, and as if they were wishing they'd stayed on the bench, far from blame.

"God, *relax*," my wife said. Jack was in her arms.

"I'm relaxed!" I screamed. Then, attempting nonchalance, I murmured, "I just don't know, you know, about the whole situation with the car out there."

"Oh, Jesus Christ. Cars can sit outside for a second when they're picking people up."

How does everyone know things like this?

"I didn't get much of a chance to get the air conditioner going," I added. "It'll be sweltering. Will he be okay? Do we have everything? Are they bringing you a wheelchair?"

Abby had been ripped open pretty good. She had more stitches in her than I'd gotten when I'd fallen off a cliff on a mountain bike.

"Let's just go," she said. But then the miniature senile nurse Dolly pushed a wheelchair into the room. Dolly wasn't her real name but rather an Americanized shortening of the lengthy byzantine vowel cluster she'd been given at birth on a faraway tropical island centuries earlier.

"Hokay evbody," Dolly said. "Now we see."

She'd reappeared periodically throughout our stay in the recovery wing, usually deep into the night, her accented, choppy syntax scrambling her hospital-ordered directions into baffling nursery songs.

"I'm not riding that thing down an elevator," Abby said, indicating the wheelchair. My wife is generally fearless but is afraid of elevators, roughly the converse of my own relation to the world, in which I find elevators tolerable but everything else terrifying.

"Time go now," Dolly said. "Happy!"

"I'm saying not in an elevator," Abby said.

The interaction continued for some time, Dolly seeming to insist on the wheelchair and elevator combination as the only way to get us to our car, my wife insisting otherwise.

"Hokay little mama," Dolly said finally. "We go just some way."

"I don't know what's happening here," Abby said.

"No elvate," Dolly said.

A somewhat ludicrous compromise seemed to have been reached.

"I guess we're just going to the stairs?" Abby wondered aloud as she rode down the hall in the wheelchair, pushed by Dolly.

"No elvate," Dolly mumbled, as if to herself.

I walked alongside them with the baby. He stared with his blue eyes past me at the ceiling or who knows what. I supported his head, his tiny snappable neck. His swaddle had begun to unravel.

"Jack," I said to him. "Jack, Jack, Jack."

Jack, I don't know how to fix your blanket. Jack, I don't know what the protocol is with a car when picking up someone at the hospital. Jack, I don't know how to do your car seat with all its tiny loops and clasps. Jack, my parking skills are at this point so riddled with crippling doubt that if we don't get lucky enough to pull forward into a space in front of our building today you are going to grow up in the backseat of a car jerking back and forth enslaved by your father's eternal failed attempt to parallel park. Jack, I am praying for miracles. Jack, if there is a problem, I will be to blame.

"Hokay little family," Dolly said. We had come to a stop by a thick fire door.

Abby rose from the wheelchair. I pushed open the door with one hand while gripping Jack in his unraveling blanket with the other, and the three of us started toward the stairs. Everyone, everything seemed very fragile.

"Can you please hold on to me?" I asked.

Bonds, Barry

See Asterisk.

Boner

I need definitions, illustrations, examples. I need to know at least a few things for certain. And what kind of certainty could possibly exist anymore? The All-Time Home Run King is no longer the All-Time Home Run King, but neither is anyone else. Cataloging winning is empty, pointless, and cataloging loss is impossible. Every season, in any given endeavor, produces one temporary champion and a multitude of losers, and this multitude expands with consideration of all the various endeavors, expands some more with consideration of all the seasons stretching far back into the past, and then expands yet again with consideration of all those who aspired in every season and in every endeavor to be a part of the action but who were too flawed to make the team, too flawed to even try. When imagining trying to gather all this, give shape to it, draw a sense of order from it, the mind boggles. But that's not even the half of it. Imagine daydreams, fantasies. Imagine everyone who ever lived, all the hopes and prayers ever sent skyward, all the answering silences.

All you can know is that your life will change. Fred Merkle was nineteen when it happened to him. He'd been a benchwarmer for the New York Giants that year, all through the 1908 season, a sidelined witness to a ferocious three-team pennant race involving the Giants, the Chicago Cubs, and the Pittsburgh Pirates. Then, one day in late September, when the Cubs were visiting the Giants, Merkle made his only start of the year, subbing for Fred Tenney, who was sidelined with lumbago, a form of lower back pain. After going hitless in his first three plate appearances, the teenager came to bat in the bottom of the ninth inning with the game tied and two outs and the potential winning run on first.

When I was that age, nineteen, I was serving as the most pronounced benchwarmer on the 1987–88 Johnson State College Badgers, as far from the action as you could possibly be and still be considered an official uniformed athlete. I didn't admit to myself that that was who I was, and yet in some subconscious way I not only accepted it but embraced it. I didn't want to be part of the action. I didn't want to be responsible. I didn't want any pressure on my shoulders. *Let it be up to someone else.* This plea settled into my life like a seed into soil.

By the time the baby arrived, decades later, the seed had grown into a trunk-like thickness at the center of my being, anchored by deep, gnarled roots. What a crater there would be if it were ever removed. I could feel the beginning of this wrenching excavation at the hospital, despite the near-constant presence of nurses, doctors, visitors. When we came home from the hospital there was no one but us.

Or so it seemed at first. It's a blur to me now, that beginning, as blurry as anything I've lived through. So anything I say about it is the opposite of the kind of reliable information encyclopedias are built on. I hadn't slept much at the hospital, just an hour here or there while sitting in the chair in the corner. Eventually you start falling asleep on your feet for a second every so often. Something beyond normal reality slips into the room.

"Oh, this lumbago is a dire botheration," Fred Tenney groaned at one point. He was grimacing and limping in a pained hunch out of our living room and toward the hallway. He wore a dark, short-brimmed baseball cap and a spotless white uniform with an NY on the shoulder, but on his feet were my wife's fluffy slippers.

"What?" I said. The baby had materialized in my arms.

"I said I have to go deal with my hoo ha," my wife said, hobbling along in Fred Tenney's place. "I'm fucking gushing blood into my sweatpants still. Okay?"

Abby disappeared around the corner to attend to her episiotomy wounds. I looked down at the baby, in love, exhausted, scared. My eyelids were heavy. Someone spoke.

"I wanted to play."

I looked up. A dark-eyed teenager was sitting opposite me in the La-Z-Boy, dressed in a baseball uniform like Fred Tenney's, though he wore spikes instead of fluffy slippers and his uniform was smudged with dirt and was torn at the seams in a couple of places, as if he'd been in an altercation or at the mercy of a roiling mob. He was missing his cap. I recognized his dark eyebrows, his long, narrow face.

"I wanted to play," Fred Merkle repeated. "I loved the game. I did not want the bench."

The baby started squirming. I looked down at his tiny features. He was grimacing, bug-eyed, unhappy. I should have spent the previous several years devouring instruction manuals about babies and parenting and adulthood. Instead, I spent them praying for my life to be inconsequential and internalizing an ad hoc encyclopedia of failure to replace the clear ordering of the world that had been disintegrating since childhood. I picked up a little blue rattle and shook it. Jack started crying.

"I wanted the bat in my hands," Fred Merkle said over the crying, but when I looked up from my son the La-Z-Boy was empty.

There's no one else.

Fred Merkle stood alone in the batter's box in the bottom of the ninth. With the weight of the season on his shoulders, he connected, sending a clean line drive into right field. He reached first base safely, and the winning run advanced to third.

My wife shuffled back from the bathroom. I handed Jack, still crying, back to her and felt relieved. Maybe Fred Merkle, despite his love of the game, felt a little of the same thing while standing on first after coming through with his clutch hit and passing the burden of the rally on to the next batter. It was up to someone else now.

"Mama's here," my wife murmured. "Mama's here."

Jack's tiny arms flailing, calming. A stillness in the room, something new.

Beloved life is loaded. Things can go wrong.

The next batter, Al Bridwell, slapped a single to centerfield, plating what appeared to be the winning run. Fred Merkle, running from first, neglected to travel all the way to second base on the play. This was not uncommon back then. Also, it would have been clear to the youngster as soon as the apparent winning hit sailed into the outfield that a boisterous throng was about to swarm the field—it was not unreasonable to want to avoid this unruly invasion. But a ball was retrieved from the midst of the bedlam, and when Cubs second baseman Johnny Evers stepped on second with the ball in his possession, umpires ruled that Fred Merkle was forced out at second base for the final out of the inning, canceling the apparent winning run.

The state of the field being what it was, awash in angering fanatics, it was deemed not possible to resume the tie game. At the end of the season, with the two teams tied atop the standings, a makeup game was played, and the Cubs won it to take the pennant. The incident that forced the makeup game became known as "Merkle's boner," and Merkle became known as "Bonehead." The incident struck a chord, becoming for many years perhaps the most famous of all fuckups. Life will be left undone, joy forever nullified. It entered the culture like a seed sending down roots. From *bonehead*, a numskull, comes *boner*, the product of a bonehead, a clumsy or stupid mistake. The *Merriam-Webster College Dictionary* (11th ed.) identifies the first instance of the use of *bonehead* as occurring in 1908, suggesting that the very word may have been invented, this notion that instead of a brain, an individual could have a head filled with nothing but bone, to explain and curse and exile with mockery the actions of Fred Merkle.

The two new words followed him everywhere. Worse, wherever he went they were waiting for him. In 1912 he smacked another clutch base hit to knock in the go-ahead run in the top of the tenth inning of the deciding game of the World Series. It seemed for a few moments that he would be known from then on as a World Series hero. But in the bottom of the tenth the Giants surrendered the lead and the game and the championship in part because an easy foul pop-up landed uncaught between Merkle, pitcher Christy Mathewson, and catcher Chief Meyers. The blame for the play should have fallen on Mathewson, who called for Meyers to make the catch even though Merkle was much closer, but a New York newspaper headline the next day read "Bonehead Merkle Does It Again." In 1924, when he was managing minor leaguers, he walked off a baseball field as a uniformed member of a team for the last time, the departure prompted by a young player using the word *bonehead* to refer to him.

After that, Merkle avoided ballparks. This may have saved him some grief, but it didn't help separate *boner* from his name. When he died in 1956 *boner* appeared in newspaper headlines from coast to coast. In the following years the incident would recede somewhat from its towering prominence among athletic mishaps, crowded by other, fresher versions of loss, and the word itself would shade more often toward a different meaning from the one that had darkened Merkle's life. But this shift in meaning didn't add any retroactive dignity to the newspaper requiems for Fred Merkle.

"Fred Merkle died last night," reported the *St. Petersburg Times*. "And may his boner be interred with him."

Booing

The baby wasn't sleeping that first week. There were occasional exceptions to this rule. One afternoon it seemed he might nap. My wife had him in the bedroom, and it was quiet in there. I had to search for a while, but eventually I found the television remote beneath a cushion on the couch. Oh sweet nothing TV. Oh TV, my opiate, my concubine. Oh the canceling suction of your idiocy. These prayers of gratitude surged through me in the time it took to thumb the On button. The screen filled with fans booing, many with their hands cupped around their mouths to better project their virulent dissatisfaction. I'd missed the moment that inspired the uproar, and the announcers were choosing not to rehash it. It went on for several seconds, shot after shot from various vantage points, a stadium acridly united, thousands and thousands booing, booing. Then the bedroom door flailed open, accompanied by an exhausted sigh from my wife and the cries of our unsleeping baby. Before my wife got to the living room to pass me the boy, I turned off the TV. Everyone was still booing.

Brister, Bubby

Later there was a thunderstorm. Abby was on the couch nursing Jack. A beautiful, sweet mother, holding him and kissing him and talking in a soft sing-song to him. I stood nearby at the big picture window. It was in the evening, but there was still some light in the sky. The storm turned the light filtering through the leaves to the street we live on into something else, something hushed and glowing. We were inside, safe, and the thunder rumbled. The three of us. That light. It made me ache to say what it was, to hold onto it. I don't know the words. It's not about winning, but it's not about losing either, not exactly.

I've been adrift my whole life, as if afraid to attach myself to anything that might cause me to feel that ache. I spent one whole

year swimming laps, back and forth, back and forth. Another
year I frequented a driving range with borrowed clubs and swat-
ted thousands of pale yellow orbs out into a field. It seemed stupid, meaningless, but now I miss it. I miss it all. I miss commutes
I don't have to do anymore. Someday I'll miss the commute I
have to do now.

It's an absurd daily tedium, involving multiple modes of
transportation and several hours every day, more evidence that
I'm authoring a ridiculous life, but since Jack's birth and the
financial statements related to it, I now thank whatever there
is to thank that there is a small cubicle out in the western suburbs with my name on it. The name is on a nameplate in a slot
designed to enable easy removal. I've seen other name slots go
blank overnight. Picture lifting a thin slice of rye out of a toaster.
That's how easily my name will disappear.

Until that happens I start my long commute every day with
a bike ride past a massive cemetery. As far as the eye can see,
graves. Stone markers, cubicles, names: sooner or later everyone is an also-ran, adrift. I miss everyone. I miss Bubby Brister.
Shittiness infinity, shittiness pure. I can see him yet—stumbling,
feckless, attempting to escape a crumbling pocket late in a
meaningless freezing-rain loss sometime in the 1990s in a half-
empty concrete structure in a swamp in New Jersey.

Sometimes I drift through the Google newspaper archives.
I'm not looking for anything in particular. Below is the kind of
thing that snags me, that brings on that ache. It's the last para-
graph of a wire report recap of a season-ending loss sustained
in the Meadowlands by a 3–13 edition of the New York Jets. It's
from the issue of the *Sarasota Herald-Tribune* that came out on
Christmas Day 1995. My wife, my son, a glow through the leaves,
an utterly forgettable late-December football game, a backup
dropped for a loss, booze-addled loons on the loose. Some
things just make me wish I could live forever.

A day after snowballs barraged the field in San Diego's win over the New York Giants, there were no similar incidents from the sparse crowd of 28,885 (48,831 no-shows), although one snowball fell harmlessly in the end zone after Jets backup Bubby Brister was sacked at the 2-yard line in the third period. In the fourth quarter, three fans ran out on the field and were caught by stadium officials.

Bust

Most of us, despite our dreams, will not be discovered. The game will become harder and harder until it ejects us. As a high school ballplayer, *Bill Bene* was fumbling through this customary descent, his expiration date set for when his passage as a guess-hitting outfielder concluded. Instead, Bene's life changed with the kind of sudden starry visitation generally known only in fairy tales.

Former major leaguer Randy Moffitt noticed Bill Bene had a strong arm and suggested he try pitching. According to a conflicting version of the story, Randy Moffitt's father, Bill, made this suggestion. What is indisputable is that Bene was blessed by the divine intervention of a close family member of Billie Jean Moffitt, Bill's daughter and Randy's sister, who gained worldwide renown under her married name, Billie Jean King (*see* **Riggs, Bobby**). Billie Jean's relation pointed the coach at Cal State-Los Angeles toward Bene, and it was at that institution, on a pitcher's mound, that he would be discovered.

He first took the mound for his college team in 1986. From the beginning he threw very hard and yet with so much wildness as to be nearly useless to the team. Scouts began to appear, more and more all the time, drawn to his promise, ignoring his flaws, much in the way one falls in love. His college stats were not good, as shown most succinctly by a career ERA of 5.62. He walked more batters than he struck out. Still, the scouts swarmed.

"We had fifty-five scouts at one game," Bene's college coach, John Herbold, said, adding for the sake of comedic hyperbole, "and we had so many radar guns going at the same time there was a power shortage."

Somewhere along the line the fluttery hyperbole surrounding Bene began to coagulate into something more solid. By 1988 Los Angeles Dodgers general manager Fred Claire, who by the estimation of awards givers at the end of that year would be deemed the keenest executive in all of major league baseball, was saying that Bill Bene had the "best arm of any prospect in the country."

In the spring of 1988 the Dodgers selected him in the first round with the fifth overall pick of the amateur draft. At that time I'd just spent the winter warming the bench for the 1987–88 Johnson State College Badgers. After many years of defining myself in terms of how I did—or perhaps more accurately in terms of how I *might* do—while wearing a team uniform, it was my last season as an athlete in organized sports. This punctuated what should have been apparent for some time: even though I loved playing sports above all else, it wasn't what I was meant for.

In the latter stages of that last season, right around when Bill Bene was being identified as having the best arm in the country, I participated in a poetry reading. One of the other readers was a friend, Mark, who was the school's reigning acoustic guitar troubadour. His presence bulked up the turnout beyond the skimpy norm for poetry readings. He got the gathering warmed up by cushioning a couple of his poems with his two campus hits, one a ditty about being too lazy to do his laundry (to the tune of "Good Lovin'") and the other a Neil Young–saturated ballad about environmental destruction ("Yesterday I saw mother nature cry / down by the water side").

People whooped and pounded their hands together when Mark was done. I went on after him with the room loose and buzzing, and I read a poem about atomic bombs. I didn't admit to myself until a long time afterward that I had lifted all the imagery in the poem straight out of John Hershey's *Hiroshima*. I also didn't consider until much later that the mildly positive response by the pot-addled, guitar-warmed audience to the chunk of fakery wasn't necessarily the unequivocal message I first thought it was and that I clung to for a long time as if to a piece of driftwood.

"Yeah," someone said amid some clapping.

"Woo," someone else said.

This is it, I thought. *This is what I was meant for.*

I'm still clinging to that piece of driftwood, decades later, a proofreader in a cubicle on the second floor of a sprawling corporate office building out in the western suburbs. I get a small paycheck, some benefits. I had a week of paid parental leave just after the baby was born. It went by in a blur, and I found myself back in the cubicle, dazed. Life went on, hazily. A friend at work came by with a box of some of his unwanted baseball cards. I pulled out the 1989 Topps offering featuring Bill Bene. I'd never heard of him. The card identified him as a number-one draft pick. A number-one draft pick? This guy?

"He's all yours," my coworker said. "I don't want him."

Getting back to the routine of working didn't add any clarity to those first days with the baby. I'd be sitting in the cubicle and then, without noticing any moments in between, I'd be standing in the living room with my arms at my sides, watching my wife hold this strange and volatile new boy in her arms. She was battered, exhausted, still bleeding sporadically from the episiotomy, a beleaguered army of one who nonetheless was all softness and love with the baby, and in the occasional moments when he slept and gave her a chance to think, her mind raced with worries that something might happen to him, to his tiny fragile life.

Meanwhile I was coming down from the first high of the kid being born, when I thought I would be a different guy altogether forever, someone able to give myself over totally to complete holy sacrifice all the time, Gandhi in a replica 1970s Red Sox cap, transformed by love. Turns out I was the same as always, just more tired. I didn't sleep, not as I've understood sleep all my life. I neared it, verged on it, but it was always truncated and shot through from start to abrupt finish with insecurity and worry, a shallow, famished thing, exhaustion a kind of hunger. One afternoon, driving down Ashland, I felt in the light of day as if I had taken some low-quality but powerful narcotic, everything murky but capable of sudden unpredictable motion—2 p.m., 2 a.m., life was steep. I don't really know why, but I found myself in rare stray moments searching the Internet for traces of Bill Bene, the number-one draft pick.

The number-one draft pick struggled. Early in his minor league career he had so little control over his pitches that he was demoted to remedial instruction outside of official action. In a simulated game, in which the only other participant was a teammate standing in the batter's box, a pitch got away from Bene and broke the teammate's wrist. The coaches further modified Bene's remediation, replacing the human batter's box attendant with a department store mannequin. Bene drew a mustache on the mannequin. He named it Harold.

While working with Harold, Bene's pitching briefly seemed to improve, but this didn't last. You can dream of being discovered, of being told you have a great gift, but if this dream does come true, eventually a second discovery will threaten the first. This latter discovery is the one you pray to avoid: that your place in the world has been secured erroneously, and you will be revealed as a fraud and cast out.

In 2006 the former number-one draft pick, now many years removed from the revelation of what seemed to be a rare and beautiful gift, began using an online alias, Dan Stern, to sell hard drives containing counterfeit karaoke songs. He must have

imagined, as he ignored copyright restrictions and evaded paying taxes, that he was invisible, immune to discovery, but the
FBI eventually caught up with him. He was arrested, convicted,
imprisoned. I found myself standing around in my home, my
arms at my sides, wondering what happened to Bene's accom-
plice, the mustachioed mannequin, **Harold**. A bird thumped
head-first into one of our windows.

"Jesus," I said.

"It keeps happening," my wife said. "We need to do
something."

It's a big picture window. The bird was just flying along
and . . . *wham.*

"God, imagine what that's like," I said, pitying birds.

But then I thought about it some more. We can only ever
guess. Every single step. Faking it. And sooner or later we'll
smack into something. We'll be stopped.

Can't

A newborn can't do much. A newborn can grip with tiny fingers and hold on. I don't know what I can do. I know what I can't.

I can't fix things. Things break, I'm fucked.

Just before Jack was born, when my greatly swollen wife could barely breathe with the boy crushing her lungs from within, a heat wave descended and our central air conditioning unit broke. This malfunction and the costly and nerve-racking process of getting it fixed deepened my already pronounced distrust of the devices on which our lives depend. I no longer had any faith whatsoever in any of the things humming and groaning in my home—the dishwasher, the fridge, the microwave, the computer: on Jack's arrival, on his presence intensifying the importance of life to not devolve into pure shittiness, each thing seemed on the brink of having some small, cheap, vitally important cog snap and cause the whole mechanism to seize up and go silent.

I can't keep demoralizing thoughts out of my head.

I've lived a meandering life, awake only in stories, never forging any kind of direct, pragmatic connection to actual events, and my tendency for anxiety feeds into my literary dreaminess so that every possible setback seems not simply one problem to solve but rather an omen foreboding the inevitable unraveling of daily life into a tragedy, as if a clogged bathtub drain will lead, eventually, to me freezing to death on an ice chunk in Antarctica. More than once in my son's first few weeks, whenever anything showed the slightest sign of devolving—a knob falling off a cabinet, the front door lock sticking, a car tire low on air—I found myself dwelling on Cormac McCarthy's *The Road*, the horrifying masterwork in which the whole of human civilization as we know it is shown in smoldering irrevocable cinders, in a state of tragic fall, and a father and a son walk through it together, barely surviving.

I can't assemble rudimentary shelter, spearfish in a brook, fend off gangs of postapocalyptic marauders.

I turn and have always turned to stories. With Jack's birth I tried to channel this tendency into something productive, pragmatic—I attempted to read books about parenting. I only ever got a few pages into most everything before panicking but was able to focus a bit longer than that on a book claiming to offer a method for calming unhappy babies. The story in the book was that several methods must be mastered and executed perfectly or there will be a house full of suffering. I tried to bring the story of the book to life but kept getting the sense that I wasn't quite doing it right.

I can't follow directions.

My own son felt awkward in my hands. I kept reading and rereading the book, hoping that doing so would help me bridge the gap between the ideal story in its pages and the real fakery of my life. One morning, on my way to work, I tried to go over the book again on the bus but kept getting my attention coaxed away by two guys talking nearby, trading stories of things gone wrong to the point that litigation ensued.

I can't focus on anything.

The story one of the men on the bus told involved a man with cancer in one eye who went in for surgery to get the eye removed, and the surgeon mistakenly removed the other eye. Later, at lunch, I thought about that story while reading an article my father sent to me that traced the roots of some riots in London to a sense of profound societal desperation, the riots a grab for power by the powerless. Eye cancer, shitty air conditioners, and the roots of riot. I didn't get much work done after lunch, which eroded my already frayed sense of job security. I exited the building with the anxious sense that I was about to smack into something invisible. *I'll be stopped.* This feeling followed me to the bus stop. When I boarded the bus I tried to cancel my unease along with the duration of the ride by falling asleep. The bus got more and more crowded, and then it seemed that we were headed somewhere where we wouldn't be bothered, somewhere painless. The passenger at my side leaned so close I felt his unshaven cheek on my own.

"Hey," he murmured, and the bus began to speed, as if toward impact. I came to. I looked out the window. We hadn't gotten very far, still short of the stop at the community college, which wasn't even halfway. I stared at the white line on the shoulder of the road and thought about Schiraldi, Calvin Schiraldi, that look on his face as he stood on the mound in Game Six of the 1986 World Series with everything crumbling all around him. The moment too much. I thought about losing, about disintegration, about *can't.* The origin in my body of that word.

I can't stop looking backward.

It came to life inside me, that word, a few years before I'd ever heard of Schiraldi. I was on a junior high basketball team in a small town in the middle of Vermont, 1979 and 1980. We were so bad that, looking back on it, I've sometimes wondered, in the manner of a paranoid mental patient, whether the whole thing was some kind of social experiment, the world's purest laboratory of losing. I don't know the experiment's hypothesis. I don't know of any conclusions. I know we were edging out of childhood and we lost. Occasionally some philosophical reflection occurred.

"The best is a knob job," our point guard Eddie orated in the locker room one day. "Boys, knob jobs are what it's all about."

I can't recall whether we were reeling from or bracing for another beating. I remember Eddie propping his foot on a bench in the manner of a team captain—knee bent, forearm on thigh—as he kept repeating the term "knob job."

My bus ride home seemed to go on and on, as it always does if I can't lose myself in a story. We rode past shopping centers and malls and Jiffy Lubes. Sometimes there were low dim homes at the fringe of the busy road, all of them looking like flawed repetitions. Some had American flags. They blinked in and out of sight in a homely, dragging rhythm. There's a conjugated chant of affirmation at the heart of the myth of America—*yes, I can; yes, you can; yes, we can.* The triumph defining the American Dream *can* be realized, but it is based wholly on your unwavering belief.

Eddie wore red, white, and blue sweatbands. He had feathered brown hair and was the oldest guy on the seventh grade team because he'd been left back a year. The rest of us sat on benches and stared up at Eddie. Our pale limbs jutted from our uniforms, fraying junior varsity hand-me-downs from various eras in the school's history. Some shirts said "Randolph," some said "Braintree-Randolph," some said "Galloping Ghosts."

"Yeah, I'm telling you, knob jobs," Eddie said. "Put it this way. If anyone ever asks about me, you tell them, 'Eddie? Yeah, I know that guy. Fuckin' *lives* for knob jobs.'"

"Look," he concluded, pausing for effect, a pubescent Rockne, "you just *got* to get yourself a knob job."

He was gone the following year, along with some others, but we picked up Steve, who had been left back to repeat eighth grade. Steve played electric guitar and had feathered blond hair. I remember Steve propping his foot on a bench in the manner of a team captain—knee bent, forearm on thigh—as he talked about a girl who sat near me in social studies and dotted her i's with hearts.

"The best thing about her," Steve orated, "is her cunt."

The bus pulled into the terminal, and I was discharged along with a few other end-of-the-liners. It was dark out, and I still had to ride a few miles on my bike to get home. My route went down Clark, a narrow avenue crammed with buses and speeding cars, drivers anxious to get home, out of the shittiness. I put on my helmet, the cheapest one they'd had at the sporting goods store. I turned on the little red blinking light below the seat. I prayed for the cars to not kill me. I prayed to pay attention. I started riding. My mind wandered backward.

As a Galloping Ghost, I was baffled by knob jobs, cunts. I tried to focus on basketball, but this is hard when all you do is lose. The losses got more pronounced as time went on. A virus seemed to follow us all over central Vermont, afflicting our shots, our passes, our ability to look one another in the eye. Scoreboards loomed above the action as if victimized by partial stroke, one side tallying numbers in a rhythm like a pulse, the other side sickly, immobile. As the losses piled up, plaque began to accrue inside me around that core American word, *can*, changing it, distorting its shape, increasing its size, its weight, its stalactitic fragility, until finally a compound fracture occurred. Somewhere in that experiment, deep into the winter, deep into a loss, a rebound up for grabs, I felt this happen, a snap in my chest: *can't*.

A little over halfway through my ride through the darkness I turned left off of Clark and slipped onto quieter streets for a while. By then my heart rate had risen, so I glided through the dark awake, feeling the day leave me, feeling by its absence how much it had been smothering me, how I go through most of my waking hours just partially alive. Finally I rounded the last corner and got off my bike. The big picture window that birds kept slamming into was covered with a blind, but the lights glowed through. The glow of a newborn who can't do anything, needs everything. I stopped walking my bike toward that glow and just stood there on the sidewalk in my cheap helmet, my heartbeat slowing to an old ache, the little red light below the bike seat pulsing. Anything, everything, anything, everything. Sometimes I can't even move.

Coleman, Derrick
*See **Whoop-de-damn-do**.*

Dayton Triangles

Throughout the first decade of the NFL, the 1920s, the Dayton Triangles endured despite sliding rapidly to the floodwater lowlands of the standings, endured despite drawing so few fans to home dates that they began playing all their games on the road, endured despite being surrounded by the constant vanishing of teams all around them in the league's blurry larval beginnings, iffiness everywhere, the Evansville Crimson Giants, the Muncie Fliers, the Toledo Maroons, the Oorang Indians, the Louisville Colonels, the Duluth Eskimos, the Hammond Pros, the Detroit Heralds, the Detroit Tigers, the Detroit Panthers, the Detroit Wolverines, on and on and on the transformation of the living to the defunct, endured despite being worse than all the teams they outlasted, endured despite blooming into the worst outfit the league had seen and would see, among all the decades to come of armored bodies maiming one another no mismatch so brutally pure as the one enacted with shoddy minimal padding by the Dayton Triangles in their enduring passage, punished and winless for weeks, sometimes months, sometimes years.

Finally the Triangles carried a long losing streak into the 1929 NFL season, having won no games in 1928 and just one game in 1927, continued losing without exception throughout 1929, and extended the losing streak into infinity when, at the end of the season, they were sold, moved, renamed. The resulting team was subsequently sold, moved, renamed, and the team after that was too, and so on. I've come upon claims that traces of the Triangles, many moves on, endure to this day in the Indianapolis Colts, but every time I try to follow the traces, my mind wanders and dissipates or the baby wakes and starts wailing and my mind constricts; either way the traces disappear. I have no reliable information to pass along on this matter.

This is a terrible encyclopedia, a series of traces lost. Encyclopedias should provide the resolution of reliable explanations, but this one is not to be trusted. It's rooted in the inexplicable.

"Where did you come from, baby?" we asked Jack. We kept beaming down at him and asking him this. "Baby, where have you been?"

His arrival intensified my pervasive sense of doubt, spotlighted my shortcomings, and made me wonder about the origin of doubt and shortcomings, but worse than all that, it also made me wonder about the origin of beauty. God damn it, the world is suffused with beauty! I'd always been aware of this beauty—sometimes it followed me down the street or murmured from the radio or leaked through the blinds—but I'd more or less been able to keep it at bay with Old Milwaukee tall boys and packages of Entenmann's chocolate chip cookies and television. But when Jack arrived beauty started crowding my throat, forcing me to somehow give voice to it, and the only songs I knew were benchwarmer songs. All I'd ever done is sing about sitting on the sidelines, witnessing loss. All I'd ever done is wander and digress, sifting through numbers and names, tripping on trivial detritus, gathering it up.

I always figured all that wandering through lists and newspaper archives and almanacs and encyclopedias was just a way to kill time, but maybe I'd always been looking for something, somewhere in the batting averages and points-per-game averages and yards-per-carry averages, somewhere in all the transactions and recaps, somewhere in the endless unfolding of names and teams and facts. I wanted to unhitch time and linger, just a little, on all my negligible discoveries. I wanted the feeling that there was no end to this life, that the numbers and names just went on and on, one giving way to another and another until some kind of universal connection began to thrum. I wanted to linger on the only beauty I could possibly understand.

All I can bring to fatherhood, to this new burden of beauty, is my sprawling trivial knowledge of the bench. All I can do—or all I ever want to do—is to keep on gathering. So I don't know, really, what became of the Dayton Triangles, but I have gathered that near the end of their mysteriously long enduring, the Dayton Triangles employed a 150-pound running back and drop-kicker of Asian descent named Walter Tin Kit Achiu. His nickname was Sneeze Achiu.

Sneeze Achiu?

All these years of dicking around beyond the outskirts of meaningful history, and I'd never learned of Sneeze Achiu. How could this be?

Maybe I hadn't needed to know about him until I needed this encyclopedia, and I didn't need this encyclopedia until I came up against not knowing how to be a father. When Jack was first born I didn't know how to hold him, but within a week or so the awkwardness of holding him gave way to a feeling that holding him was the thing I'd been born to do, the feeling that made me whole. The problem was that this wholeness introduced a new gap and dread below it. The transfer of love and life from father to son, the transfer of something, of everything. How could this not be bungled? How could I not fuck him up? What was I supposed to do?

The simplest answer, the truest—be present—was the hardest of all to implement. I'd always wanted to disappear into a refuge of sports facts and, more specifically, as life went on, into the kinds of facts that few could ever care about. I wanted to be at a distant remove, but I also wanted to find something distinctly, uniquely myself, something no one else could lay claim to. I wanted to find some buried treasure, and I wanted to bury myself, and paradoxically I also wanted to bring the treasure of my buried self back to the surface. What is the nature of this treasure? What is the point of Sneeze Achiu?

All I can tell you is that when I learned of him, his preposterous name, his near-complete inconsequentiality that was hedged by his historical, albeit largely ignored, significance as the first Asian player in the NFL, it made me happy. I wanted to yelp out loud. The inexhaustible beauty of this stupid life, the ache! I wanted to run down the street with a megaphone and a banner, wander dewy heaths composing Wordsworthian odes, snort designer narcotics off Kim Kardashian's ass. I wanted to smash an electric guitar in a sold-out arena, meditate straight-spined for decades in a cave, pull a locomotive with my teeth. I wanted to laugh and sob and build a cathedral.

I want to tell my son about Sneeze Achiu.

Dead Ball

My mom came for a visit when Jack was two and half weeks old. The presence of a third adult made me realize how hard Abby and I were trying to keep absolutely still all the time, hoping this stillness would spirit our reluctant sleeper into unconsciousness and keep him there. My mom tiptoeing around in a touching attempt to follow our lead—and the way my shoulders seized up like a bear trap when she so much as stepped on a loose floorboard—opened my eyes to the bristling tension surrounding this attempt at absolute stillness. It was as if we'd somehow arrived at the notion that caring for a newborn was similar to hiding in an attic from the Nazis.

Jack, surely absorbing this tension, continued to struggle through most of my mom's visit, not sleeping much, wailing. Finally, on the last full day of her visit Mom and I took Jack out for a walk in a stroller. It was his first stroller ride. Mom pushed the stroller. Jack wasn't crying. I let my shoulders relax. It felt to me like one of those brief moments in a game just after play has been ruled dead. A hand goes up, a whistle blows. Even though the game has been stopped, momentum carries the play forward, but the pressure of consequences, of causes and effects, has been removed. For a moment, no matter.

In the stroller Jack looked up at me with his blue eyes. He sneezed, then sneezed again.

"He always sneezes twice," Mom said.

I hadn't noticed this as a tendency, but it was true. *Achiu, Achiu.* It was nice to have another set of loving eyes on the boy.

"I wish you didn't live so far away," Mom added.

I never know what to say to this. I didn't say anything. We both just stared down at Jack, who blinked up at us and then turned to face the side of the stroller.

Whoever is in possession of the ball at the moment of stoppage will follow through anyway, for practice, for pleasure. A motion without meaning. I hope heaven exists, and that it's like this. Something outside winning and losing.

On the last day of her visit I had to leave for work at around the same time Mom had to catch a train to the airport. I watched her walk away, the bag on her shoulder tipping her to the left, making her seem small and unsteady as she rounded the corner and was gone. I felt a snap in my chest.

Mommy, I thought.

Deficit

Before Jack arrived we hadn't known what life was going to look like with him. But we thought we'd need more solidity. Up to that point Abby and I had lived together in several rented apartments, and each situation had come to an abrupt end with a decision beyond our control, landlords selling the building to a developer or themselves converting the property into condos. We were always moving, scrambling, the strain of the moves leading inevitably to screaming matches and to the two of us pinned to a stairwell wall by furniture and weeping. We wanted to be in control. So, naturally, we plunged ourselves into six-figure debt.

I was worrying about this deficit one afternoon. I was by the big picture window of the condo that was the cause of the deficit. Jack was in my arms. He was about a month old at this point. Abby sat in the easy chair nearby. She had the breast pump going. I'd gone to the window to try to get a hit of the hushed, glowing light I'd seen that one day after the storm during Jack's first week (*see* **Brister, Bubby**), but I ended up thinking about the large check I sent every month to the mortgage company and about how the total number, the amount we owed, never seemed to budge. It was like hacking at an iceberg with a plastic spoon. Meanwhile the number in our savings account statement kept dwindling demonstrably. As I was holding Jack in my arms and these two troubling numbers in my head, another bird smashed into the window. *Wham!*

"This is ridiculous," Abby said. She stared at the window. She was hunched forward and grimacing with sour, pained exhaustion. Her right boob was connected to the breast pump's suction cup.

"I know," I said. "Life is so pointless and absurd on a certain level."

"Oh, Jesus Christ. I mean we have to *fix* it." She unhooked the breast pump and went down to our little storage cell in the basement of the building to look for something to put on the window to warn the birds.

I stayed by the window with Jack, hoping not to witness any additional bird collisions. I looked into the room at the breast pump contraption, which had by now accrued the aura of torture. We'd been sent home from the hospital after Jack's birth with several bottles of formula and the instructions to supplement with it as needed, which we would learn much later was shitty advice. Abby was fighting against the consequences of this advice, namely a decreasing milk supply. The dull thudding rhythm of the pump had come to signify the relentless demands of motherhood. Abby never had a break—she was always working.

She reappeared upstairs with some butterfly stickers she'd found in a box of supplies from her job. For many years, up until taking maternity leave, she'd worked as a case manager and then a therapist at a residential treatment facility for teenage wards of the state, girls who had been legally severed from their parents or guardians during childhoods marked by severe poverty, abuse, and neglect. They had difficulty getting through a day without harming themselves or someone else. The facility had a tiny, perpetually endangered budget. Sputtering state funds allowed for the purchase of low-grade encased meats and mushy generic white bread, and billion-dollar private corporations occasionally donated a few barrels of caramel popcorn or upper grandstand tickets to a Cubs game. But in general if you wanted, say, butterfly stickers to use in a group therapy session with teenage girls who had been bound in a closet or burned with cigarettes or whored out for crack, you had to buy the stickers yourself. My wife put four of these stickers on our big picture window.

Abby was always solving problems like this. I had a much more passive approach to life. Though this approach had reached a symbolic crystallization during my season as the backup to the backup forwards on the 1987–88 Johnson Badgers, it had first taken hold much earlier, in junior high, when I'd been a member of the Galloping Ghosts. At a certain point in each game, sometimes even as early as the pregame layup line, something would give way. My body kept moving, making motions, but my will had surrendered. My lifelong identity in action was forged. There weren't enough of us to allow me to man the role I was destined for, that of the benchwarmer. As a benchwarmer, I can dream. I can hold onto some glowing core of holiness, or pretend I'm doing so, or call it practice, or call it faith. But in action I only know one way. The Other is bigger than I am. We both reach for the ball, but I let the Other wrestle it away. I watch the Other go, watch the deficit on the scoreboard increase.

Defunct

I want to wander forever among the defunct. An entity defunct, devoid of funct, has had its funct removed or disabled. It no longer functions. Its purpose is gone. The Dayton Triangles, the Duluth Eskimos, the Oorang Indians. Pulled free from losing. Useless, beautiful.

Abby's butterfly stickers did the trick. The bird collisions abated. I continued to worry about our mortgage, but when the sun would shine through the window in the afternoons a rectangle of light would form on the facing wall, slowly rising, butterflies afloat within. The wall where the butterflies appeared was above some carpeted stairs leading down to the lower level of the condo. After many years of living in apartments, I liked having stairs. I liked butterflies afloat in rising rectangles of light. But I couldn't afford the stairs, the butterflies. My home in the world had been secured erroneously, and in that home I was a fraud.

"Joshua, don't buy a home," my father had told me. He'd said this over the phone a few months before Jack arrived. It was just after Abby and I had decided to buy the home. Since retiring he'd devoted his life to watching old movies, slowly walking several miles to purchase organic apples, and squinting at dense offerings from the bleak oracle of World Systems Theory. The latter, as I understand it through our conversations, makes the strong, intellectually rigorous case that the current transnational hegemony is not only inhumane but flawed, unsustainable, bound for inevitable collapse.

Things collapse all the time. There is no end to the marvel of defunct teams, but even better is to ponder the defunct leagues. The WFL, the WHA, the AFL, the NASL. The Mayflower Conference. The greatest of these defunct collectives is the original incarnation of the American Basketball Association (ABA), which lasted from 1967 to 1976, from the summer of love to the Bicentennial, from the year I was conceived to the year I created Dr. J in my own imagination, aided by photos and a written story here or there—no television sightings, just myths and legends.

"The capitalist system is not designed to enable caring or to strengthen human bonds," my father told me, "but to generate profits for nonhuman entities beyond the control of any individual, even the few in positions of relatively massive power."

"I know," I said. I was talking to him by cell phone during my half-hour lunch break from my job at a corporation.

"These *corporations*," Dad said, disgustedly, "devour everything. People, nature. All for profit. The end result of a system based on the idea of endless gain—"

His hearing aid began to squeak.

"Damn it," he said.

I was standing in the large atrium of the building where I work, staring out the window at a parking lot, a highway. I was thinking about Dr. J.

"The signs of collapse are everywhere," he said.

I love pondering the last season, bills going unpaid, debris falling, debt accruing, lights going off, Dr. J still glorious, soaring amid his peerless enactment of the term that would later disperse into two separate synonyms and become defunct in its original meaning, living on only as a corporate sales-force cliché, worse than defunct: the *slam dunk*. That word was once the center of my fandom and fantasies and dream world, the thing I would most want to do, flight and mastery and certainty and force at my fingertips, like the version of Dr. J haloed in the aura of defunct, a red, white, and blue ball in his huge hand, held high over his head like a bolt of American lightning in the hand of a god.

"Whole nations going bankrupt, the so-called natural disasters of global climate change, wars over scarcity," my father said.

"Everyone is losing," I said.

There was a basketball hoop at the far edge of the parking lot, below the highway. The short Filipino guys from Systems were playing two on two. I'd had interactions with a couple of them. One sat across from me at a muted project-ending celebration at TGI Fridays and, when the awkward table conversation flagged, showed us photos of his children on his iPad. Another helped me locate some lost material in an electronic database. Some months after the game of parking lot two-on-two, one of these two Filipinos—I'm unclear on which, never firmly affixing names to faces—would have his position eliminated in a corporate reorganization. I've always learned of these layoffs by e-mail, which makes it particularly easy to imagine my own name among those who'd been reorganized into erasure. Just another name on a list.

"There's no 'upswing' coming," my dad said. The hearing aid chirped. I inhaled.

"Everyone—" I began. The device in my dad's ear interrupted, whining.

"Hm?" my dad said. "Hold on."

He tinkered with the hearing aid for a while. I imagined its malfunctioning sounds formed a code, a message to decipher. I

imagined some deliverance of certainty, father to son. As fantasies go, it didn't have much pull, so I thought some more about
Dr. J. After the ABA folded, Dr. J would star for many more years
in the NBA, but the story of his days in the NBA was of a grad-
ual, graceful descent, a coming back to earth. This is everyone's
story with varying levels of grace, but a version of Dr. J, blessed
by defunct, continues to soar, immune to gravity. His afro is
enormous and his Converses never touch the ground. Thinking
of that Dr. J, I imagined myself into the parking lot basketball
game. There I was, altering a tech-savvy Austronesian's tentative
fade-away, grabbing the carom, dribbling out to the top of the
key, eyeing the basket. There I was, driving the lane, getting a
step of daylight, leaping, rising.

Desperation Heave

In my second season as a Galloping Ghost, in eighth grade, our
ranks thinned and the losses continued. There were desultory
attempts at improvement. One evening at practice we all put on
goggles designed to improve our dribbling skills. The goggles
were lensless and had flat shelves jutting out from the bottom of
the frames. The shelves were to prevent you from seeing the ball
as you dribbled it. We all tried dribbling blindly this way. The
balls went everywhere.

That evening the undefeated varsity had a game, and we
could hear the pregame festivities over the PA system speakers
in the junior high gym. I knew from seeing an earlier game in
the team's prolonged winning streak that the songs we heard
over the speakers—the Cars' "Let's Go" and Devo's "Whip It"—
accompanied the team's layup line, all the players still in dark
blue warm-up suits, bouncing in synch and with style through
the rudimentary drill, each leaping high to lay the ball off the
glass and through, one made basket after another and another, a
ritual purification of triumph and purpose.

When "Whip It" ended, the varsity introductions began, the names of the starters coming over the speaker and into our empty gym. Cheering followed each name, more cheering as the list of names progressed, suggesting a hierarchy of caring, of winning, of worth. The hierarchy bottomed out somewhere obscure, far from any cheering, in some aimless enduring capitulation, and it peaked with the names of the undefeated.

The PA clicked off after the last starter was named, the undefeated varsity's most talented player, Schubach, and we were left to the sound of our own blind dribbling. That final utterance from the world of winning lingered in my mind. Schubach was the opposite of whatever was happening to us. He had darting quickness but was so smooth and rhythmic and balanced that he made all the other central Vermont teenagers laboring up and down the court during varsity games seem graceless as cattle. His best move, a right-to-left crossover dribble into a midrange pull-up jumper, was sudden, buoyant, flawless. I imitated it all the time, mostly when I was home alone, shooting baskets in my driveway, and there the imitation always calmed me. Puberty was taking over my body, riddling it with tics and stutters and hesitancies, making it feel unnatural, like it wasn't my own. I only felt like myself when I was Schubach.

I attempted an imitation of Schubach's crossover while wearing my dribbling goggles and drilled the ball off my sneaker. As I went to retrieve the ball I yanked down the goggles and looked around to find that everyone had done the same. Lensless blinder eyewear dangled from everyone's necks like strange tribal jewelry, and our practice had devolved, as always, into desperation heaves. Everyone was near half-court and counting down and heaving and making a loud buzzer sound while the ball was in flight. Balls slammed the backboard or missed everything altogether. I forgot about Schubach and moved toward half-court.

"Three, two, one—*eeeeeeennnnnhhhh!*" *Thump.* Again and again we heaved, as if such a shot could ever be made, or if it could ever matter. As it turned out, I would never be called upon to attempt such a shot. Any team lousy enough to allow me playing time would never be close enough to winning at the end of games for last-second desperation. But I kept practicing the desperation heave long after the tics and hesitancies of junior high, kept imagining the desperation heave and imagining its transformation into some other term from some other encyclopedia altogether, the *game winner,* the *buzzer beater,* the *miracle.*

The miracle. It had happened, just not the way I ever imagined it would. Here he was, in my arms. It was Labor Day, and I had the day off. We'd decided to cook out, which means that we'd decided to enact our periodic ritual of me trying to get the coals lit in our tiny grill until I was undone by the attempt, swearing and furious, and Abby took over. As she crouched over the grill and got the flames going, I sat in a canvas chair on our minuscule sunless heavily mortgaged deck and held Jack. He was about five weeks old, a timeframe I was mostly aware of because it was one week shy of when Abby's maternity leave was scheduled to end. Abby stood up out of her crouch and pulled our other canvas chair next to Jack and me and sat down. Jack started wriggling in my arms, and Abby reached over and grabbed him and put him on her boob. My frustration over my inability to light the coals started to dissipate. I realized we were sitting in the chairs we'd dragged to the beach the day before Jack was born.

"Cooking out is so stupid," I said. "I'm done with it."

"You always say that," Abby said.

"Why not just cook on the stove inside and bring your plate outside if you want to sit outside? Or a sandwich? What's wrong with a sandwich? All this caveman fire stuff. I mean, I just don't get the wh—"

"I'm not going back to work," Abby said.

Some coals in the grill settled, sending up a burst of sparks. "Yeah," I said. "Okay, okay. Good."

We'd talked before about what was going to happen at the end of Abby's maternity leave but always quickly abandoned the discussion. Either option seemed to point toward desperation. Before Jack was born I imagined he'd be something along the lines of an animate throw pillow. I'd work from home a couple of days a week and would be able to "keep an eye on him" as I worked, and the other days of the week we'd just piece something together. I'd quickly learned that taking care of a baby was so demanding as to be virtually beyond our capabilities, and that was with Abby staying home all the time and working around the clock as the primary caretaker. I couldn't imagine what it would be like with her gone at her job five days a week. I also couldn't imagine what it would be like without her income, with only me making money.

"I just can't see being back there," Abby said. Her work had always been different from mine. I could go days, sometimes weeks, at my job scanning for typos without even really noticing I was there. Meanwhile, every day Abby was getting cursed at, threatened, clung to. The teenagers who lived at the treatment facility where she worked were in a kind of desperation wholly beyond anything I'd ever known, and year after year Abby threw everything she had into helping them, first as a case manager and then, after she earned a master's degree at night and on weekends, as a therapist. She'd been punched in the face, kneed in the gut, spat on, laughed at, thrown into a wall. She'd been clung to and loved.

"I can't see being there," she said, "instead of here."

Jack was in her arms, sucking away. The fingers of his right hand were spread out on her boob like those of a guide hand on a jump shot. His eyes were closed. He had barely more than a shadow of hair on his head. He was wearing a white onesie with little fire trucks all over it. His pudgy legs stuck out the bottom.

"Good," I said again. I almost added, *We'll manage.* But I anticipated that Abby would answer that with *How?* So we just sat there watching the flames taper off in our little grill. The word lingered in my mind anyway: *How?*

That question stuck with me beyond our summer-ending cookout, aiming me back toward that old scenario: half court, time running out. Now there was no ball. It was just me. Mortgage payments, eroding savings, and me. I heaved myself not into learning the financial skills by which I might help my family but in desperation into the same kinds of odd digressive investigations that had long comprised my piecemeal religion. I seemed to need this, to need getting lost in learning inanities. I learned that it's hard to find anything about **Schubach** on the Internet. I learned that Steve Balboni, baseball's prototypical lumbering top-heavy brute, somehow tripled in his first major league at bat. I learned that Sneeze Achiu went from the margins of pro football to a pro wrestling career. I learned that his signature move was called a sonnenberg. This term is defunct, no longer in use, but I'm fucking holding onto its meaning. *Sonnenberg.* You heave yourself headlong into midair.

E

Ehlo, Craig

Craig Ehlo heaves himself headlong into midair. He's just gotten the ball back on a frantic give and go. At the crest of his leap he flips the ball at the hoop and then collapses to the floor as the ball nestles through the net. A timeout is called, stopping the clock. Ehlo struggles back to his feet, clearly attempting to keep weight off his injured right ankle. Despite the injury, he has scored fifteen points in the fourth quarter, eight in the last two minutes alone. Because of his efforts, his Cleveland Cavaliers now lead the Chicago Bulls by one point in the deciding game of their 1989 playoff series. There are only three seconds left to play. On the telecast of the game color commentator Hubie Brown testifies that the hobbled Ehlo has played the game of his life.

I hit pause. I'd been watching all this on my laptop on the couch while holding Jack in my lap and lightly touching the downy shading of hair on his head. He was about a month and a half old. I'd initially turned on the computer to find videos of the natural world to show to my citified son, specifically the rippling, echoing call of a wood thrush, a beautiful sound from my childhood in the country, but he'd shown no interest or even any sign that he could fix his gaze on anything. There were several other things I could and should have been attending to around the house, but instead of doing any of them I'd shifted from the half-assed stab at connecting my infant to ageless beauty to my default mode of existence, that of the fan. It gets tiresome to always be defending against ruin. Sometimes you want to just watch old footage of transfiguring reversals. On the screen Craig Ehlo was frozen in the midst of limping up-court with his team in the lead. The video was poised to climax in the next moment of play in arguably the most emblematic image of victory ever recorded, but sometimes, if you're me, you want to hit pause and imagine the loser as the hero. I leaned down and kissed Jack's head, his downy whispering of hair. My wife stomped upstairs. I looked over. She was glaring, furious.

"The cats are pissing outside the box now," she announced. Then she burst into tears.

For years the two cats had been our babies, the most important element of our shared lives. Now they were something of an afterthought, and they'd started damaging our home, fouling the air. I'd been trying and failing to keep up a constant patrol for cat puke and cat shit, playing defense against what was becoming an unstoppable onslaught. The cats had become solely my responsibility. Abby was better at cleaning up after them and taking care of them, but how could she handle this now on top of the round-the-clock work of taking care of Jack?

As my wife wept over what seemed like the new norm in our life, problems against which there was no defense, Michael Jordan was moving left on the screen in front of me, getting a step on his defender, Craig Ehlo. The pause on the video had come undone. Jordan stops, leaps, shoots. Time expires. Jordan lands as his shot falls through the net.

In ad campaigns and retrospectives Jordan, the magnificent winner, then ascends. That famous clip of victory personified is from straight-on and focuses on Jordan's fist-pumping rise. But on my screen now, a YouTube video of the last few minutes from the actual broadcast of the game, the camera angle is from the side, and you can't see Jordan's triumphant celebration. You see Craig Ehlo collapsing to the bottom of the frame, a capitulation in his chest, his arm flailing up like those of someone being flung overboard, and then he drops out the frame altogether.

Eighty-Six

For a while in the early 1990s I lived in a place so close to the Brooklyn-Queens Expressway that the floor shook. I shared the place with my brother, Ian. Every night I unrolled a narrow futon mattress on the gray wall-to-wall carpeting and lay there vibrating. Every morning our fat, aging cat, Annie, would come over and lie on my chest, waiting for me to get up and feed her. She'd been in my family since my childhood, a once scrawny black and white kitten darting around and hiding in a sunny house in the country now old and morbidly obese in an apartment laced with truck fumes. I was twenty-four, had nothing going on. It felt good to have her lying on my chest, to be pinned down by love, or at least its purring facsimile.

Our friend Ramblin' Pete called her Eighty-Six. He always said the name to her in a sing-song, a parody of innocence, and then looked at us wide-eyed, only the faintest hint of a shit-eating grin on his face, and said, "What?" He claimed, groundlessly, that the name just came to him as fitting for her, a tribute to the secret agent number of Don Adams's character in *Get Smart*, but of course that number could not have been more freighted with connotations of ball busting when uttered by a Mets fan such as Pete to two Red Sox fans.

I hated back then to even think about that year, and yet I was entirely complicit in its enduring hold on me. It's easy to shrug it off now, but the way it had all unraveled in 1986 in the bottom of the tenth, Game Six, the moment too much, seemed for many years afterward to be linked directly and irrevocably to all my failings, to that ache in my chest: **can't**. In the mirror, always: visions of Schiraldi. You'd think I would have let go of something that reflected so dimly on my life. And yet the alternative to barely being able to look in the mirror, to wincing at the mention of mere numbers, was unthinkable. I could cease being a fan, cease caring about things that didn't have any direct connection to me. But what would this leave me with? I'd be a man floating nowhere on a trembling mattress. I needed the feeling of Eighty-Six on my chest.

At some point that year, before Ian and I engaged with the landlord in a threat-laden shouting match and had to move, Eighty-Six started puking and shitting all over the wall-to-wall carpeting. We took her to the vet. He gave her steroids. It slowed things down for a while, but eventually she was shitting and puking again everywhere. One day I screamed at her for shitting on the floor.

"Stop fucking stop fucking *stop!*" I screamed.

She scuttled under the couch, frightened, and steered clear of me for the rest of the day. The next morning she didn't come and lie on my chest. Ian and I had to flush her out from under the couch. It took a while. She was scared of me. I wanted to maim myself, be gone. She finally nudged enough of herself out into the open that we could grab her and stuff her in a cat carrier. At the vet we were told there wasn't much else to do. I held her down. The doctor prepared a needle. My brother petted her on the head with just his thumb. She was purring.

I'd been in seventh grade, working on a report on lions. It was spring, just after my first winless season as a Ghost. A friend of my parents, Ehrlich, came to the door with a black and white kitten in his arms. He was trying to give her away. Nobody else was at home.

"She's real cute," Ehrlich said. He held her out to me. "What do you say?"

"Okay," I said. I took the kitten, held her to my chest. She purred. She purred all the way to the end. When it was done my brother and I walked out onto Carroll Street. Bright sunshine blared down. Ian held the empty cat carrier against his stomach, like he'd just fielded a punt. I wanted to block for him. I was never a physical player in any sport, always shying from contact, but at that moment I wanted to throw my body away, clear some kind of path.

I thought about that day years later. I was standing in the bright sunshine empty-handed, just as I had been years earlier on Carroll Street. The day had been a wreck, cat puke on the carpet, cat piss outside the box, Abby first angry, then in tears, Jack wriggling in my arms more and more until he lost it altogether and started wailing, my stomach in knots. At that point I'd taken him out for a walk in the stroller, and he'd eventually fallen asleep. I was sitting on a bench at a playground with the stroller beside me. There was a teenaged kid bombing around on a bike that was too small for him. The sign at the playground included among its prohibitions both the riding of the bike and the presence of kids over twelve, but what is a sign going to do? He kept coming within a few feet of the stroller. I felt something gathering in me. I wanted the kid to get too close. I wanted to leap up and block him. Enough with the invisibilities. I wanted a tangible threat. But the kid rode off, out of the park. The feeling remained. I wanted to provide protection.

Empty Seats

Ian and I were in the living room of the cat-befouled condo I couldn't afford, drinking beer and watching a baseball game with the sound muted. He and Dad had arrived earlier to see the baby after driving several hundred miles. Dad was tired and had gone to bed. Abby was in our bedroom just off the living room, trying to nurse Jack to sleep.

"So. How's it going?" my brother said.

Versions of this question had come my way since the baby arrived. Sometimes I had the urge to tell someone something deeper than the usual platitudes, but I couldn't articulate what this might be even to myself, and it changed constantly anyway. One minute I'd be feeling like the luckiest man to ever draw breath, and the next I'd be thirsting for death's sweet release. In between those two extremes was a sprawling, garbled encyclopedia.

"Great. But I don't know," I said. "It's great. I mean, fuck."

I stared at the game. I took a drink of beer.

"I hear you," Ian said.

As much as it had been anything, my life for decades had been a conversation with my brother, in one way or another, from when we were kids on up through our twenties living together in a series of narrow, truck-fumed apartments in Brooklyn. Even after that conversation started to trail off as we edged into separate lives, my life was still defined by it, by its murmurs and silences. And what had we ever talked about besides sports?

Years earlier we'd stood with an empty cat carrier on Carroll Street in Brooklyn in the bright sunshine. Nothing to say, nowhere we were needed. We ended up riding the subway to the Bronx, got tickets in the nosebleeds. Back then, the early 1990s, hallelujah: the Yankees *sucked*. Nothing but empty seats all around. We spread out, hung our legs over the row in front of us, sipped watery beer, watched the uniformed bodies far below loiter and sprint. Empty seats are considered a lesion, a product of losing, an illustration of uselessness, but in those days they could transform a burden to a blessing. Nothing to say, nowhere we were needed.

Was that the time we saw a lazy fly ball conk Deion Sanders in the head? I wanted to ask my brother about it now, but I had too many other things crowding my throat. Ian and my father would stay through the following day and drive home early the day after that, my brother needed back there, with kids of his own. That first evening of the visit would be my one chance to tell him how it was going, to connect my new life with the life I'd always known.

On the TV screen some guy called for a new ball. The game was a blowout. The camera panned the crowd, such as it was. Empty seats everywhere. The vision calmed me, as if my brother was putting his hand on my shoulder. I took a drink of my beer. My brother took a drink too, then put the bottle down on the table beside him.

"Welp," he began. He put his hands on the armrests and eyed the clock.

"That," I said. I pointed at the screen. "*That's* the place."

The camera was lingering on a man surrounded by emptiness. He wore a cap of a team not involved in the game he was watching and had gone slack with an almost holy disinterest. Ian settled back into his chair, reclaimed his bottle.

"Ah yes," my brother said. "Amen."

Error

There's one photo of my father holding my son. It's from the last morning of the visit, just before he and my brother started driving back home.

"Everyone always makes sure the old man is sitting down first before they hand him a baby," Dad said sardonically. He was sitting on our couch, Jack in his thin arms. Eighty-six years old and zero years old, give or take a few weeks. In the photo they look at one another, eyesight dissolving, eyesight just taking hold, a fogged connection. Both with Mona Lisa smiles.

"Call me One-Eye Lou," Dad had said during the visit, explaining the current state of cataract encroachment.

"My son is seeing now," I'd written in my journal a few days earlier. It was like when I first heard his heartbeat through a jelly-covered monitor. Where there was once nothing, now there was a tiny urgent insistence, a hungering for life, fragile and pure. How do I protect this? I can't commit any errors, but errors are as inevitable as breathing, as cataracts.

The night before, on my suggestion, we'd ordered Indian delivery. Dad was unfamiliar with the menu choices and didn't like what he ordered, some greenish lumpy liquid from the vegetarian section. It sat there on the table in front of him. I felt bad. I always feel bad for something, though often I can't name what it is. At some point he started criticizing modern music, specifically "the rap." He presented a mocking imitation.

"*Fuck fuck fuck*," he rasped while thrusting his thin left arm to the beat. The arm knocked against his plate and his food spilled into his lap.

I don't remember much else about the visit. I only remember the flub with the Indian food because I happened to scrawl down a description of it in my notebook a day or two after my brother and father left. My memory, more and more, is an invention, a creation, like I'm marking plays in a scorecard for a game I never saw, only felt. Hits, runs, errors. Especially errors. I always feel bad, like I've made an error, and I don't quite know what it is.

You can't always know where you will go wrong. Sometimes you can't even know, looking backward, where you went wrong. Identifying an error won't explain anything with any finality anyway. An error is a fiction at the heart of fandom. It offers a fantasy of clarity, of being able to measure loss in specific units. But take even the most famous of all errors, the ground ball that bounded up the first base line in the tenth inning of Game Six of the 1986 World Series. Even if the ball had been fielded cleanly instead of skirting through Bill Buckner's rickety wickets, there's no guarantee that the slow-footed relief pitcher intending to cover the bag, pear-shaped Bob Stanley, would have beaten speedster Mookie Wilson to first. And, as a World Series game will do, Game Six had by this time acquired a kind of cosmic momentum—the Sox were falling apart. The measurable significance of Buckner's error is blurred by its entanglement with the string of inept plays and dubious decisions leading up to it: one pitch from Stanley bounding past catcher Rich Gedman to the backstop, allowing the tying run to score; other, earlier pitches, straight and meaty, authored by Calvin Schiraldi, stroked into the outfield for base hits; the choice on the part of manager John McNamara to keep the customary late-inning first base replacement, Dave Stapleton, on the bench. Impossible to pinpoint where it all went wrong.

I don't know where I've gone wrong or where I will go wrong. I know in my son's seeing eyes there is the lightness of new unfettered life, the possibility of rebirth, of me being able to see a new world through his eyes. All my life I'd been trying to go numb, trying not to see, and now the world is naked and brand new and tender and vulnerable and loved beyond all words in my thin clumsy arms. How do you hold on?

I hugged my father good-bye the morning he and my brother drove home. I could feel his bones through his sweater.

Entropy

Pick a night, any night. For hours a tag-team two-on-one endures, a prolonged version of the last phase of a battle royal, the kind of spectacle Sneeze Achiu found himself in throughout his wrestling career and from which he often emerged, after unleashing a series of spectacular, crippling sonnenbergs, triumphant. But this particular triangulation is unscripted, morose, chaotic, and the conquering behemoth at its center is invisible: the sleepless misery of a baby. And the tag-team duo opposing this behemoth, buckling, staggering, thrown, wed some years earlier in a windowless room in a Marriott, a husband and wife now turning on one another, accusing, glaring, cursing, reeling, getting tangled in the ropes, groping for props, weaponry, multicolored gimmickry, parenting books, folding chairs, holds, moves, the atomic drop, the brain-buster, the wheelbarrow bulldog, anything, everything. A white noise machine churns out an inexhaustible excoriation—*booooooooooooo*—barely diminishing the echoes of a tiny human wailing, all night long and now beyond, into the gray light, daybreak no blessing. I will not let you go unless you bless me. This was the vow of Jacob at daybreak in the middle of the first human contest. He was in a wrestling match he couldn't win, had already incurred a painful, incapacitating leg injury, but he held on. Winning doesn't exist. You hold on.

Ex-

You get thrown. You get traded, demoted, waived. It's inevitable. You get tagged with that diminishing prefix, ex-. *Out of, not, former.* This is the way things are now. Everything is separating from everything else, connections fraying, disintegrating, relations defined by the difference between the present disconnections and the past relationships. Everyone used to belong somewhere else.

The disenchantment with this epidemic of continuous separation finds a focus in sports, specifically in the anger and revulsion that *things aren't like they used to be,* by which it is meant that nothing and no one ever stays the same. From a fan's perspective there's little chance to form a bond with anyone. Fans root for laundry, as in the conceit attributed to Jerry Seinfeld, though that's putting a buffer of harmless absurdity on the situation; in truth we're rooting for commercial and consumer logos, for the human window dressing of large corporations. We're rooting for, and paying for, connection to a manufactured wholeness in a disconnected world.

And meanwhile we're all separating from our youth, ex-players moving toward a permanent bench. I can feel the prefix like a hook in my flesh. It's always dragging me back toward what I thought I once was, back to some golden age, my childhood, a sense of connection with life in all its glowing light and warmth and rippling sunrise thrush-song wideness.

And then there's the future, narrowing, darkened with statistics. What guarantee is there that someone—especially one prone to disappearing—will avoid the probability of having the word ex- attached to the word husband?

You get traded, demoted, waived. It's inevitable. You fuck up. One morning after a long night Jack started crying in the kitchen. We'd been at this for nearly two months by this point and still had no idea what to do. Abby took him into his room. I kept doing the dishes. When I was finished I walked, reluctantly, toward the strangulated bursts of wailing. The unhappy baby squirmed on the changing table, the mobile above him revolving, plinking out the "lullaby, go to sleep" song. Winnie the Pooh characters bobbed and spun.

"How's it going?" I asked. There was a pause.

"Great," Abby said, not looking at me.

"You mad about something?" I said. Another pause.

Marriage begins with vows tagged by an invisible asterisk (*the majority of marriages end in the simultaneous dual creation of the prefix ex-), then endures, always asterisked, always tentative, as a series of loaded pauses. Pauses and the fantasy of replays. As if you could go to YouTube, say, and pull Craig Ehlo back into the frame, pull him up off the floor, pull back time to the previous possession, when Craig Ehlo scored the go-ahead basket on a frantic give-and-go, Craig Ehlo the hero. As if you could then press pause.

"You seem mad about something," I said. Pause. Abby inhaled, glaring at the wall. The pause button is faulty; it never sticks when you need it to.

"I feel like I'm doing all this alone," Abby blurted then began to sob.

Stung, I started shouting.

"My whole life is this baby! I've never worked harder in my life!"

"You're always just washing the dishes," Abby managed to say.

"Wow!" I said.

Then I felt drowsy. It has always been this way—as long as we've been together, whenever I get into an argument with Abby I have an overwhelming urge to go to sleep, as if I suffer from an acute conflict-avoidance disorder that manifests as narcolepsy. I nodded off for a second, dreamed I was on a bus, the sweet one-way bus to nowhere, beside me Calvin Schiraldi now cradling, for reasons unclear, an acoustic guitar. He thumbed the low E string and monkeyed with the tuning, making the note yo-yo. I came to and resumed yelling.

"Wow, I sound so horrible! I mean, god, dishes? What a monster!"

That was about it for the bitter exchange. But I continued screaming, albeit silently. My wife was weeping and my son was wailing, and I was glaring at the floor and screaming my innocence to an invisible jury. *Dishes are such an asshole all of the sudden? Dishes are strip clubs and meth binges?* The only sounds that actually came out of me were some loud breaths whistling through my nose. Meanwhile my overwhelmed, weeping wife continued trying to comfort the crying baby. I didn't know what to do about that situation, so I moved to another room, the kitchen, and noticed more dirty dishes that I hadn't seen before. There's no end to them. I started doing them.

There is no end to anything when a newborn arrives, and the core source of the endlessness is the newborn, but that core is terrifying, unpredictable, fraught with the strong possibility, the certainty, even, of endless failure and mistakes. Whenever I waded into that core, I found I didn't know what to do or that I did it poorly, which made me avoid it. However, as my wife had noticed, every time a dish was dirtied I treated the cleaning of it as urgently as I would the disposal of a live grenade. It was one thing I knew how to do. I also knew the proper approach for playing zone defense, punting a football, fielding a grounder. I knew how to keep score in tennis and execute a crisp chest pass. I knew what constituted intentional grounding. I knew Mark Olberding from Mark Landsberger, Mosi Tatupu from Manu Tuiasosopo, Eddie Yost from Eddie Joost. On and on. What I knew could fill a book, but none of the knowledge, a lifetime in the making, seemed to be of any use.

F

Fidrych, Mark, Unsuccessful Comeback Of
See Pawtucket.

Flitcroft, Maurice
See Hoppy, Gerald

Fold

On the last day of the 2011 major league baseball regular season we took Jack to his two-month checkup, where he got two shots, one in each leg. I held him as the needle went in. I had my Red Sox cap on, the 1970s Fred Lynn model with the blue bill and red crown. I was hoping that after the checkup I'd be able to punch out from fatherhood and be nothing but a fan, rooting for the same vicarious feeling of power and worth I'd been rooting for my whole sidelined life. But when we got home Jack's legs began to swell, and he started wailing. We couldn't find any way to help him. He was crying so hard he started choking.

"What do we do?" Abby said. I had no idea, felt paralyzed. Then I was wrenching at a folded stroller, unable to figure out how to open it.

"Fucking *useless!*" I roared at my hands, my life. I wanted to punch myself unconscious.

"Just—*here,*" my wife said, disgusted. She shoved me aside, opened the stroller one-handed, and belted Jack in. We set out toward CVS for some baby Tylenol. After a block or so of the stroller rolling over bumps in the sidewalk, Jack's screaming tapered off to little grunts and groans. I noticed my fists were clenched. Some may dream of one day drifting in a gondola down a canal in Venice; I dream of one day beating the living shit out of my stupid face. I let my fists open. I took my eyes off of Jack and looked around as we continued walking. Our neighborhood seemed a little ragged, half-abandoned. A poster kept appearing on barred basement windows: "WE CALL POLICE." A flier kept appearing on telephone poles announcing a candlelight vigil for a teenaged shooting victim named Dajuan.

When we got to the store Abby went in while I kept feeding the bumps up into Jack's body by pushing the stroller back and forth over a patch of cracked sidewalk. Jack's face was still pinched and unhappy, but he was quiet. My shoulders were tense, as if I'd been bracing myself to fend off some kind of attack. An El train rolled by overhead. I exhaled. I tried to relax my shoulders. Baseball came back into my mind. The Red Sox had squandered an enormous September playoff lead but, on the last day of the season, remained just barely alive. Maybe fandom is a way to waste a life; maybe it's a way to handle uncontainable worries and hopes.

"One game left," I murmured down to my son, "and we still have a chance. Win today, slink into the playoffs, maybe get on a roll, who knows?"

My awareness of my wife steaming toward us interrupted this monologue. She looked angry. Some young loiterers were slouching near the store entrance, staring at her, commenting. All of them were dressed like Dajuan, the dead kid in the telephone pole flier—baggy jeans, basketball jerseys, baseball caps askew. My shoulders tensed.

"Fuck you!" Abby shouted back at them without breaking stride. I fell in step beside her, pushing the stroller.

"What'd they say to you?" I said.

"Whatever," she said.

I'd like to think I stopped moving for a second, pondering a confrontation, but I didn't even break stride, so deep into my thin bones is the instinct for capitulation. I tried entertaining some violent fantasies, but it was difficult for me to come up with realistic scenarios in which I was able to run up toward the harassing loiterers and cause them all grave pain. I decided I'd have to rely on a lot of surprise groin kicks, as many as I could fit in before their superior strength, fighting skills, and generalized rage at the world ramped up and left me fractured and bleeding on the sidewalk. Really what I needed, I reasoned while pushing my struggling infant home, was a large, powerful weapon, not a gun but some kind of industrial-strength many-barreled taser capable of subduing with agonizing force several members of a gang of hardened catcallers, but even thusly armed in my daydream I saw myself somehow fumbling my grip on the weapon and having it used against me in horrible ways.

Finally I surrendered to that old standby of my life and of the impotent and powerless everywhere: the impossible fantasy of having superstrength. Oh, they would laugh and heckle as the pale ectomorph approached in his 1970s replica Red Sox cap and thick glasses and drab middle-aged garments, but then *wham* and *ca-crush* and *b-doouuzzzh*, bodies flying everywhere, jaws cracking, eye sockets caving in. Oh, the weeping and begging. Oh, my fearsome strength.

We got home and fed Jack the Tylenol, which helped a little. He had a rough evening, but not quite as bad as the afternoon had been, and finally he settled into a shallow sleep. I put the thin chain on the front door, as if that could ever do anything. I found the game on TV. The Red Sox brought a lead into the ninth inning. The closer, Jonathan Papelbon, was called in to hold the lead. He got two outs then surrendered one hit, then another, then another, and the worst September fold in history was complete.

You get older, you put things in perspective, learn what truly means something and what doesn't. Maybe you even mellow a little when your team wins it all not once but twice, or when your wife gives birth to a beautiful baby. But a small part of you or, if you're me, a large part of you is always the boy choking with rage over collapse. The last hit fell in front of Carl Crawford, a highly paid free agent acquisition who had played poorly all year. I believed he could have dived headfirst in an attempt to get the ball, and instead he did a cushy butt slide and was unable to make the catch. He sort of tried, but he didn't try as if everything in the entire world depended on him catching it, as if catching the ball could protect my wife and child. He didn't heave himself into midair. He didn't sonnenberg.

I wanted to boo, but *booing* wasn't enough. I found a recent Carl Crawford baseball card and ripped it to shreds. (A sickening thought occurred to me much later, which I want to but won't edit from this account: one reason I shredded Carl Crawford might be that he is the same color as the loiterers who harassed my wife.) I held the shreds in my hands, still unsatisfied. Still powerless. The image of Jack's swollen legs in my mind. Jack crying so hard he started choking. Our neighborhood riddled with harassing loiterers, dilapidated buildings, "WE CALL POLICE" posters, candlelight vigils. How am I going to protect anything in this new life? How am I going to keep anything from folding? In my hands a baseball card ripped to shreds. I wanted to do something with the pieces, rain them down over everything.

Oh, my fearsome strength.

I used our printer to scan an image of the debris, then uploaded it to my blog.

Take heed, all foes.

Fumble

A few days after I mangled Carl Crawford, my third parent, Tom, came to visit along with his wife, Susanne. Years earlier I'd started calling him my stepfather even though he and my mom had never married and had eventually split. He'd helped raise me through the years when my mom and dad were separated. Every summer he'd been the one to carry me upstairs to my bed, a loft bed he'd built for me, when I fell asleep on the long drive home from our yearly trip to see a Red Sox game at Fenway.

Tom was very gentle with Jack. One afternoon during his visit he took Jack from me as I was trying to dance him to sleep. He danced in a slow rhythm, unlike my own, which always had at the very least a hint of an urgent punk tempo, a desperation. In Tom's arms Jack softened. His eyelids grew heavy. We were downstairs by the stereo. "Madame George" was playing, with its slow, dragging baseline, the hypnotic strings, Van Morrison's aching warble fluttering and spiraling like a thrush song at dusk. I motioned for Tom to carry Jack up the stairs, and he did so, walking slowly, with care. One minute you're the boy asleep in a father's arms, and the next you're walking up the stairs behind him as he cradles your sleeping son.

I pointed Tom toward the swing in the bedroom that Jack had recently started napping in. More often than not when I put Jack down into that swing I'd fumble the handoff, and Jack would come back awake. This would always bother me, often even infuriate me, my own ineptitude in that moment, my fumbling causing Jack's eyes to snap open, as if in the great scheme of things such a thing could matter. Tom put Jack down into the swing slowly, with care. Van Morrison's voice wafted up from downstairs. *The love that loves to love.* The arms that carried me upstairs sleeping in my Red Sox souvenir batting helmet, the baby I lay down to sleep, this touch traveling from Tom to me to Jack. That's what I don't want to fumble.

G

Garbage Time

In late October I stayed home with Jack while Abby went out. He was close to three months old. I hadn't been alone with him much, just once before, and that time Abby had been at a café right around the corner. This time I drove her a few neighborhoods south to meet her friend Caroline. Jack fell asleep on the drive back. I carried him inside in the car seat and set him down on the living room floor. He kept sleeping for a while. I sat on the couch with my hands on my knees and watched him, afraid to do anything else.

The benchwarmer has only one hope of existing in, rather than just outside the margins of, a game. Meaning must be removed. There must be a beating in progress so lopsided and so late in its life that the entry of the benchwarmer into the contest will have no way of affecting the final result. Strictly speaking, the existence of garbage time is, as the name suggests, reliant on the element of a sporting event being timed. You might see the term used to refer to the later innings of a baseball game in which one team is beating another by a huge margin, but it wouldn't be a precise usage, as there is no clock in use, so the vital element of garbage time—the ticking away of seconds that have been stripped of all meaning—is not in play. The term doesn't quite fit in football or hockey, either, because each of those timed sports carry at all times, even during blowouts, an intensity resting on the keen awareness of all involved that at any moment play can result in emergency medical personnel rushing toward a body gone horribly still. Soccer also has trouble maximizing the potential richness of garbage time because scoring a goal is generally so difficult that even in a lopsided rout it will be acknowledged as an achievement of at least some note. In pure garbage time there should be no notable achievements, nothing to get excited about or even to remember. Garbage time must not in any way matter, and so it finds its truest home in basketball, which is, perhaps not coincidentally, the game I played the longest. Benches are emptied, benchwarmers arise, shots are hoisted, flung. Nothing matters, nobody cares. Most fans head for the exits. I never do. I sit there with my hands on my knees and watch, not wanting it to end.

Eventually my son's eyelids started to flutter. He grimaced and grunted, jerking his body against the cushiony interior of the car seat. Then there they were, those clear blue eyes, looking at me.

"Hi baby," I said. I glanced up at the clock. A long time to go before my wife was back in charge. Moments alone with my infant son: pure delight bullied by a border of panic.

Glass Joe

I decided the best thing to do was to take him for a walk. Put things in motion. But the stroller was in the folded-up position. I'd been able once or twice to luck into opening it before, but generally it had been a task Abby had to complete. This time I made an effort to figure it out rationally, but within seconds my pulse was quickening, my thoughts racing. As always in situations like this, rather than focusing strictly on the task at hand, I instead did the absolute opposite: breathing shallowly and thinking about my whole life and all its ineffectual tendencies.

You're supposed to want to work your way up through a hierarchy of challenges, overcoming them, winning. I started to realize during college that I was at odds with this line of thinking. It wasn't anything that happened at college that prompted this realization but more the simple fact that college was the last buffer before "real life" was to begin. I intuited without ever allowing myself to directly think about it that upon entry into that real life I was going to eat shit. I had no plan, no desire to scale any hierarchies, no sense even of what the hierarchies about to crush me might be, just that something was going to crush me, and I wasn't going to put up much of a fight.

Soon enough the situation with the stroller had escalated into a helpless thrashing characterized externally by jerky, brutish motions and internally by a self-pitying helpless rage. In short I had abandoned my attempt to methodically overcome a challenge, and I—not the infant—was hurtling toward a tantrum, a fugue swelling on the rhythm of *can't*. *I can't do this, why can't I do this, why can't I ever do anything?*

At my college there was a boxing video game in the snack bar. I was so bad at video games that I generally avoided them, but something drew me to the boxing game. I could never do any better than knocking out the first guy, the patsy named Glass Joe, before getting quickly knocked out and eliminated by the second guy. I got to know Glass Joe pretty well. I even let him hit me sometimes and toyed with the idea of letting him beat me, but in the end I could never resist responding to his puny but persistent jabs by knocking him out. Really what I wanted was for him to lower his gloves. I'd lower mine. I'd drift toward his cartoonish realm and he'd drift toward the supposedly realer world whose edges I blunted with bong hits, and we'd meet somewhere in the middle and hit the road like Jack Kerouac and Neal Cassady, and the invisible hierarchies tyrannizing our lives would collapse in the heat of our road-going bebopping ecstasies, two holy fools free of time, the two quarters I'd slid through the coin slot lasting us forever. But of course he never lowered his gloves, and so I beat him, which was always merely a prelude to my own beating, my avatar's arms flailing impotently as the guy just one up from Glass Joe thrashed me, several increasingly tougher fighters above him, the whole world minus Glass Joe unbeatable.

It made me angry to be so helpless. Stabbing the buttons on a video game. Wrenching at the levers and wheels and legs of a stroller.

"I can't do this why can't I do this why can't I ever do anything?" I roared.

The infant beside me had by this point added his own piercing cry to my tantrum, but he calmed down first, sensing perhaps that without Mommy on the scene, with just this taller, stupider, scarier Mommy filling in, he was going to have to take care of himself. You'd think seeing this would have dampened my own raging, but my mind kept jackhammering *can't.*

Finally I bashed myself in the head with a two-handed blow. The impact made me stagger backward from the stroller, blinking. This kind of assault was not unprecedented. Whenever the unbeatable hierarchy of life was smothering me, sparking a helpless rage, I punched myself in the head. I was trying to stop. I had even promised my wife that I would stop forever, and I lied to her that I had. It was my secret pathetic addiction. I was my own Glass Joe.

Goalby, Bob

For some moments before Bob Goalby was declared the outright winner of the 1968 Masters golf tournament, it appeared that he was tied for the lead with Roberto De Vicenzo and that the two would play an eighteen-hole playoff round the following

day. But then it was discovered that De Vicenzo's playing part-
ner for the day, Tommy Aaron, had entered the wrong score on
the seventeenth hole, penciling in a four instead of a three. De
Vicenzo neglected to notice the mistake before signing off on
his scorecard, and by rule the higher score, though inaccurate,
was posted as De Vicenzo's official result. Goalby was given the
championship. Though Goalby had been a highly skilled professional golfer for many years and had played the tournament of
his life, he was degraded in the public conception as someone
who had backed into a beautiful thing. Messages came his way:
You don't deserve this.

Years ago, when I was thirty-five, Abby and I moved away
from New York City to stay with her parents in Racine, Wisconsin, and look for work in Chicago. I had few marketable skills.
I could load a box onto a truck, stand behind a cash register,
check a bag, push a broom. To some extent I could also stare at a
page and notice mistakes. Months passed. I ate American cheese
slices from Abby's parents' gleaming refrigerator and drove
around aimlessly, staring out at bowling alleys, Burger Kings,
Green Bay Packer lawnware. *Why are you here?*

At some point I started killing afternoons at a driving range.
I bought bucket after bucket and drove yellow balls out into a
stubbly field. My ability to drive yellow balls out into a stubbly
field improved. Most days I was the only one there. Once, a mom
was there with her little boy.

"Someday you'll be able to hit the ball as far as the man,"
she told him.

I thought: *Man?*

Every so often in Racine I played actual golf with Abby's
dad, and I never saw any progress in the awful level of my game
in the context of an actual golf course. There are skills, and then
there are skills. Mine seemed to be entirely hypothetical, that
whole passage in Racine hypothetical, a bubble of **garbage time,**

nothing to do, nowhere I was needed. Eventually I got a call from a publishing company in the Chicago suburbs that needed a part-time proofreader. I was shown a cubicle and given some pages. I started staring at text looking for mistakes. Years went by. Without ever planning to do so, I stuck with the company like a barnacle. Most weekdays have been a Xerox of that first day. But some kind of wandering is still inside me, some mostly beaten wildness. My mind wanders at work, and I miss mistakes. They slip through. I know it's happening all the time. I worry someday they'll be discovered.

I was thinking about all this as I sat in the park along the lake with my son. Slowed by the aftereffects of punching myself in the head, dizziness, shame, I had finally gotten the stroller open. I'd walked my son toward the park, feeling like I always did after these self-assaults: dully stunned, awful, calm. I didn't seem to have the skills needed for the simplest afternoon alone with my son, and yet here I was with him anyway. I took Jack out of the stroller and pointed up at some branches, some brittle leaves.

"Tree," I said. "Sky."

I carried him to the edge of the grassy area of the park and pointed at the sandy beach. Gentle waves flowed in from a lake that stretched forever. It was a beautiful late October day, my son at the center, an unimaginable love. My head still throbbed, a repetitive message always coming my way. *Why are you here? You don't deserve this.*

Goat

The Dallas Cowboys had a chance to pull into a tie with the Pittsburgh Steelers in the third quarter of Super Bowl XII. Quarterback Roger Staubach fired a strike into the end zone to a wide open reserve tight end named Jackie Smith. Smith, who would one day be elected to the Pro Football Hall of Fame, had been a standout for several years in **obscurity** with the St.

Louis Cardinals. Before the season he had been ready to call it a career, but the Cowboys, the reigning NFL champs, had talked him out of retirement. The prospect of finally winning it all lured him back to the field. He did not catch a single pass all season, but then there he was, where everyone who has ever so much as tossed a football back and forth in the yard dreams of being: in the end zone, in the Super Bowl, all alone. Staubach's pass ricocheted off his chest. The Steelers seized on the mistake and rolled to a touchdown on their next drive. The Cowboys rallied late but couldn't recover, and the loss landed on Jackie Smith. He was the guy you never want to be. He was the goat.

The video from the fateful moment shows Smith jerking his body backward in disgust, a quick motion, as if he's being jolted by electricity, but a photograph taken at that instant strips from the intended receiver all traces of animation. It'll come up at the top of the images page if you ever search for Jackie Smith. He's a rigor mortis plank, upended, cleats in the air, shoulders and silver helmet just touching the turf, arms locked to his sides. He looks not as if he has dropped a pass but as if he himself has been dropped. One theory of life is that we were thrown from heaven. We had wings but no more, and now we're falling.

I was eleven at the time of that Super Bowl, and I was a Cowboys fan. It's probably no accident that around that time I started forging a path of avoidance. I never wanted to be responsible for anything. It seemed a horrible thing to be the goat, to be responsible for a team's loss, a sacrificial receptacle for all disappointment and pain. The deeper I got into sports, into life, the more I tended toward the margins, as if sensing that this was my only way of avoiding the destiny of the goat. I wasn't conscious in my pursuance of the margins, but I ended up there anyway, and if there's a reason for this, beyond my limitations as an athlete, it would be that I was terrified of becoming a goat. I hoped to never become anything good or bad.

I stood on the beach holding my son as little waves rolled toward us. Strings of diamonds kept forming and dissolving on the surface of the water. As Jack's blue eyes looked past me to the sky, his eyelids started to droop. When they closed altogether, when the tops and bottoms of his brittle, shining eyelashes meshed, I felt it like a soft fastening click in the center of my chest. The deeper calm of his sleeping body was a weight in my arms that I'd always been missing. In a few minutes I'd start moving toward home so Jack and I could go pick up Abby from her afternoon away from us. Not that long after that, in the great scheme of things, I'd be here, now, retracing those earliest weeks. Here, now, Jack is no longer a baby. Those days are already gone. But I can still feel the small bundle I once held to my chest, the ghost of a touchdown.

I had wings.

God

See Norwood, Scott

Volume 2:

4–6 Months

H

Harold

Where is the pitchback I had as a kid, that mesh bouncy thing with the aluminum frame that was supposed to be my friend to play catch with but that was never much fun and eventually crumpled to backyard rust? Where are the braces that were supposed to straighten my teeth but only wrenched the childhood smile from my face? Where are the dribble goggles my team, the Ghosts, used once in junior high basketball practice and never again? Where is the Leaper, that screeching plastic and metal rack, gleaming and medieval, peddled to the varsity basketball coach at my high school that was supposed to give us all the ability to sky for rebounds and windmill dunks but only made our shoulder sweat mingle and our knees ache? Where are all the contraptions and props all over the world, everything ever used in an impossible attempt to shackle or shunt or splint or redeem the inevitable expansion of doubt?

You'd think I was asking this all rhetorically, that there's no way to know where any of it has gone, that it's all scattered uncataloged in storage units and attics and landfills all across the world. But there's a specific kind of exhaustion that brings everything back, tangled. Two in the morning and the baby wailing, defeated

equipment everywhere—bottles, pacifiers, jumpers, parenting
books, strollers, Velcro swaddle wraps, clutter exponential, hallu-
cinatory, my metal braces cutting the inside of my mouth again,
my dribble goggles impeding my vision, a customary adolescent
semirod tenting my underwear. I rose from bed and tripped on a
pitchback. I was late for my required Leaper thrusts.

I stumbled onward and took the baby from my wife, who had
been up all night. I tried to calm him. I rocked him and bobbed.

"Shh, shh, shh," I hissed into his ear, as one of the parenting books instructed. The white noise was supposed to be sooth-
ing. It didn't work, and within a few minutes I ran out of the
moisture in my mouth necessary to make this hushing sound. I
emitted something like the thin buzz of a dying windowsill fly.
Jack kept crying. Abby took him back. This had been going on
for nearly four months, long enough for it to seem it would go
on forever.

I lay down and, despite the suffering and failure bristling
in the room, drifted off again, my body one more piece of
faulty equipment on our harried bedding, scrambled in with
dislodged fitted sheets, baby clothes, rattles, teethers, mobiles,
a shake weight, a grip strengthener, a novelty putting practice
cup festooned with a *Caddyshack* gopher. At some point I rolled
onto the sharp fingers of a one-armed mannequin. It was Harold, the piece of unorthodox remedial athletic ware that minor
league instructors in the Los Angeles Dodgers chain assigned
twenty years earlier as a batter's box inhabitant to a struggling
number-one draft pick: **Bene, Bill**. Harold still had the mustache
Bene had drawn on him with a marker as well as several contu-
sions from pitches that had gotten away from the guttering prospect, but he also now had marker stubble all over his face, as if
Bene, or someone, had wanted to depict some sort of erosion of
grooming habits. His left arm was missing.

I got up out of this mess and moved again toward Abby and Jack.

"Let me take the baby," I said.

"Just go sleep on the futon downstairs," she said grimly. "This is how he is now."

I took Jack from her anyway and rocked him to sleep, but he was wide awake and unhappy again within a few minutes. Abby got up with him. I lay there, guilty, drifting off occasionally only to be stabbed by a mannequin arm.

Just before five I got up, fed the cats, and ate breakfast. By then Jack was up again, and I went in and took over the jiggling from Abby. He went to sleep but was up again just minutes after I'd left the bedroom. I went toward the wailing again. That word: again. Again, again, again—the squawking hinge at the center of parenthood. Abby was getting Jack back to sleep again.

"Maybe *you* go lie down on the futon and get some sleep," I said. "I'll stay with him."

"This is what I do now."

"But it doesn't have to be that way right now," I said.

Abby said something I couldn't quite catch beneath Jack's cries, but I knew it had the loaded word "writing" in it. I was always droning on about writing, about how the baby made it so that I never had enough time to write. This was nothing new—I'd always found some way to complain about my writing throughout all the years we'd spent together. Beyond that, I'd always subconsciously woven those complaints into a passive, oblique critique of our relationship. The arrival of the baby had intensified the pressure I funneled into our marriage, ratcheting up that corrosive notion that our life together could be validated in my mind on a certain crucial level only if I suddenly transformed myself into a celebrated Dostoyevskean whirlwind of visionary creativity. Abby had always been supportive of my writing, but who in the world could withstand years of constant whiny dissatisfaction on the subject, especially if I continued to freight that word with all my hopes and dreams even as our son was wailing?

"What did you say?" I shouted over Jack.

"Writing," Abby shouted. "Shouldn't you be *writing*?"

In an ideal world, one in which I forged a measured, compassionate path through life guided entirely by love, I would have ignored the way I heard her say that word, with sarcasm-italics, ignored the sting of that perception, or misperception. I would have focused on the baby's happiness, on my wife's happiness. Perhaps later, during a moment of relative peace, the baby asleep, I would have brought up with Abby the subject of my writing as it affected our marriage and tried to work through the swamp of desires surrounding writing that had seeped into our life together and flooded it slowly and thoroughly with a sludgy unidentified muck. But who can ever act with such reserve and love and resolve, especially with a baby wailing?

Instead I took Abby's question about my writing as a shot, a bit of mockery. I took it as if she knew the truth about me, which was that since the baby had arrived any possible writing time was as often as not given over to beating off to photos of Kim Kardashian's ass spilling over the overmatched fabric of a tiny bikini. Like all who are full of shit, I was in constant fear that someone would point out that I was full of shit.

"I am balancing everything," I said. "You don't have to *tell* me to write."

"If that's what you're getting out of this conversation, you're excused," Abby said.

I remained stuck on this for hours. *You're excused?*

"What a thing to say to a guy going in there to try to help," I complained later while staring at the ceiling. I was downstairs, near my desk, but instead of writing, I was lying on the futon. My hand was down my pants, lazily, just in case things ended up going that way. I was also prepared to race from the futon to my writing desk to furiously imitate a frenzy of literary productiveness if I heard footsteps on the stairs. My eyelids were heavy, my grasp of the strike zone shot.

"She gets mad at me when I try to help," I said aloud. If anyone had been leaning down and peering in through the basement window, it would have seemed I was speaking to no one. "She gets mad at me when I don't. What am I supposed to do?"

Harold had no reply. He had fallen beside me into a collapsed pitchback, his one arm tangled in the slackened netting. We stared up at a ceiling of gray sky, clouds upon clouds. I had a customary adolescent semirod tenting my underwear. I used my tongue to poke loose a spongy crumb from my braces. SpaghettiO meatball.

Hitless
See **Velez, Eugenio**.

Hoppy, Gerald
See **Jolly, James Beau**

Hubris
I bought a Butterball turkey to cook for Thanksgiving. It was Jack's first big holiday. He was a week shy of four months old. In the past Abby and I had traveled to see my parents at Thanksgiving, our one visit a year. Because Abby had a fear of flying ever since a plane she was on dropped like a brick for several seconds of blinding terror, whenever we made our one visit to my parents we drove. But Jack was becoming increasingly miserable in the car seat. A thirteen-minute drive was hell; a thirteen-hour drive was unfathomable. For weeks leading up to Thanksgiving I'd avoided making a decision on where we'd go for the day. I'd always tried to avoid decisions, hoping that in doing so I'd also

avoid any consequences. Finally I'd called my mom to tell her we wouldn't be able to make the drive.

"Oh," she'd said. That sound, a brittle oval of heartbreak, lingered in my chest. It was still with me days later on Thanksgiving morning, though I tried to ignore it. Avoid decisions, avoid heartbreak. Find something meaningless.

"Holy shit, check it out," I said to Abby. I brandished the Butterball turkey, still in its mesh and plastic wrapping. Abby was nursing Jack by the window, watching for her parents to arrive. It would be my first time hosting a Thanksgiving dinner. Perhaps this was also a consequence I was trying to avoid acknowledging. What good could ever come from being at the center of any story? Better to stay on the sidelines.

"There's a toll-free number on this turkey," I said.

"Oh yeah?" Abby said.

"Yeah, can you believe that?"

It amused me to consider this. The Butterball turkey was idiot-proof, it seemed to me. You throw the thing in the oven, and then a few hours later the built-in thermometer pops out, and then you take the thing out of the oven. To say I was confident that I would be able to handle this without placing a call to a corporate help center would not quite be accurate. It was beyond confidence. You'll see this in sports just before the worst, most humiliating collapses. There's an assumption that things have reached such a level of certainty that they can only go one way.

"Where can we get champagne this time of night?" I'd asked some friends in 1986 when Calvin Schiraldi was one strike away from clinching a Red Sox World Series victory.

"What moron," I said several years later on the morning of my son's first Thanksgiving, "would ever have to get on the horn to 1–800-BUTTERBALL?"

"Hello?" I said, panicked, a few hours after that. "Is this 1–800-BUTTERBALL?"

Human White Flag

Sometimes the fans of a team enjoying success will identify the player buried deepest on the roster as a human victory cigar, enacting a ritual with linguistic roots in the crowing displays of the NBA's greatest and most obnoxious winner, Red Auerbach, who lit up actual cigars in the waning moments of his team's conquests. In this mutation of the Celtics boss's malodorous swaggering, the mere presence of the head benchwarmer in the action becomes a signal for cackling celebration among fans, who cheer the little-used human for demonstrating how superfluous he is and how his superfluity on the court demonstrates the certainty of a win.

I started thinking about being a human cigar while I was shooting free throws at the hoop in the parking lot of the corporate complex where I work. It was the week after Thanksgiving, when a 1–800-BUTTERBALL operator had been able to confirm that I hadn't poisoned my family by feeding them a turkey that had cooked for hours with a plastic bag of giblets still inside it. My last year in organized sports had occurred over twenty years earlier, when I'd been the backup to the backup forwards on an all-Caucasian northern Vermont NAIA college basketball team that started a melancholy six-foot-four Grateful Dead fan at center and lost unceasingly. I spent a lot of time throughout the 1987–88 Mayflower Conference season practicing free throws. This was an illogical choice, of course: any coach put in charge of my solitary practice hours would've had me frantically chugging steroids or at least learning how to draw offensive fouls in case the other guys didn't want to. But free throws were easier and in principle sounded like a noble thing for a basketball player to work on. And, besides, the coach didn't tell me what to practice.

All the practice that year, all the hours, all the thousands of free throws, everything fed into no more and no fewer than two official in-game free throws, my entire official foul line experience for the year, my last in a uniform. The two free throws didn't matter; I wouldn't have been on the court if they had. The game had been lost long before I'd gotten the call to go in. In this sense I was the opposite of a human victory cigar. I was the human white flag, I guess, although a good white-flag waving sets a standard of grace and honor not altogether applicable to my situation. Naturally, in this near-empty gym there was no one making noise about my arrival on the court. And yet, after I was fouled on a play, I sank my first free throw, and it seemed to me that there was cheering.

It thrilled me. So much so, in fact, that I tightened up and missed the second free throw. This miss has bothered me ever since. All the time I put into studying free throws, all that monastic, pure-hearted practice, and in the end the best I could do was 50 percent, the kind of percentage that gets certain NBA players mocked as millionaire layabouts, too lazy to try. The truth was that it wasn't just the thunderous sound of the cheering that caused me to miss. Even when I practiced alone I was usually able to hit only about 65 to 70 percent of my attempts, which was one reason I kept practicing—out of the sheer frustration of not being able to master the simplest task on the basketball court, a place where I'd spent more time in my life than any other place on earth besides my childhood bedroom.

After the game a blond guy I knew from keg parties came up and told me that he and his friends, two unpretty girls, had gone nuts when I put in that first free throw. This explained the cheer. The slit-eyed sardonic look on his face made me understand that it had been a cheer built mostly on irony and humor and that I was the butt of this *joke* or, more accurately, the foundation upon which the joke of imitating cheering in a situation long past cheering could be built. He also mentioned something about my form. I had indeed constructed for myself during all the hours of practicing free throws a methodical ritual before each shot, which was to bounce the ball four times and squat down on the fourth bounce, pausing briefly, readying for release. It was a solemn thing to me—the four bounces was not arbitrary but rather my earnest tribute to the Buddha's four noble truths. Life is suffering, etc.

"Fuckin' hilarious," the guy said. "We were dying."

I'd thought, to that point, that my form was smooth and satisfyingly "textbook," like watching an instructional video or an American bald eagle in flight. But my fan, or whatever you want to call him, made me understand that all the hours of practice had resulted in a comical display of beady-eyed ostrich-like jerkiness, the comedy residing primarily in the naked sincerity with which the head benchwarmer went about his tasks: as if they mattered.

So anyway, twenty-five years later, shooting free throws in gray late November on the hoop in the parking lot of the corporate complex, I was thinking back to my labored free throw form, all that work wasted, and for whatever reason, perhaps laziness, I altered my usual release point, bringing it lower. I started hitting every free throw. All those years ago I was doing it wrong. The solution had not been in ever-stricter adherence to some four-bounce ritual, to some notion that I could turn free throw shooting into a holy sutra recital, but simply in exerting slightly less energy by way of lowering my release point a little.

I hit shot after shot for a while, then put my collared shirt back on and clipped my ID back onto my belt, my fattened prechild face grinning out from the magnetized rectangle. I crossed the enormous parking lot and entered the building and spiraled inward through a pasteboard maze to my cubicle. Tacked to the inside of the cubicle were phone lists and project schedules and a piece of paper showing editing symbols, all the marks to make to note mistakes. My body was buzzing inside my business-casual clothes, my fingers still feeling the true shots, one after the other, decades too late. A red tack held up a photo of my wife not long after we'd first met, rowing me in a rowboat in Central Park, the beauty at the center of my life, always rowing us forward. I looked at my computer. There were e-mails to respond to, tasks to carry out, quality-control standards to uphold. Just to the right of my computer a yellow tack held up a big Xerox printout of a photo of my son. He stared out at me, looking stunned, beautiful, impossibly new. What was this strange victory I'd been called into?

I

Implode

I dreamed I was back in high school, way behind, a test coming up in a class I hadn't been to all year. I woke from this dream feeling trampled and clammy. I tried to tiptoe out of the bedroom, but there was a cardboard box and vacuum cleaner barrier in the doorway. We'd constructed this barrier to battle our cats' latest concerted attempt to ruin our lives. They'd started pounding on the bedroom door all night long, waking the baby, so we'd begun pushing a scare-cat mechanism, a vacuum cleaner, up against a slab of cardboard that spanned the length of the doorframe to try to keep them away from the door. It didn't really stop them, especially after they figured out the vacuum cleaner wasn't going to turn on, so its eventual effect was to give us a faltering illusion of control over the situation and to add another obstacle to me getting out of the bedroom in the morning without smashing loudly into something. So on this morning I knocked over the whole thing, Jack woke and started crying, and my wife loosed a sigh so deep and cutting it could have pierced titanium.

I fled downstairs "to write." Instead, I just sat there trying to ignore the crying through the floorboards. *Someday*, I mused in a perverse attempt to comfort myself, *the sun will implode.* But then I wasn't sure whether implode was the correct term to use for that inevitable event. Explode? I did a Google search and almost immediately got sidetracked, listing as usual toward the wide world of sports, namely an article titled, "Broncos Rally as Chargers Implode."

"It's bad," Chargers linebacker Takeo Spikes said about his team collapsing from within to blow a twenty-four-point halftime lead. "Every adjective you can come up with as far as disappointment, it covers it."

You could sit and name every term that could ever have its own entry in a complete encyclopedia of failure and it still wouldn't provide the healing satisfaction that language is intended to provide, that feeling of having something named, pinned down, known. All words that related to disappointment, to the atomization of sense and meaning, could be drawn into the implosion and disappear, and still there will be a black hole, a cosmic absence. Someday the sun will implode, or whatever. There are no words we can say that will carry beyond the implosion. Or is it the explosion? I still don't know.

I finished reading about the Chargers' implosion and moved on to another article about the subject of implosion, namely the bungled implosion of a **defunct** coliseum, the O-rena, which resulted in a piece of debris striking and injuring the leg of a bystander. Unaccountably I began fantasizing about being a bystander. They're always innocent. *When I grow up I want to be an innocent bystander.* I willfully omitted from the fantasy any injurious consequences, such as having your leg gashed by a plummeting chunk of rebar from the former home of the Orlando Magic. This absence from the fantasy was ludicrous, as innocent bystanders exist as such only in retrospect, after they have been lucklessly maimed. Eventually I went to work, found out that several coworkers had been let go, that we who remained now had to get supervisor approval to use the printer, that we were running out of pens.

Incomplete

When I think of life, of all that will be seized in midmotion, incomplete, in the inevitable all-ending implosion or explosion, I think of **Bubby Brister**, not when he was a college star or a reasonably functional member of a decent Pittsburgh Steelers team or, at the end of his NFL days, as a clipboard gripper on a two-time Super Bowl–champion Denver Broncos squad, but instead in the middle of his athletic career, when he came up against his limitations, when he was called upon to carry the New York Jets, when he was pressed into duty on a moribund mid-1990s version of that team that toiled in the shadow of another team in a stadium not even located within the borders of the supposed home state of the team; specifically I think of him dropping back in a hurry, knowing his offensive line will not be able to hold back the blitz, and I think of him throwing downfield, of the ball wobbling in flight and nosediving at the feet of the intended receiver. I think of the football bounding and rolling to a palsied stop on the artificial turf.

Is there any happening in sports more disenchanting than the incomplete pass? You have to be in the stands at a game, preferably a game that doesn't matter, preferably in the freezing rain, to really experience it. On TV there will be no lingering whatsoever on the football as it lays on the turf incomplete. Replays will run instantly from many angles, showing, for instance, the surge of defensive lineman toward the quarterback or the faulty footwork of the passer as he faded back or the imperfect route of the intended receiver, and then as the clock stoppage between plays continues there may also be hurried, urgent sideline reports or in-studio updates from other games, everything presented with a staccato seriousness.

There are always versions of this scramble of reportage and instant replay and analysis after every play in football, which is the game with the most fractured connection to the notion of continuousness of any played in the world—and also is, perhaps relatedly, by far the most popular sport in the most powerful nation the world has ever known—but the void between plays reaches its unbearable nadir with an incomplete pass. Part of this has to do with the feelings of fluidity that come from the game clock. A running play or a completed pass will keep the clock running, whereas an incomplete pass will stop it. Even when a running play or a completed pass ends with the ball carrier going out of bounds or scoring, which also stops the clock, the clock stoppage seems different from the stoppage caused by an incomplete pass. In those plays, even when the ball carrier is stopped for a loss, time seems not as if it has been broken but rather as if it is at a pregnant pause.

I haven't been to a lot of live football games, but I did go see the Jets when they had Bubby Brister at quarterback, and so I've seen an incomplete pass for real. Jack Kerouac suggested the title of William Burroughs's novel *Naked Lunch* thusly: "The title *means* exactly what the words say: *naked lunch*, a frozen moment when everyone sees what is on the end of every fork." I've seen Bubby Brister through freezing rain miss his intended receiver. The ball wobbling on the artificial turf, time not just stopped but snapped, that primary imprisoning illusion, its comfort, for one naked instant gone.

Infinity

Reference books lay strewn around the condo. The type of book was dependent on its location in the home. Encyclopedias and almanacs occupied the dim basement level, on and near the table where I would sit, in the early morning, and fail to write, these books open to pages featuring one or another of a small group of major league pitchers through history who had allowed one or more runs and never recorded an out. They had the briefest of entries in the list of names beginning—in my beloved outdated tomes—with Aaron, Hank, and in each of the entries, among the other stats, was what looked like a numeral in defeat, a flattened, toppled eight, the sign for infinity.

Upstairs it was all partially read parenting books, old baseball cards and grocery lists inside each one, marking the location of my surrender. Sometimes I'd run aground on step-by-step directions, which I'd never been able to follow in any situation, let alone one involving an infant wailing into my brain. Other times I'd be thwarted in my attempt to use the books to gain some sense of order and time. I wanted to know, like every other lemming flocking to the parenting aisle for the best-selling series of books, "what to expect."

The series of books using that phrase began with a titular twist on a meaning of the word "expecting," but because of that manual's juggernaut success—tapping as it did into a vast middle-class Caucasian anxiety in this new disconnected age when no one has any idea what to expect and everyone has to figure everything out on their own in scattered anomic isolation from village lore and wise elders and all that other kind of shit from the warm vanished days of yesteryear—the brand was soon expanded into both prepregnancy and postpregnancy directions. I often turned to the one on what to expect the first year. It had little sections on each portion of weeks throughout the first year, with bullet points of what the baby should be doing and might be doing at each stage. It turned parenting into an ongoing barracks inspection.

"It says he's supposed to 'squeal in delight,'" I said to Abby one night. It was a day or so after I'd been told at the office about the pens shortage, the firings. I was still shaken by the defining element of the departure of former employees, which was the speedy seamlessness of the removal. It was the same way each time one of these waves occurred. You'd see a few new blank slots in the black placards on the outside of emptied cubicles. You'd see a box of tissues in one of the conference rooms. Often I didn't know those who'd been removed. This time the people laid off included my friend who'd given me his **Bill Bene** card. He had kids.

"Fuck," I said, looking down at my kid. "Is he ever going to squeal in delight?" I looked back at the book of expectations.

"I don't know," Abby said.

"It's in the 'probably be able to' section."

"Stop reading that shit."

"What do they mean by that anyway—*delight?*"

"Exactly."

"It says to check with a doctor. 'The delay could indicate a problem,'" I recited. We both looked down at him squirming on the carpet beneath this contraption with bells and little cloth animals hanging from it. It seemed impossible that he would ever be able to do anything.

"He's never going to be delighted," I said. I had to bite the inside of my mouth to keep from crying. I'd succeeded in transmitting my saddened worry to Abby, who peered down at Jack looking like she might be verging on tears too. I had the urge at that moment to tell her about the layoffs at work, about how I worried that the wave of eliminations would empty my cubicle too. This was the kind of thing I was usually able to keep to myself, but now I had to fight to keep from confessing that this whole thing, providing for and presiding over a helpless child, was beyond me. To remain silent, I just bit down on the inside of my mouth a little harder. The next day I went to work, and my name was still on my cubicle. While I was at work Abby texted me with some news.

"HE ROLLED OVER!" she wrote. This skill was, I remembered, in the vaunted "may possibly be able to" bullet list. Later, when I got home, we tried to get him to recreate the precocious feat, but he just lay there.

Over the weekend we walked to the park by the lake to take a family picture in the sun. Still brooding over the layoffs at work, I ended up snapping at Abby about her impatient remarks as I fumbled with the camera and Jack began to jerk and whine. After that flare-up I pushed Jack in the stroller across a wide grassy area of the park, moving quickly to get him to stop crying, and because Abby was mad at me or I was mad at her or both, she lagged back instead of racing to keep up, so she ended up walking alone past another in the neighborhood's endless series of young homeboy woman-harassing packs and was duly harassed, and it was my fault in that I should have been beside her or, more generally, should have found some way at some point in my life to be a sturdy middle-class adult capable of providing an oasis of security and calm, if not delight, and a white picket fence and serenity far from our seedy environs. But these times are bad, and I'm forever distracted from attempting to make a sturdy middle-class living by my ruinous attraction to forging some impossible order through the act of writing, and anyway, there is no middle class anymore, and I'm barely clinging to a job that barely covers or does not cover the costs of a family, and so one wrong move, one accident, one bad day, and into the imploding abyss we go. We're headed there anyway, with our new condo in a neighborhood fraying into poverty, which was the only place we could afford a condo, which means my son remains unprotected by me from a breakdown in humane social custom, if not in the form of bullets then in a tangentially related series of crises, one after another, some humiliating, others worse. There was nothing in the parenting books about any of this.

Still, that evening I was playing on the carpet with Jack when he rolled over. It was something to see. I put a check mark next to "roll over" in the parenting book. The 1975 Bill Hands baseball card marking my place in that book is still there, as if the feat of rolling over, the first complicated motor skill plateau, signaled a point beyond which words could not offer any ordering. Things began to develop more quickly after that, it seemed. Soon after learning how to roll onto his stomach, he learned how to roll from his stomach onto his back. At first he did this in a way that caused him to tumble down too quickly and bump his head on the carpet, but then he started doing it more smoothly. The development staggered me, as it revealed a process of trial and error, of refinement, and showed that he was not simply being moved along through various bullet-point stages of development by instinctual evolutionary imperatives but was instead turning things over in his whirring little mind. He was experimenting, asking, growing.

A new, deeper vulnerability set in. My son was charging forward through time. Someday he would get to his feet. Someday he would walk. Someday he would run. The possibilities, suddenly, seemed endless, a scary new version of everything beyond our ability to know what to expect. I stopped reading the parenting books. I couldn't stop looking at my encyclopedias.

Someday my son, it stands to reason, will ask me about infinity. This is a concept that used to frighten me as a child. It still does, in some ways: the idea that time and space go on forever, that within this forever we are tiny, finite, without any permanence whatsoever.

If my son asks, maybe I'll tell him about how in baseball earned run average (ERA) is used to show how many earned runs a pitcher would give up in any given nine-inning span. Though the mathematical formula used to determine ERA cannot produce infinity as a result, it does allow conceptual space for what may become of a pitcher who gives up runs but does not record any outs. Math be damned, it is agreed that in such cases the player's ERA is infinite. As far as ERA is concerned, that pitcher will never record an out. The game will go on forever, run after run after run crossing the plate until the end of time.

Of the pitchers with a career ERA of infinity, Doc Hamann faced the most batters—seven—without recording an out and also is the only member of the infinity club to add a wild pitch to his appearance. But he didn't end up with a loss. Of the three pitchers with an infinite ERA and a winning percentage of zero, Harry Heitmann allowed the most earned runs to score, with four. This is in some way irrelevant, though: all the pitchers in question will give up an infinite number of runs. In my view it was Marty Walker who had it the worst. He faced six batters, more than anyone but Doc Hamann, and took a loss as well. He walked three and gave up two hits; a sixth batter evidently reached base, presumably on an error. This means Marty Walker had a chance to escape infinity—he'd done his part. But a teammate—either Don Hurst or Pinky Whitney, both listed by baseball-reference .com as error makers in that game—foiled this chance.

The members of the infinity club are guardians of eternity, of a specific and singular version of eternity, the only version I could ever dwell on without wanting to scream. I like Marty Walker's version of this guardian of eternity the best because he is the only one aided in his guardianship by a teammate, possibly one named Pinky, someone to help carry the burden. We are finite in an infinity. All we can do is bungle ground balls, trying to help.

"We're all in this together," I'll say to my infinity-terrified son.

"But what happens when we die?" he will ask, I assume, because I used to stay up nights thinking about this, sitting on the stairs, asking my brother. My brother would ask me baseball trivia to calm me down. What with genetics and all, what with the eventual unavoidable crossing of thresholds of awareness, the question will probably come back to me through my son.

"Did you know," I will say, "that Marty Walker's full name was Martin Van Buren Walker? He's the only player to be named after the eighth president of the United States."

"But what is infinity? What does infinity mean?"

"Marty Walker's nickname," I'll reply, "was Buddy."

It Is What It Is

"I don't entirely believe in what I do," I said to Bubby Brister. "My job, I mean."

He and I were over by the lake, near the site of my wife's most recent harassment, and I was complicit in a process, primarily acted out by the former quarterback, of feeding footballs into a machine that catapulted them one by one out into the gray water. I had my hands in my pockets but seemed, by relative proximity, to be in charge of the cache of footballs, which were in the reusable bags I sometimes remembered to bring with me to the grocery store.

"I edit these tests," I said. "Multiple choice, mostly, all day long. I sit in a box honing devices to make people fit into boxes."

Catapulting the footballs out into the lake seemed wasteful, risky in a certain special sense: I was worried we'd get caught. An ominous hush settled over everything, the spine of this silence the dull rhythmic thumping of the football catapult. Bubby Brister seemed to be bristling with an anger that I feared I was agitating, if not the sole cause of, and yet I continued to babble.

"There will be a reckoning, maybe, but probably not," I said. "I mean for being so useless. But probably life will just go along like always until it verges on ending, at which point I will suddenly want it to continue. *Wait, wait. Not yet.* That's what I'll be saying. Am I right?"

Bubby Brister turned to me and, with some dramatic deliberation, opened his mouth wide. It was in terrible shape. He let me have a nice long look then narrowed it to a smile, his eyes like those on a mannequin. He spoke, a familiar phrase that jolted the whole moment, the lake, the footballs, to nothing.

I bolted to a sitting position in my bed beside my wife and baby, seized by the nauseating fear that I might lose my job. It had been a couple of weeks since the layoffs, the warnings about the printer and the pens, but I was still waking every morning to this dread. The thumping of the lakeside football catapult had changed to the sound of the cats banging on the cardboard-and-vacuum-cleaner barrier outside the bedroom door. I pulled myself out of bed, into my life, haunted by Bubby Brister's proclamation, his ruined teeth. His teeth had all either been knocked out altogether or existed only as jagged remains. His words formed a motto that had in recent years gained permanence and ubiquity above all through sports, the flat incantation spreading like a deadening viral invasion throughout our only widespread public rituals of doubt and failure. Mistakes, complication, loss—all began sometime in the early twenty-first century to get waved away by this circular meaningless press conference bludgeon.

"It is what it is," Bubby Brister had declared.

Jackson, Bo
*See **OFP**.*

Joke

One day in ninth grade at the end of gym class a girl named Mindy ran to me. Yes, that's how it seemed: my dream of having a girl *run to me* was finally coming true. She was laughing, her white teeth shining. She grabbed me by the arm! The sudden sunny attention was thrilling, and that night and for many months onward, even after I better understood the context of the situation, Mindy's touch, the brief squeeze of my puny biceps, would work its way into my nightly orgies with the women of the early 1980s television landscape. It was the most physical contact I'd had with a girl since fifth grade, when one wearing a George Harrison button on her jean jacket had driven her sneaker into my nuts.

"We want to play you," Mindy said. It took me a moment to realize what was happening, that I was being approached not to be freed from the crushing burden of loneliness but as the emissary of my terrible ninth grade basketball team, that it was another challenge, even worse than the one that had happened the year before, in eighth grade, when the seventh grade boys squad had challenged us and then, laughing throughout, beat us.

What could we do? We had to play the girls. Laughter riddled the proceedings, the girls on the court with us giggling, the sidelines and bleachers pocked with cackling peers. Each team had difficulty scoring, so the game was close for a long time, laughably, ulcerously close. Finally our smallest player, Jon, a good athlete who was during regular games too slight and quiet to avoid being swallowed into invisibility by our collective ineptitude, discovered he could strip the ball from the other team's point guard. He stole it from her and scored a layup, then did it a couple of more times to secure a win that changed nothing: we'd been challenged by girls.

"You got lucky!" Mindy boomed in my general direction the next day in gym. There were others within earshot. I couldn't think of anything to say. I'd always wanted to believe I was good at sports. If I wasn't good at sports, what was I?

"We'd a beatcha without Jon," Mindy concluded. I looked down at my sneakers, the gray wormy laces. A guy named Dale, standing nearby, snickered. Dale did a little bullying in his free time and had the kind of glasses that got dark in the sun and then were supposed to get clear again inside but never really did.

"What a *joke*," Dale said.

Life with a baby, among other things, is often pretty tedious. Time, that fuckhead, drags. You sit on the floor with a rattle for hours. You drift, stiffen, worry, and things long buried arise. How Dale's thin lips curled with loving scorn on that word. How, during the game, a rebound up for grabs, your elbow grazed Mindy's small left breast.

"Oh, Mindy," I moaned that night and every night for a long, long time.

Jolly, James Beau
See Paychecki, Gene

Juggling

I never knew what to do with Jack. That thought, which I'd been trying to keep from myself, crystallized one afternoon in mid-December. Jack was about four and a half months old by then. Freezing rain was pelting the big picture window, driving home the point that going for a walk outside was out of the question, and winter was settling in; we'd be sitting inside and staring at one another on the little square of living room carpet for the next several months.

There was a rattle and some clean, unfolded laundry between us. The rattle had already proved itself useless. Were some guys just born knowing what to do with a baby? I tried dangling a pair of my underwear in front of Jack, as if he were a cat. He stared at it then started fidgeting, his body stiffening. I'd seen this before, recognized that if I didn't do something, he'd start jerking his head back, flailing, wailing. I put the pair of Hanes on my head and pretended to sneeze, dumping the underwear from my head into Jack's lap. The joke flopped. He flung himself backward and started to cry. I put the underwear back on my head, but then, panicking further, I instead tried juggling three loosely balled-up socks. They instantly unraveled. My wife, who had been attempting to find a few minutes alone in a bathtub, conferenced into the situation by way of screaming.

"What are you *doing* out there?" Her voice knifed through several walls.

"Handling it!" I yelled, underwear on my head. I still gripped a sock.

"Just bring him in here!" she screamed. I picked up the boy.

"There, there," I cooed, wanting to hurl myself into a wood chipper. He wailed and jerked, and that's when I almost dropped him. I managed to deliver him in one piece to my angry, soapy, naked wife. Despite the situation, I ogled her like a starving man staring into a bakery.

"Mama's here," she said, and Jack immediately began to calm down.

Returning to the living room, I exhaled and underwear slid off my head. I sat on the couch and tried to hide from all my thoughts behind the vision of my wife's naked body, but the feeling of almost dropping the boy lingered in my hands. From the start the feeling of holding him had been indistinguishable from the anxiety of almost dropping him. Just when I'd been getting used to having the impossibly slight weight of the entire universe in my hands, he'd started this new thing of spiking his meltdowns by suddenly jerking his body like a boated stingray. I'd almost dropped him down the stairs. I'd almost dropped him on concrete. These exceptions had multiplied, becoming the norm. A lifetime of hesitation and doubt intensified and narrowed to one unceasing question, my life stuck in the in-breath gasp that comes just after a ball has been bobbled, juggled—not an error or an incompletion, not yet.

Among the most famous instances of this kind of on-field juggling came in the latter moments of the 1980 World Series. The Philadelphia Phillies seemed on the brink of shedding the burden of being the longest-tenured team in the league without a title, but then, late in the clinching game, reliever Tug McGraw loaded the bases and catcher Bob Boone and first baseman Pete Rose converged with alarming confusion in the vicinity of the presumed landing area of a foul popup off the bat of Frank White, a chilling echo of the fateful 1912 World Series snafu involving a foul ball landing between catcher Chief Meyers and first baseman Fred Merkle (see *boner*). Boone, in later years, bristling at the role in the play that history foisted on him, would point out that Rose erred in not handling the chance himself, which was indeed much closer to first base than to home, and, failing that, in not even venturing to communicate with Boone as the play unfolded. Without this direction, and fearing that Rose would barrel into him, the hustling catcher made a tentative last-instant lunge for the ball and bobbled it. The ball popped out of his glove and into the air. Rose, as if he'd orchestrated the whole thing, appeared just then, a dashing mop-headed brute, a hero, and snatched the juggled ball from the air.

I was thinking about all this while staring down at the unfolded laundry at my feet. Fucking Pete Rose, I was thinking. Always saving the day, and flying headlong through the air for triples, and racing to first on walks, and shattering catchers in collisions, and mauling middle infielders in brawls, and surpassing immortal records by sheer force of will. Some people never seem to hesitate or doubt. And yet who would want his life now, exiled to forever hunch beady-eyed behind folding tables, scribbling his name again and again like he's signing for a bill that never stops coming? No immunities, no exceptions. Everyone's bound to this book.

Junkin, Trey
See Snap, Bad.

K

Klotz, Red
*See **Losing**.*

Klutz

I dreamed I was trying to juggle but had forgotten how. I lurched around a cramped, suffocating cubicle, knocking over stacks of papers and schedules. An ache in my chest. To have that thing so long with me gone. I woke up on the couch, unfolded laundry at my feet. There was always unfolded laundry. My wife, naked from yet another interrupted bath, another attempt for a few minutes alone, sat across from me in the recliner, nursing Jack.

"Nice nap?" Abby said. She glared at her fingernails. Soap was visible on her body. She must have had to come out of the bath in a hurry, having to attend to a crying baby because the baby's father was snoring nearby on the couch.

"I couldn't juggle," I mumbled. "Do . . . do we?" I got up. I was not very far from crying.

"*What?*"

"We have tennis balls, right?"

There was a catch in my throat. It was suddenly the most important thing in the world to reaffirm that I could juggle. I stalked around the house searching for tennis balls. I bumped into things, clumsy. I found the first two tennis balls in opposite ends of the main floor of the condo. Was everything like this now, dismembered by *entropy*? I went down to the basement. Abby followed with Jack attached.

"What is happening here?" she said.

I was on my hands and knees, peering under a stack of furniture I'd been meaning to lug to the storage closet. Entropy, clumsiness, to-do list always undone. I looked up at Abby. Jack was in her arms. He was naked too. The light fixture in the low ceiling had one of its bulbs burnt out, and the soft light made the dried soap all over her body resemble fading scars.

"You are so beautiful," I said.

"What's wrong with you?"

"I don't know, I can't explain it. It was this dream. I have to . . . "

I got up and went back upstairs. Who would marry a writer? It's like chaining yourself to someone needing, as if it were life-saving medication, to juggle. God, if you exist, hear my deep gratitude to have found someone willing to tolerate my idiotic wanting. Abby put Jack down in a belted high chair and joined the search. She found the third ball behind a bureau.

"Here," she said and stomped toward the bathroom to shower off the bureau dust and dried soap. As I watched her naked ass disappear around a corner, I ached like a fellow in a sonnet of yore. It had been roughly one billion years since we'd fucked. Must everything be subject to worsening change? I turned to Jack. I held the three tennis balls. All I'd wanted to do since waking from my brief slip into unconsciousness was juggle, but now, because the dream had felt so real, something so long with me gone, I was afraid to start.

I hadn't juggled since some time before Jack was born, but I'd been juggling for most of my life. When I was ten my grandmother had gotten me a book called *Juggling for the Complete Klutz*. Attached to the book was a small red mesh sack with three square beanbags inside. All things outside of sports that required trying and failing repelled me, but in this instance I'd kept trying to get all three beanbags aloft at once, a faint, alluring pull in the ongoing failure of something almost happening, as if the latch of a locked treasure chest was on the brink of giving way. Finally it happened, all three beanbags flying. I lost control of my throws almost as quickly as I had all the other times before, but this time the slight difference was unmistakable. I'd *juggled*. Learning to walk must have felt the same way. Learning to ride a bike. A moment **adrift**, the laws of gravity loosened. I ran downstairs to find someone. Tom was in the kitchen flattening balls of dough into tortillas.

"I can juggle!" I said. I managed a very brief but discernible demonstration. Tom's eyes widened with delight. This reaction repeated itself with everyone in my family. But then I marched off to school with my three square beanbags, envisioning kids chanting my name as they carried me on their shoulders through the hallways; instead, everyone I juggled for smiled, then asked over rapidly encroaching boredom whether I could juggle four things, then turned away to other more interesting matters, such as learning multiplication tables or poking one of the classroom gerbils with a pencil. This reaction was a letdown that could serve as a prototype for all subsequent letdowns in my life. Eventually I came to understand that I had devoted myself with uncharacteristic tenacity to learning something so gaudily useless that it could, were it necessary, be used to illustrate the very concept of uselessness.

I kept juggling. It became a solitary practice, like most of the other things I did or would do or still do, like reading, writing, walking, mulling fantasy sports rosters, jogging, shooting baskets, meditating, beating off. I learned how to juggle bowling pins, big plastic rings, sneakers, marbles, clods of dirt, tennis rackets. Anything, everything. I learned to flip things under my leg, around my back, off my head, my chest, my knees, the walls. However, as if to highlight the gulf growing between me, the juggler, and a hypothetical audience, a possible connection, I never was able fulfill the inevitable ubiquitous request of anyone who ever saw me juggling—*can you juggle four?*—with any regularity. I juggled three things, just three things, in increasing seclusion. I tried to imagine that it was some kind of a spiritual practice. At my wintry college, my Zen pretensions at their most pronounced levels, I juggled snowballs outside the classroom before big tests "to focus." I'm sure I secretly hoped that I'd be seen doing so and admired, but no one ever said anything about it, at least not to my face. Once at this college I juggled three basketballs during a lull in a practice for the Mayflower Conference doormat on which I was the backup to the backup forwards. Our terrible coach, an English teacher in wrinkled clothing, noticed this display.

"Wonderful," he said. "All our troubles are now at an end."

It was my last foray into public juggling. Soon after that I also made my last appearance as a uniformed athlete. What is immune to the motion leading to these endings, to all endings? Sooner or later everything is separated from everything. When I was very young my father was separated from the rest of us, becoming a stranger to me, a guy in thick glasses who visited sometimes and seemed unusually clumsy. Surely one reason I'd plunged into sports was to avoid becoming like him, a klutz, as if that's what caused him to get separated. But there's no avoiding separation. Eventually Tom and Mom separated from one another too, and some years after that my brother and I, who clung to one another deep into our twenties, stopped sharing an apartment and then gradually stopped talking with one another as much, moving into other phases of our lives. Eventually even stranger things started happening, reconfigurations, my mother and father coming back together as aging housemates, moving close to my brother and his family, and I found myself far away from this new core and from Tom too, unable, with the new baby, who couldn't bear so much as ten minutes in a car seat, to visit for Thanksgiving. Now Christmas was approaching, the thirty-third anniversary of getting the *Complete Klutz* gift from my grandmother, and I was standing near the infant son I kept almost dropping. I found myself holding three tennis balls, needing to juggle.

So I juggled. It was the same as always, nothing special. But after a few tosses I noticed that my son, who had been gnawing on the corner of a cloth book, was watching me. The book slid quietly to the floor. Jack was smiling.

"Hey there," I said. "Hey, sweet baby."

I kept juggling, turning to him.

Juggling for my family for the first time, for Tom as he made tortillas, for my brother when he got home from basketball practice, for Mom after her day as a paste-up artist at the local newspaper, for my dad on one of his brief Greyhound bus visits, for my grandmother who'd gotten me the *Klutz* book—that was the feeling at the center of juggling, the connection at the center of my life. I could feel it again. I'd been juggling so long that I didn't have to look directly at what I was juggling. I could do it by feel. I could watch Jack's blue eyes follow the rising and falling arcs of the tennis balls. I could feel in my fingertips the faint pulsing buoyancy of his smile.

L

Laugher

Most words used to identify pronounced single-game defeats carry connotations of domination and woe. The losers are routed, whipped, thrashed. But there's something beautiful about losing. Hallelujah for the exception in this subcategory of the lexicon of failure, the laugher, the loss so sprawling that all meaning and intensity dissolve, one team scoring with the rhythmic constancy of a conga line, the other staggering unevenly in no particular direction. Every day with the baby was a laugher, lopsided, too much, and one blurred into the next until life itself was a one big laugher. Whatever I once assumed to center my being—gone in the fog of the laugher. Memory goes screwy. I can't pull from the laugher any one specific moment when Jack first figured out how to change his imitation of laughter, that smiling unbroken "uuuh" sound, into laughter itself. One day it was just there, as if it always had been, a pealing staccato report of voice and breath and joy, a ringing, and it was instantly so central to my life that it's no wonder I didn't notice its arrival. When do you first notice your own heartbeat?

Legend Without a Ring, the

Near the end of Dan Marino's record-shattering career, my
friend Ramblin' Pete got a pair of free tickets to see the Jets play
the Dolphins in the Meadowlands. It was late in the season, and
both teams had been eliminated. A couple who lived down the
hall from Pete's parents had season tickets, and in those years
it became something of a yearly tradition come late November
and December for these Jets tickets to become so unappealing
not only to the season ticket holders themselves but, even at the
marked-down price of nothing, to everyone in their family, all
their friends, all their neighbors, the doorman, the pizza guy, anyone, everyone, that they fell to Pete, the last stop on the flowchart
before the incinerator, and although Pete was an outgoing fellow
with a wealth of friends, it seemed to always turn out that I was the
only person in his life willing to accompany him to such a game.

To get there we had to take a bus from Port Authority. On
the bus to the game against the Dolphins a man wearing a notable piece of headgear bellowed again and again, "Danny Marino,
baby, the legend without a ring! Danny Marino, baby, the legend
without a ring!"

What bothers me is that I can't quite remember the specif-
ics of his headgear. It was either a dreadlock wig or a multicolored many-pointed bell-tipped jester hat or some combination
of both. For a long time I had these details fixed in my mind, but
I seem to be losing my grasp on the past. All I remember now,
for sure, is that the man kept up his refrain for the entire ride,
his voice a dragging, boozy foghorn.

Danny Marino, baby, the legend without a ring!

Of the game I remember nothing. But nowadays, online,
you can search for and find impersonal traces of everything
you've ever touched. I would have guessed that this game would
have been in Dan Marino's final season, when it was certain he

would be leaving the sport without a Super Bowl title, but that year, 1999, I wasn't living in New York, nor was I the year before, and the year before that, 1997, the Jets had their first winning season in nine years, which makes it impossible for the tickets to have fallen to Pete and me. It must have been the last game of 1996, on December 22, the final game in the worst season the Jets ever had, before or since.

According to a box score available online, Dan Marino had 262 passing yards and three touchdowns that day, helping the Dolphins end their season at a keenly pointless 8–8. Afterward, just before the bus driver pulled the door shut to start what seemed would be a morosely quiet ride back to Port Authority, the fan in the distinctive headgear boarded, still jingling, still bellowing the same thing over and over, the chant slightly slower now, his voice hoarse, as if he had not stopped booming his enigmatic assertion the entire game.

Danny Marino, baby, the legend without a ring.

We found it impossible to tell whether he was saying this triumphantly, in celebration of Dan Marino, or mockingly, as if to puncture his enduring glory. You would tend to think it was the latter, but there was something else about the chant: there was some kind of joy in it. How else could you keep repeating such a thing all through a bus ride to a game no one really wanted to attend and all the way through such a game and onto the bus ride home? Would he ever stop chanting his chant? Is he still chanting it yet in some monastery for holy fanatics, the bells on the ends of his jester cap or dreadlocks jingling with each syllable? You would assume that there had to be love in the chant, perhaps for Dan Marino and his spectacular but stingingly incomplete career, perhaps for the incompleteness itself, the feeling of not quite getting that final salving victory that makes everything all right forever.

Several years later, to the day, December 22, I was at the wheel while my baby wailed in a car seat in back. My wife was beside him.

"What do we do?" she said. She was on the verge of crying. We hadn't made it to my family's house for Thanksgiving, but Abby's family was closer, only an hour and a half away, so we were headed there for Christmas. Cars full of other families speeded all around us on an icy highway. I hated driving, had always hated driving.

"I don't know, I don't know, I don't know," I said.

The baby cried so hard that he started choking for breath. My wife unbuckled her seatbelt to climb over the top of his car seat to breastfeed him. It was the only way to make any progress with Jack in the car, but if we got in an accident, Abby would fly through the windshield. I'm not meant for this, I was thinking. After a lifetime of losing, I'm not meant to be at the wheel. I should be a passenger, benumbed. A bus from the Meadowlands, a jingling psalm, life in all its pain and sweetness undone.

Lochhead, Harry

When I was thirty-three I went to a party with my girlfriend. It was around five years after the Dan Marino game. We'd been together for a few months, about as long as I'd ever lasted with anyone. We'd gone to parties before that one, but they'd all been cramped, forgettable beer scrums. This party was in a loft with high ceilings, a big dance floor. If we'd danced together before, I don't remember it. I liked the way she danced, something in her shoulders, a lightness and softness in the way she moved them to the beat. I liked the way she smiled up at me as we danced. Up to that point the message of my lifetime win-loss record had long seemed clear to me. But then that smile. She wasn't intending anything in particular with it, but something about it was different from any way I'd been looked at before.

It'd be nice to say that we drifted on air from that party and have been floating together through life ever since, but things don't work that way. I don't know how they work. On the cab ride home there was some kind of drunken flare-up, a fight. I can't remember the particulars, and even if I did, it wouldn't help me understand how things work. It's odd to write an encyclopedia when you do not know anything, but that's not quite true. I do know stuff, just not anything important.

One thing I can recite with authority—and I do this aloud sometimes, like a prayer, to keep at bay the feeling that I'm losing my grasp of any facts at all—is the winning team in each World Series going back to 1946, and then going back farther than that I can probably get about nine out of every ten winners correct to 1903, the first World Series, at which point baseball history starts to resemble, in its fogginess, my own past.

I do know a little about the 1899 Cleveland Spiders. At the beginning of that year Frank Robison, who owned both the Cleveland and the St. Louis franchises in the National League, transferred all the capable Cleveland players to St. Louis. Every part of the Cleveland roster was gutted, but nowhere so deeply as at shortstop. The longtime starter, Ed McKean, was sent to St. Louis, as was his young heir apparent, future Hall of Famer Bobby Wallace. Just before the season began, the team still needed a body to anchor the infield, so they signed a minor league shortstop from California named Harry Lochhead.

Lochhead went on to lead the team in games played with 148 and errors with 81. He seldom reached base and had no power, tendencies that produced a team low .540 OPS. He's been referred to as the worst player on the worst team of all time. Although this is unfair, given that he and not any of his fellow Misfits or Exiles, as the Spiders were also known that year, manned the most crucial defensive position on the field, the sheer quantity of Lochhead's negative contributions—his mangling of grounders, his wild throws, the ubiquity of his uselessness with a bat—argue in favor of him as the team's epitome, the best representative of the team that lost more games in a season than any team in any sport ever has.

In all, the Spiders amassed 134 defeats against just 20 wins, finishing the season 84 games out of first place and 35 games behind the league's next-worst team, a putrid Washington club that managed a .355 winning percentage despite the benefit of 14 games against the Spiders. At a certain point the Spiders stopped playing home games, just like their football cousins in benchmark failure, the *Dayton Triangles*, losing and exile somehow interlocked, and after the season the franchise was erased. Many of the players who had filled out the roster for the Spiders never appeared in another major league game. Harry Lochhead, proving he really wasn't the worst of the worst, managed to get into 10 more games in the renegade American League in 1901, but that was it for him, and he was out of the majors by age twenty-five. He died just eight years later, at thirty-three, a month after getting overexposure from wandering lost in a desert.

When I was thirty-three I went to a party with my girlfriend. On the way home there was some kind of a fight. I wanted to get back to the good feeling of the party. Back at my apartment, the fight over but still simmering, I went to hug her. She tried to shove me away.

"You shouldn't be with me," she said. "I'm a fucking mess." She started crying.

There must have been a moment just before Harry Lochhead got lost in the desert. He could have turned one way and still been okay. Instead, he turned the other way, and that was it. Throughout my life up until that moment, whenever I had been given a chance to turn one way or the other, I'd always turned in the direction of my losing lifetime record, toward isolation, exile. Maybe I didn't want to do that anymore. Maybe I was drawn to fucking messes. Maybe her smile as we'd danced at the party in the loft with the high ceilings had knocked me loose from all my asterisks.

"I love you," I said. Neither of us had said this before to each other.

You get used to being covered with asterisks, all those little burrs digging into your skin, linking you to every diminishment. You imagine that a moment free of them would sing. But it's more like losing a popup in the sun. You stagger, blinking, bracing for the impact of a new error. You open your arms and hope.

"I love you too," Abby said.

It's blinding, the brightness. You're lost in an unsortable expanse.

Lose

Jack's first Christmas Eve, he fell asleep early. He never did this. My wife and I didn't know what to do with ourselves. We were in Wisconsin, having survived the icy drive up from Chicago. We sat in a bed in her parents' guest room. Jack was in a swing in the corner that made a faint clicking noise as it swayed. The white noise machine hummed, and sleet ticked on the roof and windowsills. A window facing the street had frosted over. Every once in a while the headlights of a car lit up the ice.

One Christmas Eve when I was a kid the windshield of our VW camper froze over like that. The defroster had broken. We were driving through the dark, and every once in a while the headlights of a car lit up the ice. I sat in back with my brother. Up front, in the passenger seat, Mom pressed one end of a tube taken from a vacuum cleaner against a floor heating vent and held the other end up to the driver's side of the windshield. The heat through the tube had opened a tiny circle in the ice. Tom peered through this circle and steered. No one spoke. Everyone watched the tiny circle. To lose it would be to all fly off together into nothing. We couldn't afford to lose it.

I don't remember whether I was scared. I probably was, but if so, that feeling dropped out of the memory pretty quickly. Throughout my adult life memories of that tiny circle in the ice brought back only a sense of togetherness and care and adventure. For a long time I assumed that such feelings were behind me, that I'd lost them, that my own life was in some crucial way frozen over, that I'd lost that tiny opening. For a long time I couldn't tell whether I was flying off into nothing or not moving at all.

But then here I was, part of a new family, huddled in Abby's parents' guest room, watching headlights light up the ice. The fleeting shadows they created made it seem as if the room itself was swaying along with my gently swaying son in his swing. I reached over and squeezed my wife's hand. I was intending only to make some kind of a gesture to communicate my gratitude for being with her, cocooned in this moment, this careful new life, but touching her in any way has a certain inevitable effect. A part of my anatomy becomes that most annoying type of benchwarmer, one who does not know to be cool, detached from the action, but instead is constantly engorged with peppy schoolboy enthusiasm, leaping up at any provocation to show a readiness to sprint into the action.

"Well," I said, "here we are."

Even if my wife didn't notice the bulge in my sweatpants, it was obvious what I was getting at, as I was always getting at it. It had been a billion years since it had gotten any results.

"Yeah, yeah," Abby said. But then she said the words all men long to hear.

"All right, we might as well get this over with at some point."

Throughout my life, whenever I've been afforded the rare chance to have sex with another human being, my starving urgency hinders any sensitivity and tenderness. Most of the time sex with me is not altogether unlike having a duffel bag full of hockey equipment fall on you. However, on this night, thinking of all the weeks my wife had to limp around with her holiest of holies wrapped in gauze, I moved slowly, carefully. This went on for many, many seconds. Afterward I lay on my back and stared at the ceiling as if through a tiny opening in the iced-over world to heaven, or, you know, as if I'd just gotten laid.

"How was it?" I said. My wife said the words all men long to hear.

"Well, it got a little less excruciating as it went on."

I wrote the line in my notebook the next morning. It had made me laugh, and I didn't want to lose it. More generally I didn't want to *lose*. I didn't want to lose this feeling, which, yes, very much resembled the afterglow of sex but went beyond that to include the relief and safety and connection afforded by looking through a clear circle in an iced-over windshield and still seeing open road. I thought I'd lost it a long time ago, but it was coming back to me now, my wife and son sleeping nearby, all of us in a careful new life together. I'd woken very early, just as I'd done every Christmas morning as a kid. Back then I'd spend the pre-dawn hours working through the contents of my stocking, a long white sweat sock, which had been magically filled during the night with little toys and small chocolate footballs and chocolate coins. Eventually I'd reduce the candy to crumpled tinfoil husks, and all the spinners and spark makers and miniature pinball machines would be played out or broken, and the sweat sock would be just another sweat sock. Then I would wait for the moment I waited for all year every year: I'd wait for my family to wake.

I waited for my family to wake now. My notebook was still open on my lap. Fueled by that most volatile of substances, happiness, I got a Big Idea. The key identifier of a Big Idea is that it manages to crowd out all memories of the nothing to which all previous Big Ideas amounted. I would write a book—no, a book-length *psalm*—about the 1976 AL Rookie of the Year and fleeting cultural icon Mark "the Bird" Fidrych. I would free myself, I decided, hyperventilating, from my tiresome directionless encyclopedic sorting and instead write a crisp, linear fable of pure joy. I started mapping it out furiously. "To my son," I imagined writing on the dedication page. The book about the Bird, his one season of ebullient glory, would be my way of passing along to Jack the happiness of being alive, a happiness his arrival had passed along to me. The book would burst with sunlight. It would sell! I'd written books before, but they'd all been complicated hesitating whimpers. This would be a thundering gleeful yawp, and the lemmings would fall all over one another to buy copies at such an explosive rate that traditional talk shows and monetized hipster podcasts alike would begin rabidly clamoring for the blessing of my presence.

"Josh Wilker, thank you *so much* for being here," Terry Gross would finally say.

I'd get used to frat types bellowing my name from afar as I moved through airports. I'd cross demographics. Teens, Asians, retirees. A scene would repeat itself at the grocery store or post office or wherever, a pretty woman inching toward me hesitantly.

"I just want to tell you how much you mean to me," she would say. Then she would begin to cry, just a subtle moistening around her big eyes.

I'd quit my job and on my last day insist on treating my coworkers to a celebratory lunch at one of the nearby deep-dish chains, and I'd raise a glass of Dr. Pepper and thank them for being so kind to me all these years when I seemed to be nothing special, and they'd express their amazement at being cube neighbors to such a massive simmering volcano of cultural influence.

"To life," I'd say. The first sip of Dr. Pepper would bring me back to childhood days, to the first time I'd ever tasted it: a summer afternoon in the backyard, my brother and me playing outside until long after sunset, everything still left to lose.

Losing
See Klotz, Red

Losing Streak
When you look up the word "losing" in an encyclopedia the entry should say *See Klotz, Red*; when you look up Red Klotz in an encyclopedia, the entry should say *See Losing.* There should be in the encyclopedia reader's experience something like the actual experience of losing, that faltering sense of narrative, that faltering grasp on the possibility of going through and being done with losing, losing beyond the ordering of facts, losing doubling in on itself, exponential, infinite, no up or down, beginning or end.

Red Klotz has to be the figure at the center of this encyclopedic reproduction of the vortex of losing because Red Klotz was the figure at the center of losing streaks that went on for decades. He was the coach of the Washington Generals, the opponents of the Harlem Globetrotters. It was his job and the job of the anonymous bodies on his team's transient roster to play as hard as possible—to try to win—within the dooming parameters of a performance that included allowing several undefended gag baskets by the Globetrotters per quarter. He understood it as a job, not as a reflection on his worth or lack thereof, and this awareness of his place in the world allowed him to embrace his lot in life with indefatigable cheer, as evidenced by these remarks from a 1995 *Sports Illustrated* profile: "I don't worry too much about being the losingest coach in history. It's like if you come home at four in the morning and you hear the milkman whistling on the job and you wonder what he's so happy about. It's because he understands his purpose."

I read this article when I was twenty-seven and had dropped out of my arbitrary, half-formed life in the city to spend a summer in Vermont trying to write a novel. I had not yet held a real job, had not embarked on a career and didn't want one, not a real job, not a career. I didn't want to embark on my life's losing streak. I wanted to write a great novel and win. I wrote nothing but shit that summer and barely endured the days by reading old copies of *Sports Illustrated*.

I fantasized then and again at other particularly threadbare times in my life of running away to join the Washington Generals. I understood that the players on the Generals, though charged only with appearing to be decent at basketball, were probably much better players than I was or had ever been. They'd probably played college basketball and were goofing around for a few months before going to law school or taking that job at their uncle's shoe store. Though I'd played college basketball too, this had been a fluke of circumstance, a result of landing by chance at a place with a basketball team that was the worst in the Mayflower Conference, the least competitive cranny of the NAIA, the secondary national collegiate athletic association in the shadow of the NCAA that always featured in its title games, televised in the afternoon on auxiliary sports cable channels, two teams stocked entirely with angular pink-cheeked lummoxes who looked as if they'd been whisked via time machine directly from getting fresh crew cuts at a barber shop in a small town in Indiana in 1952. If I'd ended up at any other college in the country, I would have just kept doing bong hits in my room while listening to Bunny Wailer and not even dreamed of trying out for the team.

And I didn't even make the roster of that team during tryouts. At the end of tryouts everyone filed one by one into an office. It wasn't the office of the English teacher serving as the basketball coach, as he didn't have one at the gym, but instead belonged to the athletic director, who was also the coach of the school's dynastic soccer squad. There were soccer trophies everywhere. There were pictures of the soccer coach and various teams of his posing around various trophies. His players all had spiky Steve Perry mullets and hot athletic girlfriends and were always sleepily shuffling around campus in postcoital flip-flops and pajama pants.

"Josh, Josh, Josh," the English teacher said, "my writer."

I'd been in one of his classes, some intro to journalism thing, a shamble through the days and then everyone gets a B. My enthusiastic term paper on famed muckrakers had edged me up to a B+. He'd been in the newspaper business and now was in some kind of disheveled retreat from that life. You wouldn't necessarily notice he was retreating from something within the dim hues of a classroom, but it stood out in stark relief in the soccer coach's office. The trophy hoister in all the photos was a young, chiseled guy with a full mustache; the English teacher was older, doughier, and his much sparser upper-lip covering seemed part of a general sense of dilapidation, along with his thinning hair, pale complexion, faint acne scars, and wire-rimmed bifocals that were always slipping down his nose. He pushed up his bifocals now and gazed at me for a while across the soccer coach's desk.

"We're going to do something where you will be one of the alternates," he said. I didn't know what he meant, and then after he explained it for a while I still didn't quite know, but later, when I compared notes with the other mediocre aspirants who'd been told they were alternates, I got the picture. The English teacher didn't have the heart to cut anybody, so instead of the customary twelve-man roster, there would be ten real members of the team and six leftovers who would rotate on and off the active squad as the eleventh and twelfth men. At home games we would all sit on the bench, though only two of us would be in uniform, depending on whose turn it was to benchwarm, and for road games only two of us would make the trip.

This arrangement caused me to miss out on the team's most storied moment, when our leading scorer, the melancholy Grateful Dead fan, Nick, poured in forty-six points in a dramatic triple-overtime away game loss to a conference foe who had a star, a black guy, also erupting for over forty points. An actual black guy! This was a real college basketball game!

"It was huge," one of my teammates, the backup point guard, Rat, told me while we were shooting around before practice a day or two after the loss. "Everyone played, everyone pitched in. Nick was epic, but all of us were part of it. *Everyone.*"

"Yeah?" I said. "Everyone?"

"It hurt to lose that game," Rat said, his voice thickening. "But we grew."

I became a permanent member of the roster in the second semester. Imagine being the backup to the backup forwards on a team in the middle of a relentless losing streak, and then imagine this role as a promotion. After the Christmas break some of our players had dropped out or flunked out. In their absence I became a college basketball player in full standing, which, if nothing else, in later years would provide some thin fumes of plausibility to my fantasies of running away to join Red Klotz and the Washington Generals. We lost unceasingly, and so my official playing days came to an end with a long losing streak. It was different from the losing streak of Red Klotz because Red Klotz was doing his job. He knew what he was. He knew his role. I was involved in something more formative. I took it personally, as more in an extended series of evidence that in life there's a fundamental, intractable difference between those bound for happiness and those doomed to flounder. One day well into my team's losing streak I overheard the school's championship soccer coach as he stood outside his trophy-clogged office. He and his all-conference goalie, Jimmy, were cackling about my basketball team.

"Some people know how to win and some don't," the soccer coach concluded. "They don't have any winners."

M

Mandarich, Tony

I hacked at windshield ice with a plastic scraper. Freezing rain fell. Slush leaked into my sneakers. It was a Sunday morning in January, and I was a few minutes away from disappearing into a vision of Tony Mandarich. Certain questions were bothering me. Why had I put on sneakers? Why did I live in Chicago? Why anything? I had not made good choices, or any choices at all. Even the scraper in my hands was subpar, ineffective. How did it even get here? Who decided? And now there was someone, an innocent, sure to suffer as a result of all this lifelong spineless wandering: my son.

Some people know how to win.

I was hearing those words again, the celebrated soccer coach assessing my inept Mayflower Conference basketball squad. For years I'd been in the habit of imagining I'd reacted to these words differently, which is to say, done something instead of nothing at all. I imagined myself instead whirling around the corner with glares or curses or, my favorite, the benevolent gaze of an enlightened mystic. *I have transcended your pitiable obsessions, your trophies and abundant brisk coeducational poontang, your grasping, your infantile sorting of life.* Oh how they would suffer to be so benignly and thoroughly appraised. But eventually I'd settled into years of never turning the corner at all, instead accepting my original response as unchangeable, my adult existence a slide down the wall into a semifetal crouch to revel perversely in the notion that I didn't know how to win and so would never win, *could* never win. That last part was the key: because I couldn't win, the pressure was off. I stopped hearing the chattering of the champions; the pronouncement had entered my bones. But now I was hacking at windshield ice with a piece-of-shit scraper, and the words were coming back.

Some people know how to win and some don't.

I'd been hearing the words resurface elsewhere too. I'd be holding Jack in my arms, dancing and murmuring songs, trying to get him to sleep. Or I'd be walking him in a carrier through my menacing worn-down neighborhood, his warm body pressed against my chest. Or I'd be at work, staring at a photo of him that I'd tacked to my cubicle wall, the thinness of the wall on my mind, not even a wall, barely anything. The Big Idea to write a best-selling celebration of Mark Fidrych had been punctured. I'd run it by some people who'd helped me get an earlier book of mine out into the world, and the response was muted. *Crowded marketplace, nominal subject appeal, blah blah blah.* My own feelings that the biography of a one-season wonder could somehow soar to the heights of great literature also flagged, resulting in the common coda of all Big Ideas: *What the hell was I thinking?* Also punctured by this time was the blind, groundless hope that the money from my job would be enough to cover our bills. All my flaws, my habitual submissions, my tendency to fold, how could this not affect my child?

The cheap scraper in my right hand broke. By then I'd managed to open a small gash in the windshield ice. I got in the car and tossed the pieces of the scraper onto the passenger seat and

stared out through the gash and tried to start driving to the grocery store but was only able to move a few inches before the wheels
began spinning in icy slush. The front right corner of the car
stuck out into the street. Other cars would have to slow to a crawl
to get by. I would be the asshole of each crawl-by. I pressed down
as hard as I could on the gas and listened to the high, burn-
ing whine of the tires. I stopped, the whine still going in my
head, combining with the whines Jack had been producing all
morning and the sounds my wife had been making in response,
that sound of hers, an expulsion of annoyance, exasperation,
exhaustion, connected as if by a thousand tiny electrical wires to
a twistable bundle of tissue at the center of my head: *uuuuggghh.*
I wanted the car to come unstuck so I could drive it into a brick
wall. I stared at the gray world through the windshield opening.
Was I going to have to leave the car jutting out into the street
and walk back into the house without any groceries, with nothing accomplished at all?

Some people know how to win and some don't. They don't have any
winners.

I got out of the car and went around to the back and got
down into a kind of a stance and put my shoulder to the bumper.
As you imagine for a moment a weak, stooped man in his forties
with rain-opaque glasses bracing himself on the bumper of a
car and pushing while unable to retain steady footing in ruined
versions of the black suede sneakers that were in fashion in the
early 1970s and again, among young slouching nostalgic iro-
nists, in the 1990s, it might be useful to know the particulars of
the vision of Tony Mandarich that was overtaking the man from
within and causing him to expel sorrowful animalistic roars
from his shredding voice box.

This vision first began to manifest in the world in 1987,
when Tony Mandarich made the All-America team as a junior at

Michigan State. He led the Spartans to their first Rose Bowl win in over twenty years. The following season he won All-America honors again while becoming a national phenomenon. He was an offensive lineman, and if he had played on the offensive line in the usual way, he'd have remained as anonymous as any other offensive lineman. Being an offensive lineman means you stand guard and attempt the hopeless task of keeping all attacks at bay. You don't matter in terms of individual achievement. You are at best invisible and at worst—when, inevitably, something goes wrong—you are to *blame*. Pressure is constant. Tony Mandarich seemed to have found a way to absorb and distill this pressure into a volatile explosive embedded in the bulging muscles of his massive six-foot-six frame. He turned standing guard into a way to attack. He roared and boasted and taunted. He pancaked motherfuckers, ate their soul. He bench-pressed 545 pounds and ran a forty-yard dash in 4.65 seconds. He was impossible, an armored tank fast enough to win the Indy 500. How could he lose? In a caption accompanying a cover shot of Tony Mandarich bare-chested and enormous, *Sports Illustrated* proclaimed him to be "The Best Offensive Line Prospect Ever."

That cover was the pinnacle of Tony Mandarich, the vision. Just after it appeared he was selected second in the NFL draft, behind only future Hall of Fame quarterback Troy Aikman and just ahead of future Hall of Famers Barry Sanders, Derrick Thomas, and Deion Sanders. Many years later Mandarich confirmed that he had been taking steroids throughout his legendary college career, and he further explained that he had stopped doing so upon becoming a professional due to the NFL's stricter drug testing policies. His failure to be of any use to the team that drafted him, the Green Bay Packers, suggested that the steroids had been the sole reason for Tony Mandarich the vision, the unstoppable destroyer. However, Mandarich himself pinned his demise on an addiction to painkillers. Upon entry into the NFL he began injecting himself several times a day with Stadol, which is often administered to women in labor. The addiction hollowed his raging desire to conquer and destroy. He stopped giving a shit about anything but numbness.

"It was euphoric," he said of Stadol.

"You guys could sell this shit on the street," my wife said of Stadol. She said this just as it was first coursing into her body through an IV tube a few long hours before Jack was born. A nurse and I laughed at the quip, but Abby wasn't laughing. She explained later that the drug was an instant unwelcome riptide in her body, but ultimately it couldn't touch the pain she was feeling. Instead, it just pulled her away from being able to speak, sealing her off from everyone.

"It was awful," she said of Stadol. "I kept having these waking dreams. I was back on the street I grew up on, and everything was made of plastic."

"Like the trees?" I said. "The grass?"

"Everything."

You're isolated, in pain. Doubt corrodes what you thought was real into an imitation. In 1992 the Packers cut Tony Mandarich not long after the same national mythologizing entity that had canonized him publicly derided him: a caption on the cover of *Sports Illustrated* proclaimed him to be "The NFL's Incredible Bust." The cover included an inset of the earlier cover, as if to mock the version of Tony Mandarich that used to be considered real. The larger photo on the cover was of Mandarich kneeling on the sideline, glum, balding, useless.

After getting cut he was for a while nowhere but in his addiction. The superficial collective apprehension of Tony Mandarich ended there, with his fall, with him being, as he is often conjured in this new superficial age of endless internet list making, arguably the biggest NFL **bust** of all-time (however, *see **Next Ryan Leaf, the***). His greatest victory, getting sober, as well as his admirable return to the NFL as a serviceable offensive lineman for the Indianapolis Colts, is not a part of the most commonly told tale of Tony Mandarich. He was fixed in place as an object of derision, a poster boy for steroid use. I can't join in that derision because if there were a steroid for fatherhood, I would be its poster boy. You'd see me in the before and after and after-after pictures. This is always the three-step photo slideshow for steroid poster boys.

Before: the user's vulnerable natural state.

After: the bulked up unbeatable behemoth.

After-after: a sallow man-boobed outpatient wearing an Aunt Jemima kerchief to hide alarming purplish lesions and hair loss; or court hearings, beady-eyed denials, a noxious misting aura of generalized shame; or simply a vanishing, in its wake a mockery, the vision of an unbeatable monstrosity now lampooned as a fraud, an unparalleled disappointment, retroactive asterisks blooming into a stinging poisonous swarm.

In my case the first picture, the Before, would show me watching my newborn cry on a cold metal table as a hospital orderly cleans him of blood. I'm the only one watching, as my wife in that moment is plowed under by exhaustion and pain and the after-effects of spinal anesthetics and terrifying intravenous visions of plastic trees and, more specifically, is in that moment getting the deep rips in her vagina sown up. It's just me, and I'm happy and worried and want my son to stop wailing, but how? In the next picture, the After, I would be—what? Crushing a fastball six hundred feet? Breaking the world record in the one hundred–meter dash? What would be the very picture of undefeatable fatherhood? All the bills paid, all the broken things fixed, all the heavy things carried to where they need to be, all the dishes washed, all the laundry folded, all the worries calmed, all the struggles and burdens shouldered, all the joys spotless, unmarred. A happy wife, a son always laughing, a growing mountain of money in the bank. Who gives a shit about the after-after? I have been weak too long; make me powerful now. Make me into the vision of Tony Mandarich, the most powerful protector who ever lived. Many years after this vision was punctured, in a 2008 interview with the *Arizona Republic*, Tony Mandarich, the man, distilled the draw of steroids to one word:

Q: How did the steroids make you feel?

A: Bulletproof.

This kind of power, the power of certainty, invulnerability, is most often manifested throughout our asterisked world in fantasies of unstoppable disruption. This doesn't quite mesh with the core demands of fatherhood. Being a father is like being an offensive lineman. You stand guard, try to keep all manner of attacks at bay. Pressure is so constant as to be itself invisible, impossible to locate and defeat. When I try to describe the feeling of failure in fatherhood I can't point to anything specific beyond that pressure of always either being nowhere at all or in defeat. I want to grow so incredibly strong that I not only withstand the pressure but go on the attack against it. I pancake that motherfucker. I eat its soul! I am Tony Mandarich before his fall, Tony Mandarich, huge and fearless, the dream of Tony Mandarich, bulletproof.

So when I hear those words.

Some people know how to win and some don't. They don't have any winners.

When I hear those words I turn the corner, and I'm the vision of Tony Mandarich. I drive the two longtime residents of my mind, the celebrated soccer coach and his spike-haired disciple, down the hallway and through a cinder block wall and out across the snowy fields, and they're screaming and begging for mercy, and I drive them right off the edge of the fucking earth. Then I pancake that motherfucking void. I eat its soul! I am Tony Mandarich before his fall, Tony Mandarich huge and fearless, the dream of Tony Mandarich, bulletproof, annihilating doubt. I am in the freezing drizzle on a cold Sunday in January, roaring, driving my shoulder again and again into the back bumper of a gray 2005 Ford Focus that will not move.

Marinovich, Marv
See Marinovich, Todd

Marinovich, Todd

If I manage to get any truth at all into this alphabetization, let it be that every morning when I woke and dragged myself out of bed and moved toward the bedroom door I turned back before leaving the room and saw the most beautiful thing I'd ever seen: my wife and son together, safe in sleep. Their chests rose and fell with slow, calm breaths. I opened the door and stepped with care over the cardboard and vacuum cleaner barricade we'd set up to try to keep the cats from scratching on the door. I wanted to protect the fragile, beautiful sleep. I want to protect my son's beauty. I want it to endure so that he sees it in himself always and so that his whole life unfolds in some kind of dance of beauty and not, as mine has, in a meandering arrhythmic series of retreats and hesitant lunging mistakes. But it's unavoidable. Everyone is bound to a life of mistakes. This was easier to accept before I became a father. But when I began starting every day by seeing the most beautiful thing I'd ever seen, I fell into the hope that beauty can endure. This is a core hope of fatherhood, the basis of every father's attempt to steer his child away from the kinds of mistakes he made.

There's a mug shot of Todd Marinovich taken from just a few months before he became a father. After many years of ravaging drug addiction the former NFL first-round draft pick had finally gotten sober, but the pressure of the impending birth of his first child, a son, caused him to relapse, and he was arrested for failing to report to a court-mandated drug treatment program. In the mug shot it's hard to see beauty. See pain, see doubt. See a father. See *Marinovich, Marv.* See the man whose failure to stick in the NFL in the 1960s inspired him to devote his life to training techniques, to discovering how and why he failed, who applied all he learned about maximizing athletic potential to the relentless training from infancy of his son, Todd, to be a beautiful football superstar. See crippling pressure. See obsession. See a father who sees himself as valuing his role as a father above all else in life.

"Some guys think the most important thing in life is their jobs, the stock market, whatever," Marv Marinovich once said. "To me, it was my kids. The question I asked myself was, 'How well could a kid develop if you provided him with the perfect environment?'"

How could you fault someone for valuing fatherhood above all else? How could you fault someone for valuing his son's development and for wanting to create a perfect environment? You could parse the man's statement and perhaps take issue with the language, the way it is subtly casting children into the role of commodities, equivalent to the products of a job or a stock market killing. You could even raise questions about the idea of perfection, how striving for such a thing is always going to lead to unrealistic idealizations, which in turn will lead everyday life into continuous disappointment.

It's a little unfair to pick apart the word choices of a father ready to try as hard as possible to do what he thinks is right for his kids. Still, I find myself going along with everyone else in wanting to vilify Marv Marinovich. He's worse than us, right? He's worse than I am as a father, right? Surely his mistakes are beyond the scope of any I could ever make. This is probably true, simply because, when you get right down to it, I am half-assed.

Thank fucking god I'm half-assed. Thank god I am someone prone to giving up and giving in and not really trying my hardest, someone always looking for the easy way out and hoping every day above all for an easy time of it and to eat twenty chocolate chip cookies and drink whiskey and have a nap and watch TV. To make a really big mistake, you have to do something. The only thing that separated Marv Marinovich from other loving fathers was a total unbending commitment to his goals. He was and is great at what he does, and what he does is train elite athletes, such as Troy Polamalu, Tyson Chandler, and Jason Giambi. Another of his trainees, B. J. Penn, arguably the greatest pound-for-pound mixed-martial arts fighter ever, summed up Marv Marinovich's talents: "I honestly believe nobody has dedicated their life to athletic performance more than he has. He is the best I have ever seen in my life when it comes to sports performance."

The passion and genius he brought to his calling were based in personal failure, in his own inability to last in the NFL. He had been a college star, but upon entry into the NFL he overtrained with no subtlety, lifting more and more weights, which caused him to become too bulky and slow and to injure himself. After this failure he studied Eastern Bloc training methods and became a visionary believer in flexibility and speed. When his son Todd arrived, he wanted what all fathers want: to see their children succeed where they had failed.

When Todd Marinovich was born he was beautiful, surely, just like all babies are, at least to their parents, and this beauty endured and manifested in the world thanks, in a way, to his father and thanks to Todd Marinovich's own brutal devotion and sacrifice. The father started working with the son in the crib with exercises designed to improve strength and flexibility. The training never relented. By the time Todd Marinovich was in high school he was nationally famous as "Robo Quarterback," a reference to the movie *Robocop*. The stunningly exhaustive, unrelenting practice regimen designed by the father and embraced seemingly without hesitation by the son, coupled with the son's record-breaking on-field performance, suggested a teenager somehow beyond human weakness and doubt.

The standard story about Todd Marinovich jump-cuts from this vision of metallic teenage invulnerability to a montage of controversy, failure, squandering, strife: a bitter rift with his college coach; his resulting early departure from college; his predraft bust for cocaine; his brief, drug-addled NFL career; his many years of criminal arrests, wandering, and vagrancy; his occasional stabs at more football in the Canadian Football League and the Arena League, the former undertaken at least in part with hope that it would be a steppingstone back to the NFL and the latter purely to scrounge up money to buy heroin. The moral of this montage is usually: see Marinovich, Marv. See the results of an overwhelming pressure for perfection, for beauty, that the father exerted on the son.

I vaguely remember watching Todd Marinovich play in college for USC and remember that the nickname that had been pinned on him didn't seem to fit. Robo Quarterback implied the stiff motions of the relentless half-cyborg in *Robocop*, but Todd Marinovich wasn't stiff at all. You can see what I'm talking about in his most famous on-field moment, the winning play in a legendary 1990 shootout against UCLA. With nineteen seconds on the clock and his team down by four and twenty-three yards from the end zone, a tall lefty takes a snap, darts backward, sets, and, an eye-blink before getting leveled by a blitzing defender, fires a perfect spiral to receiver Johnnie Morton in the back corner of the end zone. The scoring play begins and ends in an instant, but that instant is a distillation of a lifetime of passion, practice, sacrifice, blessings. There's balance, speed, precision, vision, poise—all things that could perhaps be programmed into a robot—but there's also bravery and a racing, human fuck-you rhythm (encased in emphatic permanence in the aftermath by a photo of Todd Marinovich, still on the turf, giving a UCLA defender the finger), and everything is electrified by lightning-bolt grace. See ease under pressure. See a conduit for beauty.

See the most beautiful thing I've ever seen. My wife and son together, sleeping, my wife on the edge of our bed, Jack in a bassinet beside her. Sometimes her arm rested on the edge of the bassinet, her fingers touching his rising and falling chest. She breastfed him during the night, and sometimes when I left the room and looked back they would still be together on the bed, my wife still on the edge but turned inward, toward Jack, who was in the middle, curled toward his mother and she toward him, two parts of one being, the gentlest and most beautiful being alive. I had just been part of that beauty, on the other side of Jack, another layer of cocooning warmth and protection around him.

One day in January the cold eased up enough so I could take Jack to the beach. I carried him against my chest. When we got to the lake I turned sideways so he could look out at the water. Another father was nearby, his daughter in a stroller. We exchanged the usual info: names of babies, number of months the babies have been in the world. The two babies had been born within a week of one another, both about six months old now.

"It's brutal right now, huh?" the father said. "Getting them to sleep in their room alone. Every night, just a *battle*."

"He's, uh, still in our room," I said. "He's still . . . " I paused, as if the word I was about to say was something unseemly. "He's still breastfeeding."

"Oh yeah?" the guy said. "Really. Huh."

I began to realize that we were going to be the weird ones. Right around then a billboard went up in a nearby city, Milwaukee I think. We must have seen it online, a photo of a baby sleeping next to a large, gleaming meat cleaver. I forget the exact words of the accompanying caption, but it was something like, "You wouldn't let your baby sleep with a knife, so why would you let her sleep in the same bed with you?"

Abby and I laughed it off, the shrill conflation in the billboard of the risk factors in cosleeping (smoking, drinking, formula feeding, mushy mattresses, puffy comforters, etc.) with cosleeping itself, the benign, survival-supporting norm for the vast majority of the many centuries of human life on earth. But it was just another hint that we were starting to make choices that were veering us and our son away from the beaten path. Before Jack arrived I assumed without even thinking about it that I'd be the farthest thing from Marv Marinovich. I assumed I would not be a father making consciously unusual choices for his son. I assumed things would just flow along the path of normalcy, that such a path would present itself as the way to go simply because it was the way most people were going, like when you get off the subway and don't know the direction of the exit and so just fall in step with the crowd. But it wasn't like that. It was more like the line of scrimmage was crumbling. You scramble, try to see.

Mathematically Eliminated
*See **Playing Out the String.***

Mendoza Line, the
I tried to see another book. My Big Idea for a Mark Fidrych masterwork was dead, but another Big Idea grew out of it. I'd been clinging to one thing I'd learned during the brief frenzy of research on the Bird: in 1980, while in the minors and trying to make a comeback, he had undergone treatment from a

hypnotist. That story floated out of my imaginary Fidrych biography and into a story of the 1980 baseball campaign, which seemed, the more I thought about it, to be an unsung and highly valid choice as the most exciting year in baseball history. It featured two blistering divisional races, a rookie sensation so colorful as to rival the 1976 unveiling of the Bird, the Bird himself embracing hypnosis in bush league desperation, a hidden but pervasive influx of cocaine, the unveiling of Billy Ball, a golden-haired superstar flirting with a .400 batting average, and, finally, a World Series championship for a team that had never before, in all ninety-seven years of its existence, finished the year on top. I came up with a title and a sprawling subtitle: *The Highest Season: Racing for the Pennant, Chasing .400, Philly Soul, Super Joe, and Blow.*

This Big Idea fizzled even quicker than the previous one. I scrawled lists of people I should interview, but then within a few days of creating these lists I crumpled them up and tossed them. What, was I suddenly David Halberstam? When would I even conduct these interviews with Dallas Green and José Cruz? During my half-hour lunch break at work? While holding a screaming baby?

And yet I couldn't stop researching it for a while. The last thing I clung to from that year was not its pinnacle, embodied by that famous shot of reliever Tug McGraw leaping with joy the moment the long-suffering Phillies won the World Series, but its nadir, the Seattle Mariners, who lost a league-high 103 games. I was drawn to the fact that during this disastrous effort Mariners shortstop Mario Mendoza had the strongest year of his career with the bat, and yet this personal best made no impact on the fortunes of his team. Worse, it seems likely that the 1980 season was the one in which Mendoza's name started to become synonymous with poor hitting.

Most histories of that term bearing his name, the Mendoza Line, trace its origins to 1979, when Mendoza's Seattle teammate Bruce Bochte noticed that the shortstop always seemed to be at the bottom of the Sunday batting averages, next to a mark hovering around .200, sometimes just above, sometimes just below. Bochte coined the term to describe the border demarcated by a batting average of .200. Seattle teammate Tom Paciorek then passed the term along to George Brett, and Brett (who would spend the 1980 season in serious pursuance of the polar opposite of the Mendoza Line, the .400 mark that has proven itself elusive to every major league hitter since 1941) passed it along to ESPN broadcaster Chris Berman, who passed it along to the world. ESPN aired its first broadcast in September 1979, so even if Berman had debuted the term during the last month of the 1979 season, it seems probable, given the term's newness and the fledgling network's limited reach, that the notion of the Mendoza Line wouldn't have begun taking root in the culture until 1980.

I was twelve that year, which perhaps explains my adult urge to freeze it in book form. It was my last year in little league, the year I was one of the big kids in our small town, the year I hit a home run and made the All-Star team. It was the last year, given this modest athletic success, in which I knew with any encyclopedic certainty who I was. From there the defeats began to proliferate, fortifying the idea that I was in some way made for defeat. This idea has endured. Consider what consumed me throughout the beginning of my new life as a father. I was drawn to the idea of a scuffling Mark Fidrych trying to be hypnotized into believing he still had electric stuff. I was drawn to the Mendoza Line.

I'm drawn to defeat. When does something like that take hold? Maybe sometime after 1980, but maybe in some ways it started before that. My faulty memory only goes back so far. Before memory, according to a few pictures, there was a fat, startled baby. Before that, life on a cellular level, no conscious-ness whatsoever, just one tiny cell splitting into two, then two into four, and so on. Before that, who knows? All we can consider is life, and life is a constant process of denigration, of division, of one thing splitting into two. The dawn of consciousness is a grasping of this process of division, of duality. There is self and other, good and bad, right and wrong, life and death, winning and losing. It's a wound, duality. Maybe you find ways to numb the division inside, that feeling that you're not quite cutting it, that you're falling below some sort of definitive threshold or, worse, that there's not even a threshold, that there are no definitions or directions, no borders, no lines, that there's not even a falling.

Murphy

The alphabetic sprawl of all major leaguers through history includes forty-one Murphys. One is known only as "Murphy," no other name, first or last. Murphy played one major league game, on August 16, 1884. That day, for the Boston Reds, Murphy had four plate appearances and reached base once, by a walk. At catcher, Murphy made two errors, perhaps prompting a switch to left field, where no balls were hit his way. He is my favorite character in my favorite narrative, the one I first started to study back in childhood.

The first baseball encyclopedia in my life didn't actually venture in detail back far enough in time to include Murphy in its story of the game, so it wasn't until my twenties that I dis-covered Murphy. It was when I was living with my brother, Ian, in the apartment that trembled when trucks rolled by on the nearby BQE. Ian was working as an editor at a company that pro-duced an encyclopedia that included all major leaguers, even those from before 1900. I was leafing through it one day, losing myself in my favorite story, which never exhausted itself or set-tled into any lasting solidity. I came upon Murphy. Murphy was not alphabetically the opposite of Aaron, Hank, but for me he was the opposite of all that greatness and order in the world. He was anyone, no one.

In a few hours I'd go to my job on the evening shift at a liquor store. It was one of those nameless days. The short entry for Murphy made me happy: his marginality, his brevity, his errors. After the discovery I got on with my day: shower, subway ride, ring up some liquor sales, lock the gates, subway ride home. I wanted to be a writer, and the idea I had for my life at that time was that before each day at the liquor store I'd work diligently in the service of that dream. Some days took the shape of that intention, but more often I sat around in my underwear eating toast and engaging in what most people would classify as wasting time. But is it a complete waste of time if on one of those days you discover Murphy? I got this feeling every once in a while back then—sometimes when I thought I was in love, sometimes when a particular song had a hold on me—that there was something so beautiful in the world that it made me want to shout, this desire like a collapsing star in my throat, obliterating all the words I might ever be able to say. The fucking wonder. Murphy was nobody, Murphy was here.

Jack's arrival in my life ended any possibility of sitting around for hours eating toast, but I still managed to find ways to waste time. One day in late January, the morning that Jack turned a half-year old, I started researching Joe Charboneau, 1980 American League Rookie of the Year, whose rapid demise was made official with a 1981 demotion to the minors after grounding out while pinch-hitting for Jerry Dybzinski, who, a couple of years later, became the *goat* of the 1983 American League Championship Series by failing to advance a runner on a crucial bunt attempt, instead reaching on a fielder's choice, and then ending his team's rally altogether by running to a base that was already occupied (*see **Pulling a John Anderson***). I don't

know why I'm drawn to Murphy, and to Charboneau, and to
Dybzinski, but on the morning my son turned six months old
I found myself not planning some kind of a celebration of the
milestone or attending to any number of responsibilities and
problems emanating from my new life as a father but instead
sifting through the Google newspaper archives to research
Game Four of the 1983 American League Championship Series,
the Dybzinski game, and I couldn't help but roam even farther
from that already pointless roaming, veering off of an article
on Dybzinski's mistakes to read other articles in the old newspaper. That pull—away from what I'm supposed to be doing, to
something else, to everything else, to what I imagine I might be
missing—is the defining aspect of my life: to digress, squander,
dick around, wander, waste, disappear, go missing. I ended up
reading an article about the Atlanta Braves, who used to be the
Milwaukee Braves, who used to be the Boston Braves, who for
one season shared a city with the short-lived Boston Reds, who
for one game employed a man known only as Murphy. In the
article Atlanta Braves manager Joe Torre voiced regret about
not speaking to Phil Niekro directly when the Braves released
the aging knuckleballer. In the article the word "something" was
misspelled.

"With all that's gone on and all that's been said, I felt
uncomfortable calling him, but I knew it was somnething I had
to do," Torre said, according to the AP report.

I got that feeling, that private irrepressible wonder. I wanted
to shout. *Somnething.* It's the kind of error that doesn't get missed
anymore due to SpellCheck, the automated tool embedded in
word processing programs that instantly displays a squiggly line
below any misspelling (so long as the misspelling is not also a
word). I see it underneath mistakes onscreen but feel it everywhere. A squiggly line seems to run beneath everything, a constant tremor of uncertainty, fixes needed. How could it ever be

any other way? Human life begins to form when one microscopic sperm cell among hundreds of millions (or billions and billions, counting all the platoons sent day after day for decades on suicide missions to socks, tissues, shower drains, etc.) slips through a virtually impenetrable series of impediments, an exception to the rule so outlandish as to be a definitive mistake, something miraculously missed. All my life a series of misfires and missing and disappearing and then this: my inexplicable somnething, my son.

Volume 3:

7–11 Months

New England Patriots
See **Asterisk**.

New York Mets, 1993
See **Young, Anthony**

Next Ryan Leaf, the

A used Dodge Intrepid looms over my life with Abby. It first materialized years ago, just after we'd moved out of New York City and were staying at her parents' place in Racine while looking for work in Chicago (*see* **Goalby, Bob**). We needed a car. Neither of us knew anything about cars. Neither of us knew anything about what our new life together was going to be like. We were grasping at an idea that the used Dodge Intrepid was some kind of an encapsulation of what we thought our new life had to be. It was dark blue and clean and big and seemed sturdy. It was bland, apparently capable, midwestern, a regular American car for a regular American life.

Neither of us ever got comfortable with it. Abby, a fan of the space program of the 1960s, that high point in American capability, put a NASA sticker on the bumper. A few weeks later, while I was driving back to Racine from a writing conference in Vermont, the car broke down. The transmission was shot. The replacement transmission pawned off on me by smiling mechanic-shop criminals in upstate New York where the car had stopped working turned out to be another lemon and conked out a few weeks later. At that point, after thousands of dollars of our savings had vanished down a dark blue hole, Abby's father stepped in and insisted on helping by buying his daughter a new car, a small black Ford Focus.

This car lasted for years, steady and reliable, but it was always a faint, nagging reminder to me that I couldn't quite manage a regular American life on my own. A relative to this nagging reminder was the memory of the Dodge Intrepid, a dark blue cloud that appeared above us whenever Abby and I were on the brink of a big joint decision. I don't think Abby shared my sense of guilt and inadequacy over the Ford Focus, but our Dodge Intrepid visions of decision dread were so in synch as to be a defining characteristic of our life together.

"Is this going to be another Dodge Intrepid?" we would ask, though eventually we didn't even need to ask it. We both knew it was there, hovering above our hesitant choices: a big dark blue mistake. We tried to avoid these decisions, preferring a life in which we existed in our adjacent personal decision-making solitudes, but every once in a while we had to make a large joint decision, and it always felt like we were stepping off into nothing. If all our decisions worked out, we might have been able to bury the memory of the Dodge Intrepid, but every once in a while we leaped into nothing and didn't glide or take wing but instead just crashed down hard to earth, like when we signed a lease on an apartment that turned out to be one headache after another, one screaming match with the landlord after another, all through our year there and beyond, into months of a nasty legal battle to reclaim our security deposit.

The problem was not that it had been difficult—when is life not difficult?—but that we had thought upon making the decision that it would be a good one, that we would by some dumb luck be making the right choice, that we would be happy. The problem is that we made the choice together, so when it went bad it reflected on some deficiency in our relationship, some inability to identify a bad decision, some inability to function as a viable unit, a team.

A few months before Jack was born I tested the commute from my job to the location of the condo we would end up buying. It took a long time, but as it wasn't much longer than my already absurd commute, I decided it was okay. I wanted it to be okay. To extend the fantasy of okay-ness, I got off the train and walked to the condo and looked in through the bay windows at an empty dinner table. It gleamed like the very ideal of a table in the light from a stained-glass ceiling fixture. I texted my wife as I walked back to the train.

"This could work," I thumb-keyed.

We'd hardly ever eaten dinner at a table. Our norm was to face the TV, plates in our laps. This had gone on for years. One of my few developed thoughts about parenthood before actually becoming a parent was that I wanted this to change if we had a kid. That vision of the dining room table through the bay window—how can I put it?—it was like seeing a way to the happiness you always dreamed of.

It was like seeing Ryan Leaf before there was ever such a thing as "the next Ryan Leaf," before Ryan Leaf failed so profoundly to live up to the astronomical expectations surrounding him—this failure underscored constantly by the contrasting ascendency of his one-time rival, Peyton Manning—that he became the definitive benchmark of bad decisions, the cloud of doubt hanging over every hope. Before all that, in 1998, Ryan Leaf seemed to have everything you would ever want in a quarterback. The other quarterback slated to go with the first or second pick in that year's draft, Peyton Manning, had mastery of almost as many quarterbacking tools as Ryan Leaf, but Manning wasn't quite as big or as strong—after high school Leaf had nearly decided to spend his college career as a linebacker—and, by reputation at least, Manning couldn't throw quite as far or as hard as Leaf. Manning was believed to be the more cerebral of the two quarterbacks, but Leaf had indicated a keen athletic mind of his own by running a pro-style offense brilliantly throughout his college career. The initial recommendation of the scouts of the Indianapolis Colts, the team with the first pick, was to select Ryan Leaf.

The team set up one-on-one meetings with both prospects. Manning showed up with a pen and a yellow legal pad to take ravenous notes and turned the interview around, pelting his interlocutors with questions of his own about the Colts' system and the role they imagined him having in it. Leaf, later explaining that he was undergoing a medical procedure, did not show up at all nor did he contact anyone with the Colts to say that he wasn't going to be showing up.

It's easy enough in retrospect to point to the two meetings—one quarterback attending in the most active and present way imaginable and the other utterly absent—as a clear indicator of what was to come: Manning embarking on what would be, according to his record-obliterating numbers, the most productive career ever at the most crucial, demanding, celebrated, and scrutinized position in any American team sport, and Leaf managing to appear in only twenty-five NFL games over four harried, miserable seasons, leaving behind nothing but burned bridges, acrimony, mockery. But even after Leaf's no-show meeting with the Colts the general consensus was still that both players were virtually inseparable in terms of who was most clearly destined for long-term success. It was easy to believe that choosing either one of the two prospects would be a good decision.

Both quarterbacks struggled in their first year. In the first and only head-to-head meeting between the two, Leaf and Manning were almost mirror images of one another in quarterbacking performance, both going 12-for-23 with an interception, Leaf claiming a slight edge in total yardage, 160 to 137, while Manning held the edge in touchdown passes, with one to Leaf's zero. Neither had an especially memorable or positive performance that day. But Manning kept showing up. Leaf, not so much. By the end of the season Leaf's teammates seemed to have developed a loathing for him. They were relieved when their team, the San Diego Chargers, acquired two aging journeymen at quarterback the following year and were maybe even a little happy to hear of Leaf's subsequent season-ending injury. He missed his entire second season and started just nine games (eight of them losses) in his third season, after which the Chargers released him. He bounced around to three more teams and managed to start three more games, all with the Dallas Cowboys, all losses, before retiring at the age of twenty-six. He'd had some injuries during his brief career, but he didn't seem to be suffering from any debilitating physical setback at the time of his retirement. He was simply sick of showing up. In his retirement this desire to not show up seemed to expand to include everything. Like his predecessor in colossal disappointment, *Tony Mandarich*, Ryan Leaf developed an addiction to painkillers. This addiction led to trouble with the law that was rooted variously in having the painkillers (possession of illegal substances) or not having them and trying to get them (burglary charges). In early 2013, just a couple of weeks before Peyton Manning was named the NFL Comeback Player of the Year by making an astounding recovery from a career-threatening neck injury, Leaf was moved from a Montana drug rehab facility to a Montana state prison for violating his treatment plan and threatening a rehab facility staff member.

"When I was taking the pills, I didn't have to deal with my feelings of being a failure," Leaf said, according to an article written for *Playboy* by John Cagney Nash, who was for a while Leaf's cellmate in prison. Leaf described to Nash his addiction: "I just sat in my lake house all alone. I'd be there for weeks, and I loved it. But it was so unhealthy. I got high and watched TV and slept. I just liked it. I didn't feel anything. I just lay around, loving it. Anyone who tried to stop me, I was just, 'Fuck you, let me go feel good.'"

I've always circled around a desire that I find reflected in Ryan Leaf's world-canceling mantra, the desire to disappear from all responsibilities, to not have to do a single fucking thing. It intensified, this circling, with Jack's arrival. Almost every day I would understand that I was stupidly lucky, luckier than I'd ever dreamed I could be, to have such love in my life as what I had for Jack and Abby. I wouldn't trade my life for the life of Peyton Manning or any other person on earth. But there were also certain moments when I wanted to trade with Ryan Leaf. Not incarcerated Ryan Leaf or struggling NFL malcontent Ryan Leaf or even college superstar Ryan Leaf, but lake house Ryan Leaf, numb and gone, *fuck-you-let-me-go-feel-good* Ryan Leaf, the next Ryan Leaf, yes, please let me be the next Ryan Leaf. I didn't mention Ryan Leaf by name in these moments. Instead, I would find satisfaction in imagining myself gone, removed instantly from my tangled life to some place of pure irrelevance, a lake house, say, where I would be so alone and undisturbed that I might as well not be there either, a ghost in a featureless after-life, reclining in a La-Z-Boy by a big window looking out on a flat blue infinity.

I imagined these departures when we were having a rough day, all three of us. Jack was crying, my wife was letting out her "uuuugghhh" sound, and I was—what?—wanting to be removed, wanting to take up residence in Ryan Leaf's lake house. It wasn't the sheer exhaustion of such moments that was doing it, though that was a contributing factor. It was that I was in this inescapable web, lashed together with someone, my wife, who did not in those moments seem to love me or like me but instead who seemed to find me, along with everything else, intolerable, a feeling that manifests in ways indistinguishable from loathing, and so I loathed her right back, this woman I loved, loathed her as much as I've ever loathed anything, and the impossible tangle of this situation, as if the three of us were on a lifeboat a million miles from any shore, no one for us but us, a trio of suffering and wailing and loathing, suggested that there was no way out except in my narcotic fantasies of absolute vanishing.

This is not anywhere near the whole truth, and I can't give a single concrete detail from when these moments of loathing gave way to my pathetic vanishing prayers because by that point I'd moved beyond the ability to notice anything except whatever illusion of escape I could paint on a brick wall and then ram myself into, reveling in the pain of that ludicrous contact.

I do remember the moment I realized my wife and I, at least for the duration of that moment, hated one another's guts. It was a quieter moment, not a middle of the night sleepless horror when everyone was going out of their minds screaming and stomping and panicking and blaming but rather something closer to the very dream I had of domestic bliss. Before we'd bought the unaffordable condo I'd stood outside it and looked at the front window and imagined the three of us sitting in there at a table, aglow, together. And then there we were one night, the three of us, sitting at a table, aglow. By then the mortgage payments and astronomical condo association fees had been corroding our savings for long enough for everything to start to seem shadowed by the memory of the used Dodge Intrepid. That night's leathery, disagreeable meat—I don't remember which variety or in what matter I butchered its preparation—coalesced itself, somewhere in my upper chest, into a small belch. Evidently the smell of it wafted across the table to Abby, because she groaned with disgust that was brought to the level of profundity by her exhaustion. This burp thoroughly nauseated her—who can blame her? I hated myself. Dinner continued. I took a bite of a carrot. I felt my wife's eyes on me. I understood that she hated the loud sound of my chewing. I chewed on, hating her for hating it.

What bothered me most was that this was it. For the rest of our lives here we were. I was going to be sitting across from someone, belching in her face, and she was going to remain over there, having her face belched into. What was the alternative? Head for the hills?

Heading for the hills attracted me on the level of a fantasy. And yet the hell of this situation wasn't in the loathing but in the loving. My wife and I had grown into one being. Our son was not the agent in this fusing but the final fastener. All three of us were one being. All families are this way, more or less, and sometimes the families have to separate. If this were to happen to me, as it did to the family I grew up in, I would not be able to take it. It would be unbearable to be separated from my son and my wife. Then again, if I had to, I'd eventually be able to bear it. Humans can bear just about anything. But even in the worst moments I couldn't bear the thought of it. Even in the moments of the greatest loathing, I didn't dream of freedom but something less complicated: nonexistence, blameless death. Or, if I had the luxury of more complicated fantastical thinking, of going back into the past. The next Ryan Leaf, or the Ryan Leaf from a long way back, when Ryan Leaf himself was the next Ryan Leaf.

Sometimes I imagined that I never left the cabin I lived in for a year when I was in my early thirties. It was the loneliest and in many ways most miserable year of my life, and yet sometimes

I found myself wishing I'd never left there. I could still be there harming no one but myself, living out my days, numbing myself to life instead of feeling it.

I didn't have to show up for anything that year. I didn't have anyone looking for me. I didn't have to be anywhere. I didn't have to be "here." This was the horror of that year, but when I thought back to that year the pain was lifted from the memory. I just saw myself in the woods, floating above all bonds but still alive. I didn't want to die. I simply wanted to have never ventured back into the world.

No Mas
*See **Quitter**.*

Norwood, Scott

In February, when Jack was a little over a half-year old, Abby's parents came down from Racine bearing enough beer and junk food to subdue an elephant, and I ate and drank myself into a stupor while the Super Bowl blared. I don't remember any of it. Probably at some point I pointed out Wes Welker to Jack because of the similarity of his last name to ours. But I don't even remember the game's turning point, when Welker, renowned for his reliable hands, dropped a catchable pass. It was late in the game, and the Patriots were clinging to a two-point lead. Shortly after the ball fell *incomplete* the Patriots had to punt, and the Giants rolled to a winning touchdown. So I gather. I pored over the details recently in much the same way I pored over the notebook I kept throughout Jack's first year. I've written in notebooks throughout my life, trying to catch hold of life as it passes, but the one from Jack's first year is the spottiest I've ever produced, an extended, barely legible scribble veering from self-pity to feverish Big Ideas and back to self-pity. I should have paid more attention, watched the ball all the way into my fingers.

"When it comes to the biggest moment of my life and I don't come up with it, it's discouraging," Welker said after his Super Bowl mistake. "That is one I'll have to live with."

I don't remember very much about that first year. But my inability to remember Super Bowls predates that more general amnesia. I rarely remember anything about the biggest game in America. In fact, I only clearly remember two moments from any of the Super Bowls I've ever watched. One was Jackie Smith dropping a pass in the end zone during the second Cowboys–Steelers Super Bowl in the 1970s (see *goat*), and the other was the moment just before placekicker Scott Norwood attempted to win a Super Bowl for the Buffalo Bills against the New York Giants. I don't remember the kick itself, though I've seen repeated replays of it famously missing wide right, cementing the final score at New York 20, Buffalo 19. But I remember the moment just before the kick, when the camera fixed on several New York Giants players down on one knee and with their heads bowed and eyes clenched shut, praying.

Please, God, keep us from feeling your loss.

Obscurity

Dictionaries persist in defining *obscurity* only as something uncertain, in darkness, unknown, but the language of spectator sports, my native tongue, has added vague geographical connotations. I think of it as a kind of habitat, or whatever you'd call a word like *estuary* or *gulch*. I see faltering streetlights, a shuttered downtown, a Pizza Hut by the highway. Empty bleachers. Athletes toiling. The last part is the most important, as *obscurity* will never be used in sports contexts without being accompanied by *toiling*. Obscurity is one of the main—if not the only—places that athletes can toil. It is also usually a place or state of being from which the athletes have just made a tentative escape. The following 2001 *USA Today* headline provides a typical example of the usage in question:

"After Toiling in Obscurity, Qualifiers Get Open Chance"

The article briefly profiles several golf club pros and bush league tour players who managed to gain entry into one of the biggest sporting events in the world, the US Open. One player, Tim Petrovic, recalls driving golf balls out into a swamp from the parking lot of a Pizza Hut where he was employed. Another, George Frake II, is described only as a "New Jersey club pro" who likes the Grateful Dead but is quoted saying something that supports the notion of obscurity as a vague geographical entity, a place defined by its contrast to the bright lights and glory of a Major.

"I definitely feel out of my element," Frake says. "This is beyond a dream."

This is how new fatherhood felt to me. I was out of my element, beyond a dream. I'd been toiling for many years in obscurity and was now in a different place. Obscurity has to do with remaining to some crucial extent unseen, and the minute Jack first fixed his blue eyes on me I was thus unmasked, in a new place of joy and terror. Toiling in obscurity is usually presented as the negative image of the current blessed geography, but there's beauty in obscurity too. There it doesn't really matter if you fail.

I'd first started dreaming about this place as a child, seeing it in the names of minor league towns on the backs of the baseball cards of journeymen. I imagined a life *adrift*. Tidewater, Lodi, Osh Kosh, *Pawtucket*. It appealed to me, obscurity as a revolving carousel dodge from the grim specificity of winning and losing, of adulthood. As I edged out of childhood I gravitated toward obscuring the world with drugs. I liked the feeling of not knowing where I was, that floating inebriated numbness, consequences removed. During the latter, singed-brain stages of a long acid trip at the second to last Grateful Dead show I ever attended (perhaps in the company of George Frake II), I gravitated to the fringes of the crowd. I was starting to come back to myself and didn't want to. I didn't want to be where I was or anywhere else. A barefooted woman in a peasant dress spotted me sitting off to the side as she hurried back to the concert. She shouted something at me over her shoulder with a kind of loud, bullying cheer, a cartoonish all-caps accusation. It's stayed with me.

"WHY ARE YOU HIDING?" she shouted.

Then she was gone. It was as if the remark had daggered toward me out of thin air, a message from some presiding universal authority, the carrier of this message—a cheerful woman bound for communal celebration, for happiness, community, laughter, love—appearing momentarily only as a representation of all I was missing. As with every criticism that's come my way, I saw in her rhetorical question an inarguable truth. I was, without good reason, hiding. Always! This did not cause me to stop hiding or even figure out why I was hiding. I simply continued hiding with a greater awareness that I was doing so. I preferred obscurity.

A week or so after Wes Welker didn't come up with the ball in the biggest moment in his life Jack started running a high fever. Since his birth almost seven months earlier he hadn't been sick. There'd been the time his legs had swollen up after getting shots at the doctor (see *fold*), but no sickness. I was always afraid of him getting sick, and now here it was. My wife Googled symptoms. I Googled directions to the pediatrician. We'd been there before, but I always had trouble remembering the proper approach at one key point when the two-lane street veered into two separate streets. Stay left or right? I always fucked it up. I stared at the map on the screen, our route, wanting to burn it into my brain, these roads, this route, my place in the world, so that when the time came I wouldn't make a mistake. Jack's blue eyes were on me. Now I needed to know exactly where I was.

Offside

One triviality among billions in question on the Internet, that perpetually expanding argument at our fingertips, lists and lists careening to infinity, truth implacable, mythic, flawed, is the notion that French soccer great Zinedine Zidane was never called offside. The appeal of the claim, always with its supporters in any of the chat rooms where the subject arises—zealous romantics battling caustic belittling empiricists—is that it seems to speak to a superhuman sense of control and of place, the ideal of always knowing exactly where you are in relation to everyone else. The nature of the violation and the notion that someone could be in such profound possession of himself and his surroundings as to avoid it is the key part of this fantasy. Avoidance of any other kind of infraction wouldn't be quite the same. Consider Wilt Chamberlain's feat of never fouling out of an NBA game. Coupled with Chamberlain's astonishing scoring and rebounding records, the statistic presents a portrait of an athlete with such tremendous strength and agility that he never had to strain off balance or flail wildly to impose his gargantuan individuality on the game. But to never be called offside, to never get out in front of the play—a claim based not only in Zidane being called offside so rarely that the instances are difficult to find or substantiate but also in a sense of a greater chaotic world beyond the limits of the individual, the action hurtling up and down the field being a spontaneous creation of nearly two dozen men—this is something else altogether. To think that one of these men, and not just any of the men but the most assertive and important player on the field in any game he ever played in, would never step outside the rhythm around him: almost unthinkable, sublime. The idea of a master at home in the dynamic infinite flux of all, never offside, verifies the myth of life as we wish it could be lived: the individual glowing within a golden, flowing web (*see Zidane, Zinedine*).

But life as it is actually lived is another story. There's a German word that can be used to capably describe it: *abseits*. It means aloofly, separately, distantly; secluded, solitary, isolated, cut off from other people. It is also the German word for offside. A player gets ahead of the ball, out ahead of the play, aloof, alone. This is wrong: your solitary actions are hereby disallowed. They do not matter. Everything must be done within the web of all of us; nothing done alone can matter.

Sometimes I found myself wishing we could have raised our baby within a community, like in days of old. Ah, the days of old. Extended family nearby, neighbors a synonym for friends, elders not herded into grim institutions away from the workforce but kept close at hand for their warmth and wisdom. In days of old the experts in healing were part of the community too, woven into the web from which one was never abseits. Now there's really none of that, or there wasn't for Abby and me. How could it be otherwise? My whole life had been a reaching for the dream of some cushiony obscurity, aloof, alone, a place where errors don't really matter. When Jack started running his high fever there was just Abby and me and the perpetual expansion of arguments at our fingertips. There was no end to the information on the Internet that seemed to relate to Jack's symptoms, his fever and suffering, but none of it carried with it any certainty. It could be nothing to worry about or it could be something terrible.

We decided to drive him to the pediatrician. This is what you do with a baby. He is sick? Take him to the doctor. We did this pretty quickly after it was clear that Jack was sick, but at first we did look for a while on the Internet. You want to have some answers. You also don't want to take the baby out of the home, out of the last tiny shred of warm community left. This was the main part of our reluctance. Had we lived in a different time, a doctor would have come to us. But those days are over. You take the baby to the institution, its machinations.

Not long ago I was talking with my wife about that time.

"He got better eventually," I said. "And if we'd done absolutely nothing at all . . . "

"Right," Abby said, "he would have been fine. Minus all the . . . "

"Right," I said.

"I don't even want to fucking think about it," Abby said.

I didn't either, but images of the machinations scrolled. The blood-drawing, the X-ray-machine manacles. Zidane would have known not to make the choice that led to those things.

"He would have gotten better on his own," Abby said.

Jack did get better. It was all a false alarm. It's easy in hindsight to wish we'd never left the house in the first place. Zidane would have known what to do, but how could I? Jack seemed so fragile, so close to being nothing at all, that any indication of inexplicable suffering on his part made me want to rush him to professionals. I wanted to be out from under the burden of making the right choice, the burden of having to be perfect, like Zidane.

OFP

Recently I was watching a documentary about Bo Jackson, and when the story was told of a spectacular game-saving throw he made, I started to cry. I was at work, on my lunch break, crammed as much as possible into a corner of the lower-level corporate atrium, squinting at the film on my phone, eating a salami sandwich, bawling. That Bo Jackson could do something like that, something no one thought was possible, it caught on something inside me, some buried gratitude for beauty. No one believed it could happen. The catcher on the Royals, Bob Boone, the very same guy who had featured in the Pete Rose catch (*see juggling*), was among those beginning to walk off the field under the assumption that the game was over. Boone noticed that the impossible laser throw was sailing toward him from the farthest limits of the field. When Boone made the sweep tag on the runner, Harold Reynolds, the game saved, something gave way inside me, made me weep.

This was the day after my wife and I talked about when Jack had gotten really sick. I didn't want to think about that time, wanted to keep it buried, but it kept rising up. When my half-hour lunch break was over I turned off the movie about Bo

Jackson and swabbed my face with a crumpled Kleenex. There were a few minutes left in the movie. He had just incurred a terrible hip dislocation that would end his football career and reduce his remaining moments in baseball to a hobbled aftermath. I walked to my cubicle thinking about how things can go wrong.

Jack was quiet through most of the drive to the pediatrician, and then he started vomiting. At the doctor's office they pricked his finger for a blood sample, and some high numbers in the reading prompted the doctor to order more tests at the labs in the hospital across the street. There two technicians tried and failed to get any blood from Jack's veins. They opened wounds on both arms and both hands. He screamed and cried until he had no tears.

"He's dehydrated," a technician said.

We used a plastic bottle cap to tip water at his contorted mouth. The technicians tried again to get blood. I held his feet. One technician held his arms. He screamed. My wife bent over him and tried to calm him by nursing him.

"Mommy's here, Mommy's here," she said. Finally one of his tiny veins opened.

"Hallelujah!" a technician whooped. Dark blood drained through a tube from his arm and into a container. Jack kept screaming.

The X-ray was not as prolonged or as awful, but the image may stay with me longer: my baby, still no more than a few pounds of flesh and soft bone, strapped into a Hannibal Lecter restraint, his arms pinned in an upraised position next to his reddened, scream-creased face, the technicians scurrying out of the dim room as the machine hummed and Jack howled and Abby's raw voice kept reaching and falling short of comfort, "Mommy's here, Mommy's here, Mommy's here."

There was some relief at the end of that night, a nurse from radiology who was herself a mother of small children finding us afterward and telling us that the preliminary reading of the X-ray was negative. This seems to be an element of medical crises, these little notes of mercy, people taking an extra step around the monetized, litigation-fending machinery of hospitals to give a kind word. We thanked her. We drove home, still not knowing what was wrong with our baby. I noticed the moon, huge and full and low over the buildings of our neighborhood. It was February. Concrete and metal edges poked up everywhere through a ragged, glowing blanket of snow.

Jack continued to struggle with the high fever. It went on for days. Each day would include a period in which he seemed to be getting better. His fever would come down, and he'd stop writhing and crying and he'd smile a little, even laugh. The weather got nicer. One of the days we took him out behind our building, into the parking lot that looked onto an alley, and we basked for a few minutes in the sun. There was a dripping sound of water from the snow melting on the roof. I pointed to the alley.

"That's where we'll play catch someday," I said.

It was a corny thing to say, especially as it amounted to a statement made aloud to myself, but after seeing my baby wailing with his arms strapped to his head, I needed to see something else, a future, the two of us throwing a baseball back and forth in a garbage-strewn alley. The sunny period didn't last. Within an hour or so Jack was wailing again.

"What do we do?" my wife said.

"He'll be okay," I said.

"But what do we do?"

I went to the bathroom. I didn't really have to go. I just sat in there with the door closed. I had a fantasy baseball preview magazine in there. It was filled with future projections, predictions, lists. It overflowed with the intended reassurance and solidity of numerical tools—BABIP, WHIP, OPS+. I'd played fantasy baseball for years, and for decades before that I'd leaned on sports and the numbers of sports to give some kind of a shape to life, but as I leafed through the fantasy preview with my son's wailing leaking through the door, I couldn't imagine how or why anyone could care about any of it.

The next day Jack once again had a brief spell when he seemed to be getting better. Like the day before, I reached for some sunny version of the future. As he played on the rug I went online and ordered tickets to a baseball game at Wrigley Field in June. It would be Jack's first game. I needed to see something in the future that I could predict, something good.

I'd never felt that need as strongly before, but it had always been with me in some way or another, as it is in all aspects of human life, this tendency to reach forward to something you can control or at least anticipate or, better yet, hope for. In baseball this tendency is crystallized most succinctly in the scouting metric called OFP, which is short for Overall Future Potential. OFP is generated by dividing the total ratings of a player's five tools— hitting, power, speed, throwing, and fielding—by five. In terms of guaranteeing the success or failure of a given prospect, the number is powerless. Bo Jackson, for example, had one of the highest OFP scores ever recorded. He still had to hit major league pitching, which he did with uneven levels of success—strikeout-glutted slumps broken by spectacular, legendary bursts of power—before the hip dislocation ended any chance that his overall potential could ever be realized. OFP is designed to hold power over the future and, as such, is inherently flawed, a term understood to include the sense of its own failure. No number can diagnose what will be, and anything pretending to is a fiction to hang onto in the face of there being nothing to hang onto.

The next morning, before the sun came up, we checked Jack's temperature, as we had been doing incessantly, measuring and measuring and measuring with this one thin tool at our disposal. We found that his temperature had suddenly plunged way down. An on-call doctor told us that our thermometer was probably broken.

"If that's actually his temperature," the doctor said, "he needs to go to the ER right now."

We found another thermometer. Same number.

In the car my wife sat in back, hugging Jack to her chest. I drove through red lights toward the ER. We'd been dressing Jack lightly the past few days, trying to keep him cool, but now he was wrapped in blankets and had his winter hat on. The hat was in the shape of a baseball, white with two arcs of red stitching. That's all I could see of him in glimpses in the rearview mirror. My wife's arms and the blankets and the stitches of a baseball. My world.

At the ER we were told to remove Jack's footie pajamas in exchange for a hospital gown. They didn't have a gown small enough for him, so he wore one made for a small child. Inside it he looked even smaller. They needed more blood. When the nurse saw all the wounds already on his arms and hands she had us remove his socks so she could probe for a vein in his foot. But he kept his baseball-shaped hat on. He kept it on even when he was getting punctured again for more blood, even when he was screaming. When he was screaming, a wild-haired woman in a hospital gown pulled back the curtain on our examination room. She was connected to an IV drip.

"I'll rip this thing out of my arm if you don't stop hurting that baby!" she said. The nurse had finally found Jack's vein, and his blood was flowing into the receptacle, so I knew the worst of this latest mutilation was over.

"He's okay, he's okay," I assured the wild-haired lady.

A resident appeared, a kid-sized Indian guy. This doctor was younger than the 1986 Fishbone "Bone in the USA" tour T-shirt I was wearing. He jabbed a thermometer at my son's tiny mouth, unable to get it in there.

"You've never done this with a baby," my wife said.

"Um," the resident said.

My wife glared at him, but I had to look away. I dropped my gaze to the floor and saw his shitty sneakers. They were no brand at all, the kind you see selling for $15.99 on a rack at K-Mart, except on the rack they're white. His were dirty and gray. The soles were worn down, lopsided. The rest of his visible clothing was hospital-issued, crisp and spotless, able to support the illusion of capability and authority. The sneakers said something else altogether.

I couldn't shake the message from those sneakers even after the hospital pediatrician appeared. She projected a much more reassuring sense of expertise, but while she was in the examination room with us the subject of Jack's white blood cell count came up. The pediatrician was explaining that we needed to wait for further results that would help explain the elevated white blood cell count. My wife, whose thoughts always spiral toward the worst horrors imaginable, said the word leukemia.

"No no no," I said before she was done saying the word. "Let's please not even."

"It's okay to talk about it and get it out there," the doctor said. She said more, but I wasn't able to take it in beyond that it was generally reassuring. The gist was that there would probably be other indicators if the word my wife said was involved.

"Probably?" my wife said.

"Let's just wait and see what these latest tests say," the doctor said.

"What kind of word is that?" my wife said after the doctor had left. "*Probably*."

"He's okay, he's okay," I said, but in my mind I kept seeing the resident's shitty pair of sneakers. You live for a long time under the assumption that bridges won't collapse, that manhole covers in the sidewalk won't give way. But in the end these things are all made by people: like Scott Norwood, like Wes Welker, like me. We're all wearing shitty sneakers.

"Everything's okay, sweet baby," I said to my son, gently stroking the baseball he was wearing on his head.

We waited. Twenty minutes, thirty minutes, forty minutes. I tried to move time forward somehow. My mind ricocheted with worry. There was a poster on a wall outside the exam room of a smiling hospital-gowned child with no hair. Our curtained room was right next to the nurses' station that had a speaker broadcasting static-laced reports from approaching ambulances. "Patient having difficulty breathing," one report squalled. "All limbs swollen," another said. "Patient unresponsive. Eyes rolling back into the head," said another. The wild-haired woman who had opened our curtain earlier kept yowling that she was being mistreated. A call for security went out over the loudspeaker.

"No, no, no!" she wailed while being subdued.

We wanted to be told we could leave this place. As we waited and hoped, I kept touching the baseball hat covering my son's head. I focused on that baseball, clung to it, as if by hanging on to the baseball I had the power to hold on to a world in which my son was okay.

Finally the pediatrician entered and told us the number from the blood pulled from his foot. It was a low number. I wasn't sure what that meant.

"He's going to be okay," the pediatrician said.

My wife started crying.

"You're going to make me cry too," the pediatrician said.

I felt a weight that had been pressing down on my chest rise up into my throat and stop. I wanted to cry, but I couldn't, as if a long time ago something inside me had been dislocated. To feel anything deeply I need lunch-break documentaries on my cell phone. I need things that have nothing whatsoever to do with me. I need stories of wondrous strangers. I need sports.

I was directed to the front desk to finish filling out some paperwork that we'd skipped when we'd first arrived. The front desk was near the double doors that led out into the parking lot. The sun had come up and was shining. It was going to be a warm day. There were small gray snowbanks at the corners of the parking lot, long patches of brown grass visible beyond. Winter was in retreat. When I was done filling out the paperwork I went back to the examination room to wait with Abby and Jack for our discharge papers. Abby had gotten Jack out of the oversized gown and back into his pajamas. She stood with him at the front of the exam room, the curtain open, and was murmuring to him and pointing at the many shiny machines. I took my place beside them and looked at the machines too.

I started thinking about the tickets I'd bought for the baseball game in June. The weight that had risen from my chest was still stuck in my throat. How can you know what will happen? How can you know that Bo Jackson will perform miracles on the baseball field? How can you know that, far short of reaching his overall future potential, he'll be stopped?

All those shiny machines. The world is beyond measuring, idiotic, aglow. An orderly was walking by our examination room. He noticed Jack in my wife's arms, noticed on his head the white hat with the two arcs of red stitching.

"Someone's ready for baseball," he said to Jack. On the word *baseball* I lost it.

P

Paterno, Joe
See **Asterisk**.

Pawtucket

At one point when I was in the middle of puberty I let slip the information that it is not possible for one to perform fellatio on oneself. I was in the company of a couple of fellow ninth graders, after junior varsity basketball practice, waiting for the Late Bus. We'd been disagreeing about a geographical detail in a limerick of—in terms of the ninth-grade male demographic—unsurpassed renown. The other guys stated that Nantucket was the homeland of the man there once was. I disagreed.

"There once was a man from Pawtucket," I recited, proof that even at that early age sports was already distorting my memory.

"*Paw*tucket?" said one of the guys, Larry.

"You 10A," concluded the other, Malcolm.

This ubiquitous local insult was a reference to the room at our school in which kids with learning disabilities were quarantined. The door was always shut, a poster covering the Plexiglas window in the door. Some kids, the ones who could barely speak sentences, had been there for years and seemed destined to be there forever. Others had been more recently subtracted, inexplicably, from the general population, which added an element of demotion to the concept of 10A. If it was determined that you weren't cutting it in the normal world, down you went.

"*You're* a 10A," I replied. But I began to doubt myself about Pawtucket. Larry and Malcolm moved on to a discussion of the key element in the literary work in question. I saw an opening, a way to reclaim some face, and offered my critique of this element's plausibility.

"Yeah?" Malcolm replied, grinning. "How do you know you can't suck your own dick?"

I realized with a queasy jolt what I had just publicly admitted. Worse, my authoritative tone had strongly implied that I was not letting slip evidence merely of a single instance of curious semi-accidental anatomical exploration but rather that batteries of rigorous laboratory-style testing had been performed to reach an empirically imperturbable conclusion.

I regret this. How could I not? What life lesson could possibly be learned by blurting out such an admission? Did I "grow"? No, I just became a little more crumpled with the shame that there was something wrong with me. Not that this stopped me from trying to emulate the anatomically gifted man from, as I alone believed him to be, Pawtucket. I may have cut down a bit on these attempts, both because of the clear evidence that what I was attempting was impossible and because this inadvertent public airing now solidified the perversion that the attempt implied; nonetheless, every once in a while I would give it another go, alone in the room I'd shared with my brother for years that now felt empty with him away at boarding school. I'd get upside-down in a clumsy shoulder-stand and lean my back on the wall and bend my pelvis downward as far as it could possibly go. My erection would always remain beyond reach of my—and, for the time being and into *infinity*, it seemed, anyone's—mouth.

Pawtucket, as it happens, is best known not as the land of the self-fellating but as the home to the Boston Red Sox's affiliated triple-A minor league team. If you are in the majors and failing, Pawtucket is where you are sent; if you are in Pawtucket and succeeding, you might find yourself sent to Boston. Throughout my childhood Pawtucket had signified hope, disappointment, inertia—some at Pawtucket rising, others falling, still others going nowhere at all. But in the early eighties hope and disappointment were not in balance. When once Pawtucket had been deeply stocked with young talent, such as future stars Fred Lynn and Jim Rice, now the cupboards were comparatively bare. By the time I publicly admitted to trying and failing to blow myself, the element of hope had distilled down to almost nothing.

But that almost nothing was a tiny diamond of childhood joy. Mark Fidrych, signed that year by the Red Sox to a minor league contract, was already several years removed from being a rookie superstar: he hadn't even played in the majors since 1980. As he toiled just out of sight in Pawtucket, a moribund version of the Red Sox stumbled onward in Boston, Jim Rice diminished and grounding into double plays, Yaz creaky and fading, and everyone else from the good old days now gone. It all seemed dismal to me, those Red Sox of my puberty, and so I had to believe that the Bird's return to the Show was a possibility. The occasional newspaper reports from the minors gave strong indications to the contrary: childhood was over; Fidrych wasn't coming back. Even so, there were times, alone in my room, when I aimed a prayer toward Pawtucket.

Paychecki, Gene
See von Hofmannstal, Count Manfred

Pisarcik, Joe

Not too long after Jack's visit to the emergency room Abby took him to the Brookfield Zoo. Jack was around eight months old. The zoo excursion tired him out, and he fell asleep deeply in my arms long before his usual exhausted surrender in the middle of the night. I took him to the swing we had for him in the bedroom and did the quarterback kneel.

You could argue that the most demanding job of any athlete in the world, taking into account skill level, athleticism, physical and mental toughness, analytic intelligence, quickness of thought, and fortitude to withstand in-game pressure and postgame scrutiny, is that of a professional football quarterback. And yet the moment of victory for a quarterback, the quarterback taking a knee to run out the last few seconds left on the clock, would perhaps be the easiest play in any sport for a layman to perform.

I did the quarterback kneel in the bedroom, laying Jack down, and then came out of the bedroom and eyed the clock, 7:30. Jack usually didn't go to sleep until much later, until long after both Abby and I were exhausted, and now we suddenly had a wide open evening. It seemed like the first quiet moment in months. We sat in the living room, stunned, as if smelling salts had just been administered to prod us awake where we sat. For a little while we didn't have anything to say. I racked my brain for stories from my life, but my life outside our walls was a looping clip: a bus to a cubicle to a bus to home to a bus to a cubicle. Since we'd moved to Chicago I'd gone deeper and deeper into my lifelong tendency toward isolation. I relied on Abby to bring stories home.

"How was that meet-up thing?" I asked finally. I remembered that earlier in the week, through some online group or chat room or Facebook page, Abby had invited another mother of a baby over to the house. We'd both found that parenting a newborn had an element of piercing loneliness, a feeling that the parenting was being done within a profound isolation from the rest of the world, but unlike me—and characteristic for her—she had done something about it. I'd already asked her about the meet-up the evening after it happened, but it was when Jack was awake, so the conversation only went as deep as the shallowest word in the English language.

"Fine," Abby had said. She said it again after a long pause the night Jack went to sleep early.

"Fine," she said. Then she burst out crying.

"What the hell?" I said. "What happened?"

"I don't have any friends," she said.

"What? You have a shitload!" I said. I was shocked. The only thing I had that even remotely resembled a social life in Chicago was when I attached myself to gatherings of Abby and the friends she'd made here.

"They don't have kids," she said. "It's different now."

"What happened?"

"Oh, nothing," Abby said. "It was, whatever, I don't know. She wasn't my kind of . . . we didn't connect." I started to rev up one of my useless rationalizing platitudes.

"Well, you know, who ever really knows what it is th—"

"She was asking me about the neighborhood, this neighborhood," Abby blurted. "'How do you like it here?' And I was like, 'It's, you know, it's good, it's okay,' and she was like, 'Really, you can tell me.' I could tell she was pushing at something. She was from out in the suburbs somewhere, I don't know. So I said, 'We like it, you know, it's good,' and she said, 'No, no, I know. I know what you mean. I know there's a difference between blacks and niggers.'"

Abby began crying again.

"Sheezus," I said.

I went over and hugged her, standing and reaching down to her in the chair. Sometimes she leans into a hug, but other times she stays locked up in private misery, her shoulder muscles bunched, bracing. It's like hugging a trembling, electrified rock. I let go. She blew her nose.

"I'm going to have to do this alone," she said.

But we kept talking. Her crying had created an opening. The air felt changed, a little softer. I've always relied on her to create these emotional openings, just like I've relied on her for stories and social-life shrapnel. We were allowed to talk now. I could say things.

"I'm worried," I said.

"About what?" she said.

"No, I mean I'm worried all the time. I worry so much I can't enjoy the good moments."

"The good moments?" Abby swabbed her wet face with more tissue.

"Like when we were all walking together along the lake a few days ago. I was worrying the whole time."

When I was a kid the quarterback kneel play hadn't yet developed. Teams protecting a lead would usually run a play in which the quarterback sort of crumpled to the ground, falling on the ball, which resembled the kneel play in its brevity and simplicity but lacked the clean formality of the current-day genuflection. You can see an example of this precursor to the kneel play in the first of three final plays run by the New York Giants in a 1978 game against the Philadelphia Eagles. The Giants needed only to run three plays to win the game. On the first of these plays Joe Pisarcik takes a snap and falls on the ground. The Eagles defenders battle to get to him and are even able to make some contact. There's no tacit agreement to hold back. It's been suggested that the Giants' offensive coordinator, Bob Gibson, noticed this violent attempt to get to Pisarcik and wanted to avoid it. This would explain his call for a running play on the next down, which resulted in Larry Csonka rushing for an eleven-yard gain. This left time for one final play.

"Ever since Jack got sick, the emergency room," I said to Abby. "But even before then. But it's definitely worse now. Do you know what I'm saying?"

Abby gave me a look. She'd been imagining the worst from minute one of Jack's life.

"Right, I know you know," I said. "Like there's no moment that can't go wrong."

The announcers spent the seconds leading up to the final snap thanking the producers of the telecast and reciting the records of the two teams involved as if the Giants had already won. Meanwhile there was some disarray in the Giants huddle as Pisarcik relayed the news that Gibson had once again sent in a play that called for a handoff to Csonka. Everyone in the huddle wanted Pisarcik to disregard this play and fall on the ball, but Pisarcik had recently gotten in hot water for changing Gibson's plays. The huddle confusion led to the Giants rushing to the line of scrimmage to avoid a delay-of-game penalty, and the rushed snap to Pisarcik was a little off-center, causing Pisarcik to bobble it. Csonka was a little too fast in his movement toward scrimmage. The timing and precision needed for a handoff was already marred, but Pisarcik still tried to carry out the play by shoving the unsteady oval toward Csonka. The ball bounced off Csonka's arm and fell to the turf. Pisarcik tried to dive on it, but it bounded away and into the arms of Herm Edwards, who raced into the end zone, winning the game for the Eagles.

I was watching that game, ten years old. I watched every football game I could back then, anything and everything that came into my house and eased the blank ache of a Sunday. The only station we got that aired pro football was CBS, and CBS played Cowboys games and Giants games, which was, in terms of the two teams' relative appeal, like having a channel that played only Bugs Bunny cartoons and Soviet grain production documentaries. I vividly remember dozens of the Cowboys flashy, exciting stars and don't remember a single moment in a Giants game or a single Giants player, with the sole exception of that one play and that one player, Joe Pisarcik. I didn't even remember that Larry Csonka, a player of titanic prominence to a kid in the 1970s, symbolized most clearly by his appearance on *The Six Million Dollar Man*, was involved until this attempt to understand my own slippery grasp as a father sent me back to the game. But I remember Joe Pisarcik. I remember feeling terrible for him. The game was seared into my mind from that point forward, like a fairy tale with a chilling moral. The very next week in the NFL the quarterback genuflections began and have not stopped. They have managed to succeed in all instances with only one exception, which is a whole other story (*see* **Victory Formation, the**). With Pisarcik a prayer was born. It's the same prayer I said whenever I laid Jack down into his swing. Nothing is safe, but please let this sweet small victory hold true.

Player to Be Named Later

That night, Jack woke a few hours after I quarterback-kneeled him into his swing, long before morning, and he was miserable and stayed that way for hours, and within that misery Abby and I hated all life, including one another, yelled at one another, then finally Abby stayed up with Jack and I went to bed feeling useless, a superfluous name on a losing roster, and logged an hour or two of guilt-frayed sleep and then took the car to work fantasizing that I'd come upon a previously unnoticed off-ramp to a rest area of such deep peace that it could take me in and then trade me back into my life transformed, still me but painless, arriving.

But before all that, before Jack woke, Abby and I sat in the living room and talked about our loneliness, our worries. We talked and I felt better, and then a subject that we'd managed to raise previously in one or another slim quiet moment was able to surface. Another kid. A player to be named later. On one hand it seemed like the most insane thing to pursue. As it was, with just one tiny eight-month-old human among us we were barely keeping it together or not keeping it together at all, depending on the given moment. On the other hand, any time we started edging into that conversation I popped a stupidity-enhancing **boner**. The conversation, for me at least, quickly became about the possibility of sex, regardless of what it might bring: a new baby, or bankruptcy, or years of widespread drought and famine.

All this is to say (to brag?): I fell on my wife like a duffel bag full of hockey equipment, so to speak. Midway through this abrupt collision, which would not turn out on this occasion to yield any new mouths to feed, I noticed that Abby had dried sweet potato paste in her hair, residue of some experimenting with solid food with Jack earlier in the day.

I love my wife's body, her beauty, the detritus that accrues on her as she charges through life. I wish I could fall on her like a duffel bag full of hockey equipment more often. But with a baby around, the father moves to the periphery of the roster. Weeks can go by, months. I found myself recently fantasizing about getting an incurable disease, which in itself is not novel, as I am frequently fantasizing about ways in which I might be able to become easily and blamelessly removed from suffering (*see* **Next Ryan Leaf, the**), but in this instance I was fantasizing specifically about how the incurable disease would allow me to request some heartrendingly tender "final wishes." In short, if I was going to die the next day, my wife would pretty much have to let me go to town on her.

Sorry—"make love" to her. Like many, I find that phrase "make love" nauseating, but there is something deeper than just a Penthouse Letters scenario in having sex with my wife.

There's tenderness, there's the rare opportunity to touch and be touched. There's that word, nauseating as it is to include in fuck scenarios: *love.*

There's something else too, since becoming a father. The biological involvement of a father ends, strictly speaking, with the ejaculation of sperm. You want to feel useful. You want that biologically deep reassurance that you are useful. Obviously there's never a shortage of things that need to be done, ways in which a person could feel useful. This was what was behind my frantic attachment to dishwashing (*see ex-*). Was I so dedicated to clean dishes? To the contrary, I have always been a sloppy, distracted dishwasher, prone to shepherding soapy, smeared dishes back into the cupboard. The main impetus behind all my dishwashing was a need to demonstrate to myself and maybe also to Abby that I was useful, which I only sort of was. Meanwhile I watched Abby feed our son directly from her own body. Fathers don't have this kind of primal connection after the act of conception. Fathers have boners. So I popped boners all the time and then, with a few sweet exceptions, disposed of them myself and felt even more useless than ever.

This is the lot of the player to be named later. You lurk on the periphery of one thing until there comes a time when you are shifted to another thing. An aura of uselessness can accrue. Consider Mario Guerrero, for example, arguably the prototypical player to be named later. In 1972 he was the player to be named in one of the most famously lopsided trades in history, when the Red Sox sent future Cy Young–award winning Sparky Lyle to the Yankees for Danny Cater, and Guerrero's inconsequential years on the Red Sox accentuated rather than mollified the feeling that in the Lyle-Cater swap the Red Sox had been robbed. Without making any impact on the Red Sox, Guerrero was eventually traded away straight up for a player to be named later, and then before long he was traded again, this time for a minor leaguer, Ed Jordan, and a player to be named later, who turned out to be another minor leaguer, Ed Kurpiel. Two years after that, in 1978, he was sent to the Oakland A's, who were embarking on one of the worst two-year stretches of any team in history, as a player to be named later in a massive shifting of bodies to the A's for star pitcher Vida Blue. The A's got Gary Alexander, Dave Heaverlo, Phil Huffman, John Henry Johnson, Gary Thomasson, and Alan Wirth—not a single player of distinction—for Vida Blue, who was not only the last remaining superstar from the team's dynasty earlier in the decade but also the possessor of arguably the greatest name in baseball history, his name so glorious that the pile of nobodies offered in exchange for it still needed even one more name, so a player to be named later was added, and that player was Mario Guerrero. With this transaction Guerrero's experiences as a player to be named later finally came to an end, an end that would be followed soon enough by the end of his career. But before that he played the 1978 season, a season in which he managed to score just twenty-seven times, despite getting 139 hits and coming to bat 546 times. This turns out to be a record: no one who has ever had that many hits has ever scored fewer times. Mario Guerrero, as it turns out, was historically inefficient at mattering. Hits only matter because they become runs, and getting hits without scoring runs is what he did. He was on a dreadful team, but he was also devoid of power and had little speed and little ability to increase his times on base by getting a walk; when he managed to scratch out a hit it was usually a single, and he didn't end up going anywhere. The object of the game is to score, and in 1978 he turned in a perverse masterpiece of baseball uselessness, the player to be named later personified.

Piece of shit, useless. But what are you going to do? You can't trade yourself out of your life. Or can you? Obviously there's the option for trading your life for nothing at all, but that's more like quitting (*see **quitter***). The truth is, you want to be named. This need has been with me for most of my life, or maybe all of my life, but I suppose I only noticed it when it started to intertwine with sexual fantasies, which in turn intertwined with long, sprawling romantic fantasies. Throughout puberty I used to lay in my loft bed for long stretches imagining a blurred idyllic union with some girl or another at my school, one who announced her boundless love by *running to me.* I never imagined any specific dialogue between us but just imagined that we'd be together, murmuring soul to soul, and that she would say my name softly over and over.

It was painful to be reminded every day at school how far this fantasy was from reality. I went from class to class, invisible to the girls around me. After school at JV basketball practice I ran and dribbled and shot, and after that I waited in the hallway outside the gym for the Late Bus as the varsity practiced inside the gym. My brother would have been on the varsity squad by then, but he was away at boarding school. The Late Bus pulled into the parking lot, and I got on with the others who had been waiting. It climbed up out of one valley and meandered down into another, approximating the routes of all the regular buses earlier in the day. The sky grew dark as the bus emptied one stop at a time. The driver lived near the end of the farthest possible destination on the route. I lived beyond his house. Often I was the last passenger, the only reason the bus driver had to go out of his way. Sometimes in those years it seemed the only time I was noticed all day was by this bus driver, Mr. Race, who scowled up at my reflection in his rearview mirror as he rode past his own house. At my house the bus jerked to a stop, and the door was yanked open. Neither of us spoke. The bus lurched into motion the moment my feet hit our rutted dirt drive.

"Oh Josh," I called out to myself later in the night. I was up in my loft bed. I was imagining one or another of the girls I'd been invisible to throughout the day naming me.

"Oh Josh," I call out to myself now. Now I imagine it's my wife saying these words. It's always my wife now. She is the one I have burdened with the job of calling my name.

When this is over, typically I adjust the roster of my online Strat-O-Matic 1970s baseball squad. Piece of shit, useless—those words lurk in such anticlimactic moments. While serving as the all-powerful front office ruler of my online Strat-O-Matic 1970s baseball team, I can release Mario Guerrero, pick up Ed Brinkman, release Francisco Barrios, pick up Pat Zachry. But behind all the names, that nagging shame recitation persists. Part of it is learned, I suppose. The prevailing cultural message for centuries has been that beating off is shameful, which tends to infuse the practitioner with shame. But for me the shame is primarily based not on anything external but in an unavoidable sense of loneliness. You come into your palm and there's a rush and in the wake of the rush there's this diamond clarity: you are alone. You tried to trade yourself out of your life and got traded right back, whump.

Not even Mario Guerrero was ever traded for himself. This distinction is shared by four players, three of whom were something more like loaned, or traded and then returned.

Only one player, Brad Gulden, was clearly and inarguably traded for a player to be named later who turned out to be Brad Gulden, at least according to baseball-reference.com, which I choose to consider an unimpeachable if not outright holy authority. On that encyclopedic site Brad Gulden is the only player who is specifically named within his own transaction log:

November 18, 1980: Traded by the New York Yankees with $150,000 to the Seattle Mariners for a player to be named later and Larry Milbourne. The Seattle Mariners sent Brad Gulden (May 18, 1981) to the New York Yankees to complete the trade.

Gulden ended his career with a lifetime batting of average of .200, precisely on the *Mendoza Line*. I want to name the feeling I get when I think about this perfect mediocrity. I want to sing an aria to this perfect mediocrity. I want to tell my son about the player to be named later who arrived exactly neither here nor there.

Playing Out the String

I once saw perfect mediocrity. It was, not completely without relation, also the first and only time I ever saw *David Aardsma* perform in person, though I have no recollection of anything the arbitrary starting point of my ordering of the world did that day. It was a few years ago, before my son arrived, when I still had whole wide days to burn. I went to a late September game at Wrigley between the Cubs and the Rockies, two teams I didn't care about. Both had been mathematically eliminated for weeks.

Through the first several innings I sat in a row near the back of the lower deck, next to a friend from work. Eventually rain delays and prolonged, instantly forgettable rallies and incessant pitching changes and the inability of either lackluster side to win during regulation began to whittle the already meager crowd down closer to nothing. My friend left somewhere in the vicinity of the tenth or eleventh inning.

Alone, I began creeping a few rows at a time toward the sporadic, inessential action. By the thirteenth inning I was sitting in a wet seat near the field on the first base side, no one else in my row. I could see the raindrops on the batting helmet of the on-deck hitter. A rare calm came over me. Mostly I lurk around in the back rows of existence in a low-level perpetual cringe, vaguely braced for invisible blows, but once in a while there are moments when I can imagine that time has somehow been defeated, that the matter at hand, vivid and meaningless, will remain undecided indefinitely, and I'll never have to deal with real life.

Each team kept calling in pitchers from the bullpen, one after another, in what would turn out to be, at least according to my later attempt to identify something to hold onto from the game, a record-setting procession of hurlers. In all, twenty pitchers would take the mound, which, from what I have ascertained, is the most pitchers ever used in a single game. And just for good measure a twenty-first pitcher, Carlos Zambrano, would be the last player of any kind called into the action, not as a pitcher but as a last-hope pinch-hitter. In they came, one after another after another, none but the very last leaving even the slightest trace in my mind. *Aardsma*, Affeldt, Corpas, Dempster, Field, Francis, Fuentes, Guzmán, Howry, King, Martin, Mateo, Mesa, Novoa, Ohman, Ramírez, Ryu, Venafro, Walrond, Wuertz, Zambrano.

Nowadays pitching changes occur to the accompaniment of pulsating heavy metal explosions, thick-muscled relievers charging toward the infield as if intending to shatter Joe Theismann's tibia and fibula. This was not the case that day at Wrigley, especially as the game wore on. Instead, as pitcher after pitcher trudged onto the grassy sog, the stoppages came to resemble the downbeat mound replacements of my distant youth, when fellows from the bullpen generally resembled recreational bowlers and lachrymose vice principals, and their entrances into games were somehow homely and desultory, verging on aimless, as if they might just as easily wander into the stands as onto the mound. By the thirteenth inning at Wrigley, in a kind of hypnotic trance induced by the endless parade of ineffectual twirlers, I was thinking about how, at some stadiums in the 1970s, the inherent passivity of the bullpen entrances of the era reached an apex—or a nadir, depending on your preferences—with the use of a little electrical cart. The carts were shaped like giant baseballs topped by a suitably huge baseball cap in the same design as the one on the head of the reliever within, who rode as a dazed, somber passenger, as if to cross the expanse of the outfield on foot would have sapped too much of his limited energies.

Once, when I was a kid, my father bought me a palm-sized plastic replica of the Mets version of this bullpen cart. My brother and I visited our father in New York for two weeks every summer. At our urging and against his revulsion for sports, he would always take us to a game at Shea. The day he bought me the bullpen cart I couldn't take my eyes off of it, even when the game was still going on. I don't remember anything about the game, but I remember riding the subway back to my father's apartment after the game, rolling the little plastic baseball-headed bullpen cart up and down my lap, carefully, gently. Of all the souvenirs that ever passed through my hands, it was my favorite.

In my father's apartment we all slept on the floor, my brother and me side by side, perpendicular to our father, our feet nearly touching his legs. I held the bullpen cart in my hands. From those few nights every year as a child I developed a lifelong response to being in a high rise and hearing the sound of nighttime city traffic below: it always makes me feel safe.

When I think about my vanished souvenir, the little plastic version of the Mets bullpen cart, my fingers tingle, feeling its absence. It's not a bad feeling, exactly. It's like the feeling I get all over my body when I'm lucky enough to be at some sparsely attended sporting event with two teams playing out the string and the game starts to feel like it will last forever. In the bottom of the thirteenth inning at Wrigley, as my whole body was faintly tingling, Aramis Ramírez singled off Ramón Ramírez, the twentieth pitcher to enter the game. Matt Murton came to the plate next and began working the count in his favor. It seemed like things might be moving toward a conclusion. The sparse gathering roused from near-silence to the outer limits of its capabilities: murmuring. Then there was a burst of shouting behind me, something that ended with these words:

"You'll never play baseball again!"

I thought at first it was the kind of drunken barking loosed at ballgames in a jocular pantomime of rage. Then a wiry man, bristling with anger, stalked past me down the steps of the aisle and grabbed the shoulder of a blond teenaged boy sitting three rows in front of me, by himself, like me, a fan who'd moved down close and didn't want to leave. The kid was wearing an Aramis Ramírez jersey.

"You hear me? You'll never play baseball again!" the man shouted. "Now get in the car!" The kid just sat there, staring at the game. The man hit him hard in the face with an open right hand.

I stared at Matt Murton in the batter's box.

"Get in the car!" the man barked again. "We've been waiting in the car for an hour! You think the whole world revolves around you? Get in the goddamn car! I've got kids that need to get to bed."

The man drew closer.

"*We'll leave you in the city,*" he hissed into his kid's ear. Then, using his hitting hand to give the kid's jerseyed shoulder a shove, the man straightened up and away from the kid.

In the batter's box Matt Murton took another pitch. An Aramis Ramírez jersey crossed my vision. The kid and the man who'd hit him were moving up the aisle past me, the man with a tight grip on the kid's arm. After they passed by, I heard one last thing.

"Don't think I won't break your fucking shoulder."

Matt Murton trotted to first with a walk, but then Jacque Jones stranded the would-be winning run, Aramis Ramírez, at second. On to another inning. I went down below the stands and called my wife from a pay phone to tell her the game was still going, that it might go forever, but of course it didn't, nor did I even believe it would, but I wanted it to, I still wanted it to, so when the Rockies took a two-run lead in the top of the fourteenth inning and the Cubs got a man on in the bottom of

the fourteenth inning and sent Carlos Zambrano to the plate
to pinch hit with two outs, and he lifted a fly ball to rightfield
and the rightfielder Brad Hawpe, while setting himself for what
looked like it was going to be an easy catch, skidded slightly on
the wet grass, I prayed for him to fall, for the ball to elude him,
for both the lead runner and Carlos Zambrano to circle the
bases, for the score to be healed back into a tie, for nothing to
be decided, for nothing to be eliminated, for the bullpen carts
of yore to reappear again and again through the mist, for the
parade of morose relievers evermore.

Pulling a John Anderson

Now a defunct term anywhere outside the context of baseball
history chatter, "pulling a John Anderson" was in broad public
usage for some time in the early part of the twentieth century.
John Anderson was a baseball player who was thought to have
attempted to steal a base that a teammate occupied. Recent his-
torians have discovered that this version of the play was a distortion. John Stahl's biography of John Anderson on the Society for
American Baseball Research (SABR) website locates the birth
of the term in a late-season game in 1903. With one out in the
eighth inning of a game that Anderson's team, the St. Louis
Browns, trailed 6–0, Anderson drew a walk to load the bases.
The next batter, Bobby Wallace, worked the count full. Baserun-
ners will often break with the pitch when the count on a batter is full, not looking to steal the base but to better advance
on a batted ball. But Wallace, who struck out just twenty-eight
times that year, swung and missed at strike three as Anderson
was expanding his lead. The opposing catcher whipped a throw
behind Anderson to first, and Anderson was tagged out for an
inning-ending double play.

It's difficult to trace why this pickoff play, the product
of some bad luck coupled with assertive but not particularly

unusual baserunning, would have led to the idea that John Anderson had gamboled idiotically all the way to second base before finding it occupied. Perhaps he was caught so far off of first that firsthand observers of the play felt the impulse to mock him for something, and adding moronic obliviousness as the core cause of the failure was an outcome of this impulse. Perhaps also a small incident was turned into a big one by an elaborate game of telephone, an easy feat in the early days of baseball media, when the only concrete record of the game back then would have been a newspaper box score that showed Anderson as "caught stealing" with the bases loaded.

However it came into being, the notion of "pulling a John Anderson" caught the public's imagination. Perhaps this is because it spoke to a core societal anxiety: the fear of wanting something you can't have, shouldn't have, but try to take anyway. Sometimes I think about the term Pulling a John Anderson when I'm watching Abby breastfeed my son.

I remember a long ago morning in my apartment in Brooklyn, years before Jack was born. Abby had stayed over the night before. She had either just gotten out of bed or out of the shower, and she was naked. She was cold, and to warm herself up she came over and sat on my lap and put her arms around me. All your dreams will come true! Yes, all your dreams will come true, and then life will go on. For so long I ached to have a girl run to me, and I didn't even require that she be naked when it happened, though I had plenty of dreams about that, and the dreams were so profoundly opposed to my day-to-day reality as to be as unattainable as any thought I had to playing major league baseball, and yet, eventually, a woman, and not just any woman but one I loved and was in love with, ran to me naked and threw her arms around me.

That moment! I brought it up more than once afterward. Abby tried to explain to me that she was just cold, but I refused to downgrade the moment from my initial perception, which had something to do with the softness of the touch, the tenderness, the need, the sheer fact that a naked woman was on my lap. We'd had sex before that point and probably had even had sex as recently as the night before, so it wasn't about sex as much as it was about love, closeness, and the coming true of my deepest dreams. In my deepest dreams not only would the woman running to me want me but would love me and know me and I'd love and know her.

"I was just cold," Abby insisted, tiring of my nostalgia. Eventually this explanation dropped away and I just got eye rolls. Now I keep my nostalgia to myself, and really it's not even nostalgia: it happened so long ago as if to be something that happened to someone else, like something I read in a book.

But it does still exist in my flesh. I mean I can feel it, not always, but it's there. Recently I had a dream that haunted me all throughout the following day, the kind of dream that hits the senses in such a way that they buzz with the aftermath of the contact long into the waking hours. In the dreams my wife was soft and tender with me again. It had been a long time. It diminishes, this tenderness. How could it not? There's no room for it. Mothers of young children talk about the phenomenon of being "touched out." All day long they have this little being that needs to be touched and cared for every moment. Eventually, against every instinct and emotion that tends toward wanting to fulfill this need, the mother reaches a point where she just feels exhausted by the demands, exhausted by always having to bestow tenderness, the *presence* needed for this. And then a grown man, large and bristly with unshaven whiskers and bad breath and hair sprouting everywhere and a face turning ever more severe and unpleasant with age, ugly, loud, unappealing, a grown man comes to you with a suffocating desire to be touched.

That's what I wanted, what was missing. It wasn't about sex, not in the usual sense. Who's going to run to me, touch me? Those days are long gone, and with the arrival of a new recipient of all my wife's touching, that absence has become official, permanent, and in the face of that permanence I'm receding into my ninth-grade self, praying to **Pawtucket**, daydreaming for hours on end about being named, about reaching first base, a kiss, and then setting out in a sprint to second base. It seemed entirely fitting back then that that's how my new world of desire was set out, as an advancement around the bases. I wasn't entirely sure what third base meant, and home plate was terrifying. But second base was clear and beautiful and everything I wanted. Back then the mere thought of any of the words for what second base represented—tits, boobs, rack, gazongas—was enough to give me a raging erection. In those days all I had were words, as any actual gazongas might as well have been as remote as the moon. Now, in my second pubescence, second base was much closer but was occupied. How beautiful this occupation. In my right mind it's everything, the center of the universe, my wife feeding my son with herself, and it's a blessing to be able to support and protect that. But fatherhood has rarely found me in my right mind. More often than not, I'm wanting.

"What are you thinking about?" Abby asked me one day. I was sitting on the couch and she was in the recliner, feeding Jack.

"What do you mean? Nothing," I said.

"Your face," she said. She performed an imitation of a mouth-breathing dullard. I felt like how anyone feels when they're interrupted while lost in unwholesome cogitation. Like drifting too far off base, getting picked off. I couldn't have put what I was thinking about into words anyway, short of reciting the entirety of a clammy encyclopedia containing every synonym for tits.

"I'm just sitting here," I said.

Quitter

Sometimes I wasn't the last one on the Late Bus. There was one family that lived even farther away from everything. I always felt better when one of them was on the bus with me because it meant I wouldn't be the reason Mr. Race had to drive beyond his own house. I was sort of friends with one of them, Denny, because our shared rural *obscurity* meant that sometimes, such as when the Late Bus had expelled all its passengers but the two of us, I was the only option in the way of an audience if he felt like talking to someone. Often he talked about how much loathing there was between him and the bus driver, Mr. Race. "He hates going past his house for us," Denny said. He was hunched low in his seat and murmuring, as if we were prisoners plotting to shiv a guard. "But fuck *him*."

Other times he talked about the future, how he'd return to our town a multimillionaire and impose his will on all the adults who had slighted him or his family, chiefly the bus driver but also the varsity basketball coach and others. I was always impressed with his conception of the future, simply in that he was able to conceive of it with any specificity at all. The future to me was a blank. I was impressed by Denny's past too. He went to parties and had friends. Things had happened to him.

"Carol Ann," he said to me during one Late Bus ride. "We were camping, a bunch of us, and there was a campfire, and we were all getting fucked up."

"Drinking?" I said.

"Carol Ann was next to me," Denny said, "and that's all I remember, and then I *came to*, you know. I mean I just kinda woke up and we were frenching."

"Wow," I said. I knew the girl he was talking about. She was so pretty it hurt.

"Didn't remember anything, because of rum, just bam," Denny said. "I keep hoping it happens again, that I blank out and get back there to her."

"Yeah," I said, and from then on I hoped for the very same thing, that I'd slip the pain and tedium and disappointment of the present and the burdened blank of the future by conking out somehow and waking up later in the middle of impossible bliss. Sometimes I even skipped the fantasy of coming to while kissing Carol Ann or whoever and instead just hoped for any kind of leaping advancement through time. I wanted to shed the looming feeling of everything that was still in front of me, wanted above all to shed virginity, but I didn't want to have to live through all the unfathomable, humiliating steps it would take to accomplish this. I just wanted it to have been done and to be an adult, with everything that hurt behind me.

This dream came back to me with a vengeance in fatherhood. I knew as I engaged in the fantasy that I would someday look back on it with deep regret, knowing that I'd wasted a portion of my slim pocket of time with my boy as a tiny sweet baby wishing it away. And yet again and again I wished for just that, for it all to be done so that I could be beyond it, beyond all risk and blame, beyond all tedium and exhaustion, beyond the sadness of knowing that somehow my own chronic sadness was going to filter down into my innocent son, beyond all that, resting, thinking back on anesthetized memories. Fortifying this wish for extended blackout was a growing belief that it might be possible. I kept having a certain experience that supported these fantasies. I kept losing time.

For many years I imagined my life as an unbroken line through time, A to B to C and so on, with a starting point on the left and an arrow on the right and an orderly list of Important Moments in between. It's a popular notion, that life is orderly, that there's a start and then an arrow leading somewhere, preferably away from failure and toward success. I kept reaching for this fiction even after, with Jack's arrival, it was clear that it had been obliterated. It became evident fairly early on in fatherhood that my life was no longer a continuous narrative but a series of brief, disoriented departures from an abiding existential brownout.

In the first few weeks after Jack's birth I would find myself in places with only a vague sense of where I was or how I'd gotten there. Maybe it's like this for a boxer in the middle of a losing fight. The bell rings to pull the boxer a little closer to full consciousness, enough to start a habitual movement to the center of the ring but not enough to bring back any sense of clarity or competence. I would find myself in a supermarket, for example, moving down an aisle, my hands on an empty cart, a broken wheel making it veer to the left. I wouldn't remember driving to the supermarket and wouldn't know why I was there. I'd dig into my pockets for a list and pull out a jingly cloth giraffe.

You will have fog in your head and toys in your pockets. That's how it'll be for a while, and the fog will lessen over time but never altogether dissipate. Sometime in April, when Jack was about eight and a half months old, I *came to* yet again, the first time in a while. I was in a supermarket parking lot, behind the wheel of our car. I reached into my coat pocket for a list and pulled out one tiny blue sock. This brought me back into my life. I remembered that I was heading home, that I'd see Jack, that I'd be able to show him his sock. I remembered that I'd been at work but had left early. There had been an Office Olympics that I tried to attend, but after about twenty seconds of standing mutely at the edge of a crowd of my coworkers in a large conference room, most coworkers standing around chatting while a few coworkers prepared to compete in a series of zany office-related competitions, I had to bolt. I went back to my cube, and, imagining the questions I'd have to field about why I hadn't been at the Office Olympics, I wrote an e-mail to the coworkers in my immediate group explaining that I needed to cut out early, unexpectedly. I used my child as an excuse. *You will use your child as an excuse.* I had to do it. Some people can stand around chatting with one another in rooms; I was becoming more and more unable to be one of those people. On the way home I'd stopped in a grocery store parking lot because I suddenly had a small piece of unaccountable time. I had freed myself, albeit dubiously, from work, and I wasn't expected home for an hour. So I parked at the far edge of the lot, turned off the car, and fell unconscious. It was a short, useless sleep, except for the feeling for a split second upon waking. I didn't know where I was or who I was. This is the off-ramp I'm always dreaming of. *You will dream of leaving everything behind. You will want to quit.*

What makes you want to quit is not easily definable. You are like Roberto Duran in the fight that diminished his legend, when Sugar Ray Leonard danced and juked and mocked and vanished, again and again and again, never allowing Duran to engage.

"Duran is completely bewildered," Howard Cosell reported from ringside.

"No mas," Duran finally said. No more.

You're not getting struck with blows of any measurable force but instead are being tapped incessantly, a tap here, a tap there, and each time when you move to respond, to make the tapping cease, you miss. There's some kind of mockery in the air, a Technicolor loopiness strewn, as if you're stumbling around in a room full of floppy giraffes, tiny blue socks, blocks, battery-embedded toys all cackling out nursery rhymes and ABC songs, mockingly orderly ditties, your every move lampooned, skewered, you the buffoon in an ongoing absurdity, blundering errands, hectored, unmanned, trying merely to return to your corner, desiring some peace, hearing instead the incredulous bullfrog cadences of Cosell telling it like it is and then the bell, time to move again to the center of invisible forces. You will want no more.

Relegation

One day back in the first few weeks of Jack's life Abby and Jack and I were walking past a playground and saw a young couple pushing a baby in a swing. The baby was a few months older than Jack. She leaned forward in the swing and flapped her arms up and down, and great peals of laughter spilled out of her. At that point Jack was too young for a swing. He was so brand new he couldn't even hold his own head up. Worry was wearing us out. The happy trio at the swing set seemed to be in a whole different league.

"That'll be us someday," I said. "Right?"

"I guess," Abby said.

In the following weeks and months, as late summer turned to fall, fall to winter, I brought it up repeatedly, that image of the baby in a swing, laughing. It was a talisman to hold onto through-out the earliest, most fragile part of Jack's life, an idealization of some finish line beyond uncertainty. It was a way to imagine the future as some kind of a promotion.

"Remember that baby we saw in that swing?" I asked Abby. It was the morning of the first warm day of spring.

"Oh my fucking god, you and that swing," Abby said.

Jack and I had gotten up from playing with a truck on the living room floor and were headed outside. We'd finally made it to the first spring of his life. Jack was nine months old, about as old as the baby we'd seen laughing her ass off, so I was hauling him to the playground for the moment I'd been waiting for. But when I got to the playground and jammed him into the swing he just sat there, tense as a cat in a carrier. I gave him a push.

"Whee," I said.

He started to cry. I pulled him out and perused the rest of the playground, trying to figure out something to do next. There were some other kids tearing around, older kids. One was on a little bike going fast enough to fracture bones on impact, or so it seemed to me. Another had taken command of the highest point in the central multicolored climbing structure and was pelting those below him with acorns or pebbles. The whole operation struck me as outlandishly chaotic, far too dangerous for anyone not encased in a Kevlar bodysuit. The only other baby besides Jack was in one of the other swings. She wasn't bubbling over with joyous laughter like the swinging baby I'd so romanticized, but her calm in that swing still seemed an impossible dream. She was being pushed one-handed by a man glumly focused on thumb-scrolling his smartphone. As I gazed with longing at this tableau, a kid with snot streaming out of his nose came up to us and tugged on Jack's leg.

"What his name?" the kid said. "I like him. I see him another time with some lady."

"He's Jack," I said.

"Jack!" The kid went up on his tiptoes to put his snotty face up close to Jack's face and grabbed at Jack's hand and jiggled it. "You memba me, Jack?"

The kid's mouth was hanging open, breaths gusting out inches from Jack's tiny eyelashes. Jack blinked. The blinking seemed at first to be part of a wincing, but then it was clear that

Jack was smiling. The kid with the early stages of some aggressive crippling infection saw this and pressed in closer, his drippy nose approaching Jack's.

"Okay, okay," I said. I was moving away from this kid, this playground.

"Where you go?" the kid said. "Hey Jack! Jack!"

I took Jack as far away from the playground as I could while still remaining inside the little park it was part of. I stood in a corner on some brown grass that was starting to rouse itself after the long winter beating. There was a fence and, beyond the fence, an alley with a dumpster.

The normal human tendency is to strive for elevation. This is reflected in American sports on an individual level, in the constantly renewing Alger myth of the aspiring greenhorn advancing to the big leagues, the core brightness of this myth deriving in part from its contrasting mirror image, the failed journeyman descending. Elsewhere in the world this dynamic has a collective manifestation, as in the end-of-season ritual in many foreign soccer leagues in which a few improving teams are lifted from the minor leagues to the top division and, in turn, a few struggling teams are dumped down into *obscurity*. The former is a symbol of hope, the latter a symbol of humiliation, disgrace. They call it relegation.

The distanced playground continued to whirl with activity, voices squealing and calling. I could feel Jack wriggling in my arms. He wanted. He was wanting. I held him tighter. He got a hand free, the one that the snot-nose kid had touched, and he was bringing it toward his mouth. I grabbed the hand and held it. Jack didn't like this. He began to cry.

"*Fuck*," I said.

Where was my joyous moment with my son in the swing? Where was that elevation? If I couldn't have that, couldn't I at least be relieved of the responsibility of trying to make it happen? But no. On an individual level there's some relief in being demoted, but in a family no descent is solitary. There's only relegation.

"Already?" Abby said as we were walking back in the door. She never got any time to herself.

"Some kid was fucking bubonic," I said.

"Can you let go of his hand?"

Abby was reaching to take him away. At this point we were both screaming to be heard over Jack's crying.

"That's the hand! The hand! That's—"

"I got it!" Abby said.

She started to pull him from my arms to her own, and for some reason I held on.

"What are you doing?"

"*I* want to calm him down!"

"Give him to me!"

"He's my son too!"

We were all three standing in the open doorway, a tangle of yanking and screams. The horror of fatherhood, of a family. You can't go down without taking everyone with you.

Remmerswaal, Win

In the back of every Red Sox yearbook I got as a kid the names and small grainy head shots of the hopeful were printed: the prospects, the future stars, stationed in *Pawtucket* but poised to rise. The first few years I saw those names I believed everyone listed would eventually become one of the famed regulars featured earlier in the yearbook in spectacular color action shots, another Fisk or Tiant or Yaz. But by the time the most memorable of all these names, Win Remmerswaal, appeared in a yearbook, I'd begun to fathom that most prospects tended to just disappear. It was 1980, '81, puberty draining color from the world, the Red Sox starting to suck.

I never saw Win Remmerswaal pitch and don't remember noticing him registering in a major league box score, which ended up happening only twenty-two times. But I do remember where he came from, someplace else altogether, what sounded like a shadowy fairy tale realm, a magical *obscurity*: the *Netherlands*. And I remember his name. His first name could not have been simpler, a distillation of everything life was supposed to be aiming toward, clean and clear as an ideal: *Win*. The second name felt more like life as it was revealing itself to be, meandering, complex. It was unpronounceable but impossible to resist trying to pronounce, beckoning, a magic spell if said correctly, everything about it a tangle of knowable and unknowable, remembering and swaying and wailing and All, the opposite of an ideal, the dream-drunk wooze of real: *Remmerswaal*. Who was he? Where was he? When would he arrive to bring change?

Things change. This is the message of life with a baby. One minute you're in a miserable doorway tangle of yanking and screams, and then just a little while later you're verging on hilarity, bliss. On the afternoon of my aborted trip with Jack to the swing set Jack sat on Abby's lap in a chair by the window. I got off the couch and crawled over to him. Abby saw me coming and wiggled her finger across Jack's lips, like a toothbrush. Jack knew this game: he said, "ahhhh," his voice through Abby's bobbing finger sounded like he was saying "bababababa." I used my own finger and mouth to answer his babbling with my own. I did it and stopped, then he did it and stopped, and back and forth we went. We were having a conversation! At one point he even reached for Abby's finger like it was a microphone, like he couldn't wait to reply. I had trouble keeping up my end of the discussion because I was laughing so hard. Jack was laughing too. All three of us were laughing our asses off. Every day something like this happened. Every day we played. Every day I laughed so hard my face hurt.

"Remmersmell, or whatever his name is," said Reggie Jackson in 1980, "has the best arm of anyone on [the Red Sox'] staff." Reggie was right; Win Remmerswaal had talent. He also had will. Before him no European-raised player had ever made it to the major leagues. To get to the major leagues from anywhere, you need talent and will, especially when that anywhere is, in major league baseball terms, a nowhere, a nether land. What Win Remmerswaal had in addition to the talent and will it took to appear out of the Netherlands was an uncommon connection to the thing that precedes talent and will.

He played.

In the minor league obscurity where he lasted the longest, Pawtucket, he became known and loved for his offbeat behavior. He wrote "win" on one shoe and "lose" on the other, and, according to the SABR biography of Remmerswaal by Rory Costello, Chris Kahout, and David Laurilla, "he'd hop off on whichever foot happened that day." During one road trip his team changed planes in Washington, DC, and he disappeared. He was gone for several days. On his reappearance he gave team owner Ben Mondor a box of cigars and explained, "I realized that I was in the nation's capital, and that I may never see it again. So I decided to stay for a few days and look around." While his teammates attempted to narrow their focus only to winning and not losing and maybe some downtime painkilling swigs of beer or religion, Remmerswaal read Sartre, who once opined that "the genuine poet . . . is certain of the total defeat of the human enterprise and arranges to fail in his own life in order to bear witness, by his individual defeat, to human defeat in general."

He never hooked on with any permanence in the majors, just showing flashes of his talent and playfulness, wowing Reggie Jackson with the former, displaying the latter by ordering pizza during a game from a bullpen phone. He never completely engaged the talent he was blessed with, blithely squandered his chances, meandered onward, out of the game.

It's not about going up and down, about promotion and rel-egation. It's not about misery or bliss. It's not about that word, *Win*, in its expectations and imagined solidity. A better word to describe fatherhood would be something more like the funny sounds of a boy and his parents, prelingual, a corroded combi-nation of remembering and surrendering to the whatever of life, all its squalls and swaying and wails: Remmerswaal.

Repetitive Sports Performance Problems (RSPPs)
See Sasser, Mackey

Retreat
I wanted to check one of my encyclopedias for Win Remmers-waal stories, so I sat Jack down on a Fenway Park bedspread on the floor and handed him some toys. At nine months old he still hadn't crawled. I knew from the parenting books upstairs that this was a little on the late side, but I was trying to focus on the wonders of athletic misfortune rather than on anything real. There wasn't anything about Win Remmerswaal in the encyclo-pedia I pulled from the shelf, so I started leafing through the book aimlessly, playfully, no goal in mind, drifting, curious. My son, drawn to the sound of flipping pages, pitched forward onto his stomach. The encyclopedia was on the floor between us. He began writhing and wrenching his little body in such a way that he moved crookedly, haltingly forward, getting one of his pudgy knees involved to make the forward motion into something you could call a crawl. I pulled the book a little farther away. He kept moving toward it. I edged away until I'd made it to the other side of the room. He kept coming, wanting to grab and tear at the pages of my baseball encyclopedia. It seemed like the start of

some new unrelenting phase in the face of which I would always be in retreat.

"It reminded me of the end of *The Terminator*," I said later to Abby.

"Uh huh," she said. Jack had fallen asleep while still nursing, and Abby was holding him to her boob and looking at a laptop on the table beside her. She'd lately been joining some online groups of mothers to try to feel less alone. Her face was clouded over by something she was reading on the screen.

"You know how at the end," I said, making my voice progressively louder, "when the Terminator is just this metal stumpy thing but still keeps coming? That was how Jack—are you even listening?"

Abby turned her angry gaze from the screen to me. I kept pressing.

"I mean here I am trying to tell you about our son's first fucking time kind of craw—"

Abby started crying.

"What the hell?" I said.

She reached to the laptop and turned the screen so that it faced me. I saw that at the top of the screen, on one of the online mother groups Abby had joined, Abby had posted a photo of herself and Jack. I knew the photo to be a favorite of Abby's. It had been taken about three months earlier, just a few days after Jack's trip to the emergency room, and it captured a moment that was a sweet opposite of that ordeal, a healing. She was out in the sunshine at a nearby park, breastfeeding.

I peered in closer at the photo on Abby's laptop and noticed that a comment thread had ensued below it. I leaned even closer to read it.

On and on it went.

Aw. Nice!

I'm all for nursing and whatever if you have to, but
please? You really have to do it in my face?

I agree. GROSS.

It beautiful and natural grow up, yay Abby!!

I saw 1 at Chipotle eating a burrito with her boob all out. Yuck! LOL!

Seriously if you really need to do this cover up or
go to bathroom my kids have to see this??!?

How old is he anyway-looks pretty big to be
doing this, maybe child abuse?

U peple r morons breastfed is BEST thing
Abbie and any 1 can do for baby.

Oh you are saying your a better Mom then me
because this? I am the moron? And in public?

I so agree about in public. Maybe we should begin peeing
and defacating in public too? To not be morons?

"I feel sick to my stomach," I said.

"I just wanted to share a happy moment," Abby said. "That's
what that group is supposed to be for."

"Let's move to the fucking Himalayas," I said.

I envisioned a monastery in the foothills, monotonous chanting from dawn to dusk, gruel for sustenance, towering mountains all around to seal us off from the Internet. A world away from this world. A total retreat.

Riggs, Bobby

And then my wife was famous.

She did not react to the online acrimony by retreating, as I would have. Instead, she fought back. She didn't focus on the individuals critiquing her breastfeeding picture but on the ideas behind these voices. A mother feeding her baby with herself had somehow become for many unseemly, unnatural, something to either avoid altogether or to engage in with secrecy, as if it were worthy of shame. Abby started a blog and a related Facebook page in hopes of opposing that message. It struck a nerve. Within a few weeks she had several thousand followers. Within months the number would be in the hundreds of thousands and would grow into a whole burgeoning career, albeit one that didn't generate a whole lot of income. But there were podcast interviews, a television news feature, speaking engagements.

"I just want to tell you how much you mean to me," one woman told Abby at a parenting conference in Los Angeles as I stood nearby with Jack. Then the woman began to cry. The weeping grateful fan! It was my Big Idea book scenario come to life (*see lose*), but of course I was on the sidelines of it.

Abby's new purpose—to help a growing legion of new mothers—was demanding. Whatever time she had away from Jack—namely, the rare instances when he let go of consciousness and slept—she needed to be online. My support for this new demand wavered.

"Hey," I said on a rare night when Jack had fallen asleep fairly early. I was sitting on the couch and Abby was in the recliner typing into her laptop. I was lonely, wanting to talk. And there was some extra urgency that night. I had become aware of the general parameters of my wife's ovulation schedule, and because we were still floating the idea of trying for another baby before we were too old to do it, I thought I might get another rare stab at sex.

"Hey," I repeated. "Hey!"

Abby finally stopped typing and looked up from her laptop.

"Can we maybe just unhook for one fucking second from *Facebook*?" I said, imbuing the last word with disgust-italics.

The battle of the sexes is primarily a cold war. Icy stares, the silent treatment. Invisible bonds, invisible borders. You wouldn't even notice it most of the time. But other times, of course, you feel it cleaving you right down the middle of your body. We went to bed that night angry, wordless. There are always these invisibly charged borders and embargoes and blockades. We're hesitant to press the big red button for fear of the consequences.

A spectacular exception to this rule occurred in 1973, when a fifty-five-year-old former US Open–winning tennis player, Bobby Riggs, saw an opportunity in his true calling—as a hustler. At that time the Women's Lib movement was cresting, prompting a widespread rush of awareness of the societal inequality between the sexes. Women clamored not just to be given the same economic opportunities and compensation as men but to seize control of their own gender identity, to topple the idea that the primary role of a woman was as a cheerleading sex object, marginal, passive, servile. Equality was the word most often bandied about. Women wanted to be considered equal to men. Bobby Riggs seized on this notion and mocked it, boasting that even at his age, which was beyond ancient in terms of professional sports, he could beat the top women tennis players. He wanted specifically to play Billie Jean King, who was not only arguably the best women's tennis player at the time but was one of the most outspoken public figures advocating for women's equality. When King initially declined Riggs's challenge, Riggs played another top player on the women's tour, Margaret Court, and beat her soundly. Riggs's loud braying about the win—and about the fundamental inequality of women to men—finally drew Billie Jean King into battle. King willingly participated in the circus-like shenanigans surrounding the match (for example, after being carried onto the court, Cleopatra-like, on a covered sedan chair shouldered by muscle men dressed up as Egyptian slaves, she presented Riggs with a pig to symbolize his chauvinism). But she was also clear about setting the stakes of the match. Press reporting on the proceedings described her as "militant." She said before the match, "At first, when I was becoming aware, I blamed the system, but when I began to analyze it I realized the 'system' is men."

Their match, dubbed *The Battle of the Sexes*, was arguably the biggest public spectacle in a decade unsurpassed before or since in terms of hyped, bombastic extravaganzas. Held in the Astrodome in front of the largest audience to ever see a tennis match, it reached a worldwide television audience of 90 million people. King showed no sign of being adversely affected by this gargantuan crush of attention. She had studied how Riggs had frustrated Court with lobs and drop shots, and instead of aggressively attacking the net and dictating the action, as she normally did, she stayed on the baseline, intent to calmly swat bland, serviceable returns to everything Riggs sent her way. The strategy initially seemed passive, *womanly*, but it gradually conveyed a steely, unbeatable determination: *I can outrun you, outhit you, outlast you.* King understood that all she had to do to beat Riggs was show up, to say and keep saying *Here I Am.* Riggs unraveled, crumpling in the presence of an athlete who was stronger, faster, smarter, and far more poised than him. One of the largest convergences of public attention on earth to that point witnessed a woman trouncing a man in straight sets, 6–4, 6–3, 6–3. One large portion of this audience exulted in Riggs's defeat.

"Women are better than men!" crowed one woman on an NBC news report.

Meanwhile men attempted to shrug off the whole contest.

"What does it prove anyway?" wrote AP columnist Will Grimsley the day after the match, characterizing Riggs as not an exemplary top male player but rather an aging con artist with "joints creaking and reflexes slow." This dismissal missed the point, which was not Riggs's relative ranking among male tennis players but that King had waded into a tremendously pressurized situation and prevailed, outperforming a highly skilled man. The immediate attempt by Grimsley and others to downplay King's victory reads in retrospect as desperation. The world was shifting in a way that was bound to provoke anxiety in the segment of the population that had to that point enjoyed every competitive advantage. Now more women than ever were entering the work force, competing with men.

"[Riggs] said that women should stay pregnant or something didn't he?" said another woman interviewed after the match by NBC news. "He said that they should be kept home and pregnant so you know, I'm glad that a woman beat him."

Pregnancy, of course, is the front line of the battle of the sexes. At the time of the match between Riggs and King, it was seen at least in part as a negative, the restrictive defining factor of a woman's identity, the anchor that would (and should, said Riggs) always keep a woman bound to the home, away from all competition with men. Of course, that hasn't happened, and not just because Billie Jean King beat some blowhard at tennis. Women left the home, joined the workforce, and, despite persisting inequalities in compensation and opportunities, proved time and again to be equal to men.

As Abby embarked on her new calling as a breastfeeding advocate, I learned from her that the battle of the sexes didn't end with Billie Jean King's victory or with the ensuing gains in work-force equality that King's victory symbolized. For instance, the most primal human connection, of a mother to her newborn baby, is fucked with from moment one as American hospitals operate under the principle that the mother is not the active authority in her birth but a passive subject, powerless, to be shuttled through invasive and often traumatic medical intervention during labor. I learned that what had happened to us with Jack reflected the norm of pummeled new mothers being stitched up and sent home from the hospital with abundant "complimentary" bottles of for-mula, a multinational pharmaceutical conglomerate's marketing scheme designed to physiologically undercut a woman's resolve to breastfeed. Doctors at these corporate-funded hospitals support this disempowering idea, with the full weight of their authorita-tive recommendations, that formula can be used to "supplement" breastfeeding, but there's no such thing as supplementing breast milk with formula, as the use of formula will, without exception, decrease the supply of breast milk, which will in turn increase the need for the formula, and on and on until the "supplementation" has become complete. As Abby learned this and passed it along to the community growing up around her work, I searched for my own role amid a growing awareness that the most powerful and important people in the world are the ones with the wombs. Men have importance too— everyone does—but, come on: put a man against a woman in the greater scheme of things, and it's no con-test. So what is a father? What is a man? All inherited definitions are reeling, rigid hoaxers flailing at untouchable baseline truths.

Roadkill

Near the end of my season as the most marginal player on the weakest team in the least competitive conference in college basketball, we had a road game that we'd identified as our best remaining chance at getting a win. The opponent had also been struggling mightily all year. The drive to the game was unusually tense. While we were stopped for gas, I bought a pint of Ben & Jerry's New York Super Fudge Chunk, and I wolfed it down before we'd even gotten back onto the Interstate. In the locker room I felt like I was pulling my uniform onto a mannequin. I logged ninety seconds or so of playing time and got free for an easy shot at the hoop, a layup, and missed it so badly it was as if I'd never played a second of basketball in my life. We lost by twenty.

On our way back we stopped for a late spaghetti dinner at the home of the team equipment manager. His family lived on a farm. Before dinner I stood with our team's soulful, suffering leading scorer, the Grateful Dead fan, Nick, by a fence that had some sheep on the other side. Nick reached over and gently patted the head of a lamb.

"This is God, man," Nick whispered. The lamb looked at us with dumb dark eyes.

Nick was some years older than the rest of us. He had bounced around for a while between high school and college. He had a mustache, two jobs, his own apartment several miles off campus. He drove a rusty Datsun hatchback with an AA slogan on the bumper: Easy Does It. Because it hadn't been my turn to be an alternate, I hadn't been present at his greatest moment, the early-season triple-overtime road loss where he poured in forty-six points in a thrilling mano-y-mano duel with the opposing star, a black guy (*see losing streak*). After that peak Nick fell in line with the team's general down-sloping malaise and became increasingly less sure of himself, less assertive, less focused, and alternately more agitated and *adrift*. He stared off into space, he raged, he shrugged, he blamed. I have a general memory of his skills, his fine balance, his wiry strength, his methodical poise, but I also have a general memory of all these things fraying as the season went on, and my clearest singular on-court recollection of him is a moment when his long solemn face was twisted into the sour passivity of complaint. He was running back up-court after failing to keep his man from scoring off of an offensive rebound. He yelled at the nearest presiding authority and pointed at his own arm.

"He's raking me with his 'bows, ref! He's raking me with his 'bows!"

We lost that game. We didn't have many left. Before our second-to-last home game Nick, wearing only a jockstrap, scrawled some lines from the Jerry Garcia song "The Wheel" on the blackboard in our locker room. He underlined the last of these lines several times: *Won't you try just a little bit harder?*

"That's poetry!" he declared, sounding both angry and as if he might cry. I nodded because I was the team's other Grateful Dead fan. Nick missed this assent. He had picked up his white home-uniform shirt and was frowning down at it like it was a limp, complicated map.

"I don't get poetry," announced the jovial backup forward, Lundy. He was a weightlifting enthusiast and a very good offensive rebounder. Whenever I was pitted against him in practice he was able to get by me to the offensive glass with such ease that it pained him, my weakling frame offering him no resistance whatsoever. Girls liked him.

"And, like, especially people who do poetry readings . . . why in the world would you do that? Where would it ever get you?"

He was smiling broadly as he said this, as if the idea of poetry readings was laughable. I sat there in my white home uniform smoldering. Unbeknownst to Lundy I had not only participated in poetry readings but had elevated them to a place capable of defining what I was *meant for* (*see* **bust**), and though Lundy bellowed his oblivious rhetorical question over twenty years ago, I still fantasize about delivering some ingenious rejoinder, as only a true poet could. I know the general parameters of my response: an achingly eloquent celebration of everything beautiful in the world that would pivot at the end into a barbed, adamantine insult confirming that all this beauty would remain forever beyond the meat hooks of muscle-bound, girl-plowing Lundy and his stupid good-natured smile and offensive rebounding prowess. But the perfectly worded damnation always eludes me, so I instead resort to fantasies of physical violence. But because Lundy was far superior to me in every physical way, these fantasies always end with him pinning me on the cold locker room linoleum, Stradlater-style, with a barely straining half-smile on his face.

"Hey buddy? I don't want to hurt you," he says.

Fucking Lundy (which isn't even his real name; *see tainted*). Fucking everything. Anyway, we lost that game too, as by that point we were for every opposing team nothing but roadkill, that term for a team so terrible as to be defined only by its inability to offer any resistance, any challenge whatsoever, this inability so pronounced as to signify lifelessness.

I stopped writing poetry eventually, not because I came around to Lundy's feelings on the matter but because it was too difficult. I retained some personal claims on it, however, such as when a few years after college I stated aloud to my friends as we drank away our sorrows as lonely young men that all I wanted from life was to hook up with a poet with big tits.

"Is that so much to ask? Just a poet with big tits?"

All your dreams will come true. Yes, all your dreams will come true, but you'll still be you in the middle of them. The last woman I ever had sex with before meeting my wife was a poet with big tits. We met while I was in *retreat* from my lonely city life. I was back at the college where I'd been the backup to the backup forwards, now working as an adjunct professor. I was thirty, which seemed old at the time. I had an apartment on Route 100 with no blinds on the windows, a mattress, a card table, and two plastic lawn chairs. I was like someone prepared to flee in the dead of night, but from what, and to where? We weren't together very long, me and the poet with big tits. For one thing, our chemistry was off, which manifested most clearly when we had sex. Except for one time at the very end, I came almost instantly.

"You're just so hot, I guess," I said.

"It's okay," she said.

We went out to dinner one night and drank wine, and as she was driving us home in her little blue pickup truck the police stopped us. She failed a Breathalyzer. I had recently gotten my driver's license—finally—and felt a glowing, nearly ecstatic sense of utility when the cop said that he'd let the whole thing go if I just drove the rest of the way home. A few weeks earlier I wouldn't have been able to take the wheel. I would have had to say that I didn't have a license.

My satisfied feeling of being a capable, fully vested member of society was brief, but for a moment it was there. I was at the wheel, a poet with big tits in the seat beside me. We were singing along to the radio, which was playing an old rap hit, "White Lines," by Grandmaster Flash and the Furious Five. We were sailing down a long dark road, the sky full of stars.

"Dang dang diggety dang de dang!" we sang.

There was some motion to our left. Limbs, antlers, dark flashing eyes. I swerved a little and felt a minor, glancing clatter.

"Oh God no," the drunk poet whispered.

"He's okay," I assured her. I pulled the truck over and looked back to see the deer lying on the road. His antlered head was flailing around. He was still alive. But by the time we got back to him he was dead.

We fucked for the last time that night. We were lit by a streetlamp through my unblinded windows. For once I lasted. She wasn't as into it as I was. Every once in a while a car tore by. She was shaken by what had happened. I didn't want it to matter.

S

Sasser, Mackey

I didn't want to matter. So I was in the passenger seat, and Abby drove, her big belly almost touching the wheel. This was back when Abby was several months pregnant with Jack. We were driving downtown to a lawyer's office to finalize the purchase of our condo. By then she should have been ushered protectively to the passenger seat or its equivalent in all matters, but I hated driving, especially if I didn't know the exact details of how things would go at the end of the drive. Would I have to swerve around looking for a parking garage? Would I have to parallel park? The former troubled me because I hated having to make snap decisions in the middle of traffic, but the latter caused me a deeper level of stress altogether. I pictured myself swinging out too wide, or swinging in too narrowly, blocking the street, pedestrians laughing, inconvenienced drivers behind me raging, my wife in the passenger seat making things worse somehow by merely explaining what needed to be done, her directions powerless over my unstoppable bungling of this simple everyday task. For weeks Abby had driven to most of the appointments with our real estate agent, but my need to be the passenger didn't stop there. Abby made the necessary phone calls, found a mortgage guy, an inspection guy, a lawyer, and so forth, in all ways making the purchase of our first home happen. She set up the appointment with the lawyer to sign the papers. All I needed to do was ride along and write my name.

But it turned out the amount of signatures needed was staggering. Because it seemed vital that the signature match the official identification I had brought to the signing, I did a version of my signature that used my full first name. I never signed my name this way, "Joshua." I had rarely answered to that name. The only people who ever called me Joshua were my father, once in a while, and Morty, the boss at the liquor store where I worked throughout my twenties.

"Be good to yourself, Joshua," Morty said to me more than once through all those years when my self-pummeling tendencies were at their worst. The tenderness I felt when hearing my full name wasn't altogether welcome. Is it possible to feel simultaneously loved and estranged?

"Hello, Joshua," my father used to say to me when I was a kid. This greeting, uttered whenever he rode a bus to our house for visits, joined the list of things underscoring my father's distance from my everyday life: He didn't know anything about the encyclopedia of sports roiling in my head; he couldn't throw a baseball; he used my full name in greeting. For a while he had use of a little car, a VW Bug, to facilitate his visits, but he got rid of it not long after going into a 360-degree spin on the highway in the snow with my brother and me in the car. A lifelong city dweller, he was never at ease with any of the tasks needed to operate an automobile. Merging into traffic, yielding, getting gas. Parking.

At the lawyer's office things started out okay but got weird as the tonnage of documents piled up. I started to lose control of my signature. The W began growing extra humps. The lowercase i started morphing into an uppercase I. I watched as each signature worsened, going from gibberish to a scribble to an electroencephalograph record of a nightmare. My body was seizing up, constricting, as if I suddenly had to parallel park, but worse, because it was such a simple act. I had to stop.

"What's the matter?" Abby asked.

"I can't," I said. That word again, *can't.* I held up the pen.

Some athletes have been similarly stricken with the sudden chronic inability to do simple tasks. Steve Blass was one of the top pitchers in the National League in 1972, finishing second in the Cy Young–award voting, and then in 1973 he lost the ability to throw the ball over the plate. While compiling an atrocious 9.85 ERA, Blass walked exactly as many men in 89 innings as he'd walked the year before in 250 innings, uncorked nine wild pitches, and despite the urgent truncation of his workload, still led the league in hits batsmen. His difficulties ended his career and established a new name for the struggle of pitchers undergoing similar inexplicable issues: Steve Blass Disease. A decade later this malady was joined by another, Steve Sax Syndrome, named for a second baseman who, just after winning the National League Rookie of the Year award, became unable, on routine plays, to make accurate throws to first base. Sax eventually made a recovery from a bout with his own syndrome, but another later second baseman, Chuck Knoblauch, the season after winning a Gold Glove award, developed a similar problem on routine throws, his arm suddenly unruly as an unmanned fire hose, the most famous of his misfires beaning broadcaster Keith Olbermann's mother in the stands. The all-star was demoted from regular infielder, briefly logging time as a part-time outfielder and designated hitter before being shunted out of baseball altogether.

Say this for Blass, Knoblauch, and Sax: they may have been making easy plays hard, but at least they were under the pressure of a game. The condition they had, which psychologists have termed *repetitive sports performance problems* (RSPPs), was felt more acutely and absurdly by a catcher named Mackey Sasser. In the midst of the action, when Sasser needed, say, to make a quick throw to try to nail an advancing runner, he was able to perform the difficult task effectively. It was only during lulls in the action, between plays, really, when Sasser needed to simply return the ball to the pitcher—the simplest, least pressurized live-action task in baseball—that he ran into problems. The play at that point is not quite dead, but it is as close as is possible in any sport to being so. The batter has stepped out of the box and can do nothing to influence play, and if there are any runners on base they will have given up their lead and returned to the base to stand and wait for the next forward-moving beat in the game. The catcher tosses the ball back to the pitcher, the easiest thing in the world, the first thing any baseball player ever learned to do. Picture a son playing catch with his dad. As easy as that.

Televised versions of a given game will cut away from the inconsequential nothing of a catcher tossing a ball back to the pitcher and show replays of parts of the game that matter. But as Mackey Sasser's problems surfaced, the cameras began to stay on him. He developed a hitch in his throw that got worse and worse. He double pumped, triple pumped, the ball stuck to his fingers as if it had been dunked in glue. The waiting pitcher fumed. Fans cackled and hooted. Sometimes when Sasser finally managed to let go, his arm motion was a spasm, palsied, as if he had never played baseball before in his life, and the ball fluttered up in a wounded looping lollipop arc and fell in the grass far short of the mound.

I love you, Mackey Sasser. I love you like Pete Rose loved flying headfirst through the air for a triple, like a proofreader loves discovering a typo, like a new father loves folding his son's tiny onesies. I see you there yet, Mackey Sasser, through the screen of the little television set that sat behind the counter of the liquor store where I was benched throughout my twenties, waiting for my life to begin, hoping it would and hoping it wouldn't. I see you unable to get the ball back to David Cone, who stands with his glove out, pale, beady eyed with an exasperation bordering on rage. I see my boss, Morty, coming up beside me to watch the spectacle. In my memory Morty, rarely given over to silence, refrains from comment as he watches a grown man struggling with the simplest rudiments of his profession.

Mackey Sasser was never an all-star like his fellow RSPP sufferers Blass, Sax, and Knoblauch, but his talents made him very useful, a left-handed hitting catcher who could rake, his batting average climbing through his early years, before his chronic troubles took over, .285, .291, .307. All other things being equal, he would have been a key contributor to big league clubs for a long time, if not a star. But his tic just worsened, and no one and nothing could help, and his career came to a stop.

Long after his career was over Sasser began working with a psychologist specializing in the treatment of RSPPs, Dr. David Grand, and rooted out the problem, which was a compounding of trauma upon trauma through his life. The physical trauma was no surprise, as it is the lot of the catcher: collisions, concussions, battered ribs, bad shoulders, wrecked knees. According to "The Mackey Sasser Story" by Dr. Alan Goldberg (who worked with Dr. Grand in Sasser's treatment), this litany of physical pain allowed Sasser's RSPP to surface, but the problem was anchored far back in Sasser's past, most deeply in his own version of that central motif of the American Dream, a son playing catch with his father:

> His father had always suffered from a very severe rheumatoid condition that significantly limited his activities and left him crippled with pain. This made it virtually impossible for his dad to throw the ball overhand when

they started playing catch when Mackey was just a very young boy. Instead, his father would have to flip the ball underhanded to his son. Mackey's father coped with his persistent pain by self-medicating himself with alcohol. He was described as a "quiet alcoholic" and, as a consequence, Mackey soon took on a caretaker role in the family starting at a very young age.

"The Mackey Sasser Story," Competitive Advantage,
www.competitivedge.com/mackey-sasser-story, accessed March 30, 2014

Abby had about one trimester left to go. I was about to become a father, a caretaker, just like Mackey had. I flexed my fingers and picked up the pen. In block lettering, all caps, one letter at a time, I took up the challenge.

J O S H U A, I wrote.

With Abby beside me, and with a tiny pulsing being curled like a question mark inside her, I walked one letter at a time through all my remaining signatures, fastening us all to an unreadable future.

Schubach, Ron

You can't read the future. You can't even read the past. For example, in all my delving into the archived days gone by I could never find much about Ron Schubach, the best athlete in the history of the town I grew up in (*see **desperation heave***). I'm using his real name here, following the general approach in this encyclopedia for public figures. But I don't know how public he is. To find anything about him on the Internet you'd probably have to be me. I've made a habit of searching for him, and I've only once in all my byzantine and unrepeatable chains of related key-word grasping ever found anything. It wasn't from the state championship game loss in his junior season, in 1981—Schubach struggling,

double teamed, his talents revealed as sublime but beatable—
but was from the following year, a brief newspaper recap of a
1982 postseason high school all-star game between New Hamp-
shire and Vermont. The article reported game details for the
most part in the customarily drab, functional language of the
medium, but in a single sentence the adjectives and animating
verb suddenly come alive, as if the life they represented prodded
them to do so:

> Fleet, acrobatic guards Ron Schubach of Randolph Union
> and Mike Giannaccini of Rice Memorial dazzled New
> Hampshire for 16 and 12 points respectively.

After high school Schubach went to a small technical college in upstate New York, and, at least as the story came back to
me, he quickly found the basketball coach there to be "a dick"
and quit, never to play organized ball again. Every evening after
JV basketball practice I rode the Late Bus home, and on its long
meander through the auxiliary valleys of our town it passed by
Schubach's red brick house. He had a pretty younger sister, and
as we rode by I would tell myself that I was hoping for a glimpse
of her, but I would have been just as excited to see him, returned,
even if he was just sitting there watching TV.

Snap, Bad

You can't read the future. But if you're going to become a
father, I can tell you this: you will never again simply walk in
your front door. You will always be carrying, carrying, carrying.
Parcels, sacks, structures, wheeled conveyances, plastic contraptions, lumber, beverages, medical supplies. What's the cause of
this unceasing need? Are you stocking up for the apocalypse?
Attempting to refortify the Maginot Line? You'll wonder such
things while trying to somehow work a thumb and finger free to

manipulate an array of keys. Usually one or more of the objects in transit—most commonly the bag containing eggs—will slip from your grasp. Between release and impact a sibilant expletive will bloom in your mind, your solitary vestibule version of the reaction at the core of many sports failings, the in-gasp that comes just after the bungled release, that instant just beyond correction. *Oh shit.*

I used to daydream about a life free of cringing recoil. In my fantasies I would imagine channeling Joe Montana. I'd think of the moment in Super Bowl XXIII when he paused in his masterful game-winning last-minute drive not to deliver straining raw-voiced exhortations or heart-swelling motivational lyricism but to offer the carefree observation, in between play calls, that a beloved obese comedian was in the stands.

"Hey, isn't that John Candy?" he asked a teammate.

The clock was running down, the team under Montana's control was losing, and the entire field needed to be traversed, all this under the scrutiny of the largest audience of the year, any year: the Super Bowl. The slightest flinch, and the game at the epicenter of ravening American attention would be lost. For a long time, wanting to come out of my generalized cringe, I thought of all this, thought of Montana smiling at the sight of the big guy from *Stripes*, thought of the way the quarterback sauntered from the huddle to the line of scrimmage, in no hurry, shoulders back, relaxed. Here was a man completely at home and without worry, a man walking in his own front door carrying nothing.

I don't daydream anymore about miraculously assuming Montana's preternatural ease. I'm no quarterback. I never was, but for a long time I wasn't anything else either, which allowed for a certain a kind of daydreaming. Now I'm something. I'm an overburdened carrier cursing in a vestibule. For some reason the sheer relentlessness of the carrying that has come with fatherhood has surprised me.

I don't know whether it would have helped to have been prepared for this. Maybe if there had been some sort of predraft
combine. If entry into fatherhood were preceded by an NFL-
style combine, one of the tests would surely entail the lugging
of unruly burdens through locked doors. There would probably be two versions of the test, one with only a sprawl of inanimate receptacles and objects of varying shapes and sizes to be
transported through a series of ingresses and one with all the
inanimate receptacles and objects plus a squirmy human receptacle of boundless love. But if an NFL-style predraft combine
decided entry into fatherhood, with stopwatches and clipboards
and complicated physical and psychological testing batteries assessing aptitude in the roles traditionally associated with
fatherhood—carrier, provider, protector, handyman, steadfast
chisel-jawed raiser of spirits, guardian of finances and automo-
tive heartiness, calming presence, turkey carver—my chances of
making a roster would be slim. Even into my midforties I still had
the mealy skill set of a faltering college sophomore a few missed
classes away from dropping out altogether to go sell intestine-
twisting parking lot burritos on the Phish tour—the ability to
hurl a Frisbee both backhanded and forehanded, the rudimentary guitar strumming, the general familiarity with Buddhism
and twentieth-century American poetry and three-for-a-dollar
boxes of macaroni and cheese. My only chance of becoming a
father in this scenario involving punishing gridiron drills would
be if some squad's front office had a policy of exhausting every
possibility with the hopefuls rather than cutting them upon the
first clear intimations of uselessness. Perhaps then I might be
tried in various minor unglamorous roles to see whether I happened to have an aptitude for them. Perhaps one of these roles
might in some way suit me.

Joe Montana, interestingly enough, was not a predraft combine hero, his physical gifts not nearly as abundantly clear as

those of, say, Ryan Leaf (the Ryan Leaf role of Montana's draft year played by Leaf's predecessor in spectacular stardom at Washington State University and in professional disappointment, Jack Thompson). Montana wasn't big or particularly fast and couldn't fire a football through a steel wall, all factors that led to the future legend going unselected until the third round of the 1979 NFL draft, three quarterbacks and a squat, barefoot kicker, Tony Franklin, among the many preceding him. Because football is such a meat wheel, churning up and spitting out scores of broken bodies every year, the third round, though unglamorous, is usually still the domain of players destined for an NFL roster. Occasionally a third-rounder will never make it into the NFL, but of course all Montana needed to prove he belonged was to be given a chance to show his invincible poise in game conditions. Other later-round selections weren't so blessed and had to scramble for a roster spot.

Trey Junkin, for example, taken in the fourth round of the 1983 NFL draft, would turn out to lack the physical gifts needed to be an NFL regular, but he nonetheless found an enduring place in the league as a long snapper, playing an incredible nineteen seasons (six more than Joe Montana). The long snapper is the specialist who enters games only for punts and field goal tries, and his job is to hunch forward and hurl the ball backward several yards through his legs. Someone with no prior knowledge of American football might describe the long snapper as the fellow called upon to perform, with the broadness of Kabuki, an exaggerated dramatization of violently pooping. No one has ever won an award or been celebrated in even the most glancing way for this skill. Even in the highly specialized, highly competitive world of a pro football team, long snapping stands out as the most arcane task and the one with the least opportunity for growth. It is pro sports' clearest example of a dead-end job. But it does require a special skill, and Trey Junkin had it.

The skill in question is the ability to grip a football and then hurl it accurately several yards backward through your legs as an unknown lummox hoping to advance someday to starting nose tackle attempts to crumple your spine.

But Trey Junkin's real skill was invisibility.

I have this skill too, though I'm never confident in my grasp of it. It's how I've been able for some years to pay rent and, more recently, at least approach providing for my child. I'm not a long snapper but a proofreader. Like the long snapper, the role of proofreader does not lend itself to scenarios of advancement. There is no such thing as a vice president of proofreading. I don't mean to disparage proofreading—I am grateful that there's at least one thing I can sort of do and that it is also something that suits my personality, or at least my desire for abnegation. Also, most importantly, as a proofreader I get a regular paycheck. I sometimes wake hyperventilating at the thought that this regular paycheck will disappear. In caveman days I would have to go out and slay a mammoth, but in this strange belittling world I proofread. It is a skill, sort of, or maybe merely a willingness to make a kind of surrender most others would be unwilling to make. Or maybe it's a calling.

"You do this all day long?" I've been asked.

Too boring, too *anal*, I've been told.

"I could never do what you do," I've been told.

I can't do what I do either. Some part of me tends to get snagged on the imagined joy I am not experiencing on a given Wednesday afternoon, and so I never really have my mind on the task at hand, not in the way it needs to be. In this sense every day I fail at my profession, but my intention is not to succeed, really—it is to remain invisible. My intention is for my presence to go unnoticed so I can stay employed. This intention is often at cross-purposes with another intention, one I barely admit to myself: I want to win. I want to rise up into some championship transcendence above all cubicles and bus rides. This may be the tragic flaw of the invisible.

In 2002 Trey Junkin's long career seemed to be over, eighteen seasons in the league without any championships but, more importantly, without incident, his miraculous triumph over both transience and visibility complete. But that season the New York Giants had trouble finding anyone who could serve as an effective long snapper. They called Trey Junkin. He studied the team and the league and convinced himself that the Giants had a chance to go all the way. After all these years he might be able to win.

"For nineteen years," Trey Junkin said, "I tried to be invisible in my profession."

It would be nice to imagine that he said these words over a loudspeaker during a tearful ceremony before adoring fans on the occasion of his last game. But he said it to a phalanx of reporters after Junkin's lone game with the Giants, a playoff loss in which the team squandered a twenty-four-point lead and lost when a last-second field goal attempt failed. Junkin's snap was bad. The holder couldn't get it down in time for the kick and instead scrambled and threw a game-ending incomplete pass. A field goal attempt earlier in the game had also failed in part due to Junkin's low snap, which may have contributed to Junkin being unusually conscious of his motions on the final attempt. Years later he cited a teammate saying something to him just before the attempt that lodged in his mind. The teammate told him to just go nice and easy. Though it may have seemed like good advice, it only made Junkin think about something that had always been performed with an ease and confidence beyond that of the grasping, conscious mind. The teammate would have much better served Junkin by pointing out John Candy in the stands. Such an observation would at the very least have done no harm, and perhaps it might even have lessened the burden of the moment, freeing the mind to let the body do what it knows how to do.

Instead, Junkin went into the final play doing the opposite of going nice and easy: thinking. When he made the snap he must have known instantly that it was bad. He was the world's foremost expert on long snapping. If anyone would have known instantly that the snap was even a fraction off, it would have been him.

That feeling, that recoil—*oh shit*—I know it well from playing sports. But it's been a long time since I played sports, so the *oh shit* part of my life is more generalized, a floating pulse, constant, sometimes on an off beat but sometimes thrumming loud.

One day during Jack's first spring I was forwarded an e-mail at work from a client. Jack was close to ten months old. The most recent layoffs that had occurred at my job were now a few months in the past. For a while no cubes had emptied. The e-mail from the client pointed out that one of the materials that had gone through me for proofreading contained a sentence with a repeated word.

"Just curious, are your people doing a QA check of these?!?!?" the e-mail yelled.

The repeated word—that—is occasionally repeated in suitable fashion, such as when Abraham Lincoln dedicated the battleground at Gettysburg to "those who here gave their lives that that nation might live," so it is not something that a SpellCheck, the proofreader's unreliable, frequently misguided assistant, will catch. The instance that had slipped past me was not one of those instances but simply a case in which the typed word had been typed again. For the rest of the day and, to some extent, as with all failures for the rest of my life, *that that* pulsed in my mind. It was the pulse of me hating myself, the pulse of me worrying about my job, worrying that I'd lose it, that I'd doom my family, that there was something wrong with me, a proofreader who can't notice errors. The pulse of *that that* connected to a greater, more general pulse in the center of my being, the one that goes *oh shit.*

That night, in the vestibule of my condo building, carrying a huge receptacle of cat litter and bags full of seltzer and towering oatmeal canisters and a bulk-sized toilet paper cube the size of a golf cart and various other bags and, while trying to work my keys free, I dropped one of the bags, the one with the eggs. There was the split-second *oh shit* in between dropping and impact, but this widened out when the reassembly of my burden allowed me the chance to notice a piece of paper taped to the vestibule wall.

> **SECURITY ALERT—It has been brought to manage-ment's attention that there was a suspicious person in the common areas and a unit had an intruder come in through a screened window into the living room a few weeks ago. Tenant was home and surprised the intruder who then ran off.**

There was a bit more info on the paper: no one was hurt, be sure to keep your doors locked, call police and inform manage-ment upon noticing any suspicious individuals, be vigilant, care-ful, aware, etc. I added it all to everything else I was carrying.

I managed to get everything through the front door. Jack was on the couch with Abby, and when he saw me he squealed with delight. You will never again simply walk in your front door. You will walk in, and sometimes, no matter what, you'll feel like you're carrying nothing at all.

Snodgrass, Fred

A little after Jack turned ten months old I got an e-mail from my friend Dave, a philosophy professor I used to work with at a liquor store. I knew without opening it that the e-mail was a funeral notice. The subject line read, "Morty."

I used some credit card points to return to New York for a memorial gathering. There were photos of Morty on the wall. Morty out in front of his store, arms crossed over his chest, the bald, fearless seventy-year-old World War II combat vet. Morty at the back of the store, behind his desk, the retail-business survivor, gnawing ferociously on his pipe and pounding on an adding machine. Morty yelling, Morty screaming, Morty cackling with laughter. Morty standing beside his friend Larry, Eighth Street behind them, both of them with chins upraised, unbeatable.

The best photo was a simple close-up of the man. Everyone at the gathering gravitated toward it, had a moment with it. The photo showed just his bald head, his face, his eyes. Beneath all the toughness, the Yiddish insults and obscenities, the screaming, there was always something utterly gentle and watchful in his eyes. This came through in the picture. Morty was there when you most needed him. He took care of us.

"Be good to yourself, Joshua," he would say to me. "If you won't be good to yourself, Joshua, who else will?"

Most of the people at the gathering were ex-clerks like me, hired in our twenties, now all middle aged. Morty's silver-haired friend Larry came too. The two of them used to sit in the back of the store together every day. When he saw the close-up of Morty he said, "I miss you, you old fuck," and began to cry.

A little later Larry asked me about my father, who lived around the corner from the liquor store and used to stop by sometimes. My father and Morty were about the same age.

"Still kicking," I told Larry. "Walks a few miles every day to read Marxist tomes at a Whole Foods café." Larry wasn't listening to these details. He was in that state of keen, grieving awareness that we only ever access once in a while: you're either alive or you're not.

"Hamish," Larry said quietly. "Very hamish, your father." I made a mental note to look up the word when I got back home. Later I talked to the philosophy professor, Dave, about parenting. I remember when his first kid was born. He'd come into the liquor store and told us that he'd written a poem about his newborn's perfection. I'd last seen that boy when he was three. I was at Dave's house watching a Knicks playoff game. It didn't seem very long ago, but Dave's son was now in college.

"Get the goddamn ball to Ewing!" Dave had roared.

"Daddy, you're scaring me," his toddler whimpered. Not long after that Dave's wife popped out two more boys, twins. He'd lived through everything I ever had and far beyond.

"You shouldn't complain so much," he told me at Morty's memorial, remarking on some recent writing of mine about having a baby around. "This is the easy part."

"Oh yeah?" I said.

"Just wait until the teenager gets there," Dave said.

You don't remember what it was like, I thought. I kept gnawing on that thought like a canker sore for the rest of the night and into the next day as I raced from the airport straight to an event sponsored by a Chicago breastfeeding group. Abby gave a speech there, and after it was over we took some helium balloons home. For days we had balloons floating around. At some point I remembered to look up the word Larry had used to describe my father, *hamish.* It wasn't in the dictionary, but I found it online. Yiddish for *warm and loving.* I called up my father and told him about Morty's memorial. I told my mother too, and my brother and Tom. Everyone was still alive. My Facebook avatar is a photo from the day I got back home from Morty's memorial. I have Jack in one arm and a rainbow bouquet of helium balloons in the other. This is the easy part. When will my hands ever be so full?

The point of all this is not that Fred Snodgrass allowed a fly ball to slip through his hands in the bottom of the tenth inning in the deciding game of the 1912 World Series. His Giants led by a run, three outs away. After the error Clyde Engle, who'd hit the fly ball, stood on second base, but the Giants still had the lead. Snodgrass then made a spectacular catch of a long drive by Harry Hooper. This is what everyone who has ever made a mistake could ever hope for—instant redemption. If life were fair, Snodgrass's ledger would have been instantly cleared, one ball he should have caught but didn't canceled out by the ball he shouldn't have caught but did. The Giants continued to bumble, however (*see* **boner**), and eventually surrendered two runs and the World Series championship. Snodgrass's great catch was forgotten; his mistake lingered.

"Hardly a day in my life, hardly an hour, that in some manner or other the dropping of that fly doesn't come up, even after thirty years," Snodgrass said in 1940.

The point is that one day you'll be empty-handed. It's not that you missed it. It's that you can't get it back.

Soetaert
See **Winnipeg***.*

S___ B___ Incident, the

In June, when Jack was about ten and a half months old, we took him to his first baseball game. But first we went to a chiropractor near Wrigley Field. Jack was getting treatment to realign his spine. The chiropractor believed that his inability to endure even a few minutes in a car seat without wailing as well as the periodic weeklong stretches when this wailing invaded our bedroom, riddling the hours between midnight and dawn, was due to his spine being wrenched around during his pharmaceutically induced birth. When the chiropractor had first explained this to me a couple of weeks earlier, using the word *trauma*, I'd had to bite my lip to keep from crying, and then I handed over my credit card to purchase an expensive yearly plan. You spend your whole life recovering.

We got to Wrigley in the third inning. Maybe because I was overtired—we were in the middle of one of the stretches when Jack wasn't sleeping at night—I almost started crying again when we went through the turnstile. I managed to hold it together, but I still had a swelling feeling in my chest as I carried Jack through the concourse under the stands. Life is full of trauma, but here we were, healing, moving together toward the sunlight. I was carrying my son toward his first glimpse of a major league baseball field, carrying him toward that magical moment when the green glowing field first comes into view. But who can ever tell the trauma from the healing? The moment we stepped out into the sunlight the sound of the crowd whomped into Jack and he started wailing. That sound, the crowd, all those voices forging into one huge eyeless roar—it's horrible. You get used to it, but a baby knows the truth.

Eventually we managed to calm Jack down and took our seats. A grade-school-aged girl in a T-shirt that said Sweetasaurus took a picture of us with our camera, the little happy family at the game. By then the Mets had taken a lead on a Daniel Murphy home run. I made a mental note of it and wrote it down in my journal the next day so that someday I could tell Jack. I envisioned him looking up Daniel Murphy in an encyclopedia and finding him nestled in with all the other Murphys, forty-one in all, including the one known only as *Murphy*. I saw Jack finding the kind of fandom I'd found, a healing and a hiding, a mostly solitary wandering to weird little joys.

Daniel Murphy homered again a little later, as did his teammates Ike Davis and Scott Hairston, the latter connecting for a grand slam. Jack missed all this, instead gnawing on a carrot and eyeballing Sweetasaurus and her friend, Candy Makes Me Happy. I spent the whole time worried we'd be hit by a foul ball screaming into the stands. It was a remote possibility but one that I was fixated on anyway—I always imagine the worst. The Mets just kept scoring and scoring. By the time a beer vendor yelled near Jack's ear and made him inconsolably wail, signaling the end of our visit, the Mets led 16–1. They tacked on another run by the time we got home. At the time of the loss the Cubs were sporting an atrocious record, on pace to have the worst record of their history. It was, in that sense, the worst beating in the worst season the Cubs had ever had. The team improved slightly as the season went on to avoid a franchise-worst campaign, but it doesn't change the particulars of the moment. Jack's first baseball game and my first as a dad was by certain quantifiable parameters the lowest point in the lowest season in the most failure-saturated franchise in baseball, if not all sports.

This is a subjective distinction, though, and the much more generally acknowledged low point of the Cubs, Jack's home team, was some years earlier, on October 14, 2003, which brings us, finally, to the specific subject matter of this entry in the encyclopedia of failure.

It is an unfortunate fact that encyclopedias are never complete. There's no way I could have included all relevant subject matter in an encyclopedia of failure. This is a shame because choices need to be made, and I don't know how to make choices. Still, I have somehow lived a life. Choices have been made in it. At one point, for example, I became a Red Sox fan. I don't recall this as a choice. My brother had decided he was a Red Sox fan, and what he did, I did.

Becoming a father has forced me into the position, an uncomfortable one for a benchwarmer, of making conscious choices. Nearly every moment you have to choose, and typically there's not much time to think about your choice. You try to prepare, to rehearse your choices, such as when I was at Jack's first game and trying to keep myself ready for a foul ball. But what about the moment it comes hurtling toward you? It's always different from whatever you imagined, so it's always a surprise. I've never been able to get so much as a hand on a foul ball, but I'm sure if I were near enough to make an attempt, it would be for me like it is with almost everyone else: I'd try to catch it, but, my hands too stiff, too tense, I'd fail. Someone else would get it off a bounce or grab it off the floor. Still, I imagine myself choosing to stay relaxed, making a smooth grab, and furthermore choosing to be valiant after my catch, handing the ball to a nearby boy, who once was anonymous in these fantasies of a perfect choice but who is no longer so since the arrival of my son: I'd make the catch and hand the ball to Jack.

This entry concerns a fan, probably the most reviled fan in the history of my son's home team. I have chosen not to name this fan even though you probably know who he is. I choose not to add to the weight coming down on this person, who made a split-second choice that anyone else would have made. I believe anonymity is what he wants, considering that he has nobly declined all opportunities, financially remunerative and otherwise, to comment on his part in Cubs history. No one can speak for him, but the following seems to me to be the only message he hopes the world will hear: you go to a game, a ball is coming toward you, you reach out your hands.

This fan's story unfolded during the eighth inning of the sixth game of the 2003 National League Championship Series. The Cubs had a three-run lead over the Florida Marlins in the game and a 3–2 lead in the series. They were five outs away from advancing to the World Series, which they hadn't appeared in for fifty-eight years and hadn't won for ninety-five. A runner was on second, and Marlin batter Luis Castillo lofted a fly ball down the left-field line. Cubs left-fielder Moises Alou pursued the ball, one hand reaching into the stands to glove it. Before he could get to it, though, the foul ball hit the hands of one of several fans reaching out for it, bouncing harmlessly away and keeping Luis Castillo alive. Alou, convinced he could have made the catch, had a tantrum, spiking his glove on the grass and briefly, angrily berating the fan. Given new life, Castillo drew a walk. The next batter singled, plating one run, and the batter after that reached on an error by the Cubs shortstop, Alex Gonzalez, which loaded the bases. The Cubs' rattled ace, Mark Prior, surrendered a double that tied the score, and he was replaced by a reliever, Kyle Farnsworth, who allowed four more runs to cross, at which point a third pitcher in the inning was summoned, Mike Remlinger, who yielded the eighth run of the inning, capping a complete implosion, the team that had been five outs away from victory pitching and fielding as if palsied.

Someone had to be to *blame*. One thing I can tell you with complete authority after a life of fandom is that the feeling of blame is intimate, personal. Blaming a stranger for your woe is the sickly beating heart at the center of all rituals of fandom. It's a way of transferring some unbearable burden from yourself. Usually this blame is leveled at an athlete, but something is always lost in the transfer when this happens because the athletes are on the other side of the wall, almost another species altogether. But a fellow fan? He's *you*. To be able to blame him is to isolate everything about you you'd want to remove.

So debris rained down on this fan. Chants rained down.

"Asshole! Asshole!" everyone roared. The telecast trained its cameras on the seated, staring fan, who deviated from a shell-shocked stillness only to wipe away thrown beer from his cheek as if it were tears. The activity of angry bodies around him bristled and roiled. Eventually a phalanx of security guards arrived in the seats to remove him from the game for his own safety. Footage of the part of this removal that involved this fan being hurried like an assassination target through the concourse— the very same concourse where I would, moving in the opposite direction, years later carry my baby toward his first glimpse of a major league game, my heart swelling with notions of the green glowing field, baseball a lyrical emerald vision, fathers playing catch with sons, all the pompous arcadian bullshit I've ever embraced—is sickening, humanity at its worst.

"We're gonna kill you," one anonymous voice calls out.

"Put a twelve-gauge in his mouth and pull the trigger," another calls.

Not including the name of the target of these vows in this encyclopedia, wishing for him the same anonymity that has been afforded to those who would in that moment have had him murdered, is nothing but impotent ceremony. But what power do we ever have anyway? What choices do we have? I would have made the same choice as all involved. If I had been the fan, I would have reached for the ball. If I had been the left-fielder, I would have had an incendiary tantrum. And I've spent a whole lifetime chanting, *booing*. *Asshole, asshole.* I've rained debris. I've hated and blamed. I've felt the losses of my team in my bones, felt them closing my throat, twisting my spine. The mob is not sickening because it's something obscene outside of me but because it's within me. Jack's life—his trauma, his healing—is ultimately beyond the power of my choices, beyond my control. But sons often follow their fathers. Why would I want him to follow me into this? Why would I carry him straight into such obliterating need?

Volume 4:

11 Months–

Tainted

None of this happened. How could it? It's a pressurized mixture of memory and fandom, symbiotic fictions in flux with each passing feeling, each new need. Some names have been changed, others haven't. I want to be truthful, as if I'm staring into the blue eyes of my son and telling him what I know of the world, its victories and defeats, its mysteries and solidities, its facts, but if even facts aren't beyond the possibility of becoming tainted by forgetfulness and bias, what hope is there for objective truth in the phantasms of fandom and memory?

My first memory is of chasing after my brother, in Willingboro, New Jersey. It is an unusually early memory: we moved away from that town when I was two. Before we moved, a car hit my brother and broke both his legs. I witnessed it, so I'm told, but I don't remember it. I've never associated that first memory of running after him down the sidewalk with him getting hit by a car, but it's possible it happened that day, that the memory ended with the accident, and that the accident was too much for me to retain, that I had to rid myself of it, my conscious life beginning in a drastic revision.

This would provide an alternative explanation as to why there's an implacable feeling of longing in the memory. I'd always thought it was because I wanted to catch up with my brother so I could play with him. Maybe it's because I want, in retrospect, to stop him, to save him, to save myself too, erasing that memory before it had to be partially erased by the imperfect, compromising sorting of the conscious and subconscious, some measure of the event existing as an *asterisk* behind all memories to come: my beloved everything brother, four years old, slammed to the ground, motionless, coming back to life only to wail in immeasurable and terrifying pain, the two-year-old watching powerless.

There's no way to know whether my first memory was once attached to that event, but what can't be denied is that for a very long time I wanted to follow my brother everywhere. Even longer than that I wanted to avoid all risk. There's a hesitation in everything I do, a permanent separation. Something similar occurred to one of the key figures in this encyclopedia (*see Sasser, Mackey*):

> The second piece of personal history that Mackey shared was as a 7 year old, witnessing his 5 year old brother run past him and his sister at a crosswalk and get hit by a car. The vehicle struck the boy in the chest and threw him some 100 feet in the air. His brother was "dead at the scene" but the EMTs managed to revive him. According to Mackey, his brother was never the same physically or emotionally after this accident and that it seemed to ruin his life. Even though he was just a seven year old at the time, Mackey was wracked by guilt that he had somehow failed in his responsibility to watch over and protect his brother.

> *"The Mackey Sasser Story," Competitive Advantage,*
> www.competitivedge.com/mackey-sasser-story, accessed March 30, 2014

Hesitating with every step is a stunting way to live, and, more than that, it creates distortion, a remove from life that acts like a breach into which fantasies and anxieties and longing flow. In other words, it lends itself perfectly to fandom, to living at a safe remove through others. What's missing from life itself exists in shadow form in fandom, in the devotion to a team for a game, a season, a lifetime. My brother and I became fans together, fans of everything, the wide world of sports, but fans most specifically of the Red Sox, who, throughout our childhood and many years of adulthood, disappointed us. When the team finally won it all, my brother and I were in our thirties, finally after a long hesitating delay edging off into separate lives, and we reunited for the victory parade. I have a picture from the parade, my brother smiling, confetti on his Yaz hat. The duck boats carrying the champs have just rolled by. In the years to come, through investigations, suspensions, rumblings, and hearsay, asterisks began to descend on some of the passengers of those boats. The burrs of an asterisk snagged on the fringes of the championship itself.

"You know all those guys were juiced up in '04," was how a fellow passenger on a Pace Bus put it to me. He'd noticed my Red Sox cap. I'd been trying to take a nap, to catch up from another night in the stretch of sleeplessness for Jack that had continued after our trip a few days earlier to Wrigley, but I'd only been able to verge on unconsciousness. Calvin Schiraldi had been strumming a guitar and trying to harmonize the Everly Brothers' tune "Bye Bye, Love" with *Harold*, the mustachioed mannequin assistant to *Bill Bene*, the dummy only able to produce a sound like that of a white noise machine, which then turned to the sound of *booing*, then to the groaning sound of a bus. The passenger who had spoken sat across from me. He had on mirrored sunglasses. He pointed at my cap.

"All juiced up," he repeated. Schiraldi and Harold were gone. I felt like I'd been dropped into my seat from a jarring height.

"Everybody was," I snapped.

"Sure, sure," the man across from me said, and then before I had fully recovered consciousness he had steered the conversation, which soon revealed itself to be a monologue in which my role was to periodically nod, to the magnificence of the 1985 Chicago Bears.

"Never see a team like that again," he said again and again. He recapped in chronological order the regular season and each playoff game, emphasizing the terror opposing teams experienced, occasionally highlighting some particularly crumpling hits by Singletary, Hampton, McMichael, et al. He was an older guy, big and loud, with the mulleted shoulder-length hair and stonewashed jeans of a younger man from the 1980s. He took off his mirrored sunglasses at one point, and I saw that there was something wrong with his eyes, one of them looking past me, the other through me. I was still smarting about his comment about my championship team and had been looking for a chance to shoehorn into his monologue some biting speculation about the asterisk-meriting substances flowing like a filthy anabolic Ganges through the locker room of an NFL squad in 1985, but when I saw his eyes I swallowed that thought down. It wouldn't have stopped his love for his team anyway.

"Never see a team like that again," he concluded, then rose abruptly and got off the bus, not even looking my way, let alone saying good-bye. As the bus pulled away from him he walked in one direction for a few steps and stopped, then turned and started haltingly in the other. My face ached from the polite smile I'd plastered on it throughout his detailed season recap. He knew everything about that team. You're going to tell him everything is tainted, everything is blurred? He knows that anyway, even if he doesn't know which way to go when he rings the bell and gets off the bus. Everyone knows it. Nothing is untainted but what is sacred and nothing is sacred but stupid love.

Uggla, Dan

One day in late June: pure mercy. I walked over to the lake with
Jack strapped to my chest. He'd been in a rough stretch, crying
all the time, not sleeping. I'd hoped the sight of the wide water
of Lake Michigan would help. It didn't. Jack grimaced and wrig-
gled. But there were some people playing tennis nearby. I imitated the sound of a racket hitting the ball, our faces inches away
from one another.

"Thock," I said.

Jack brightened and laughed. I said it again. He laughed
again. You'd need to be Kandinsky to capture that laugh, its
merciful release: flocking wheeling colors, love-struck jazz.

"Thock," I said again, and again Jack laughed.

I wanted Abby to hear it too, so I called her. She listened.
Then I called myself and left a message. I wanted to hold onto it.

Later that day he was crying again and, as I held him, jerked
his head back and smacked it on a doorframe, something that
I'd let happen before and had vowed to never let happen again.
The impact made him cry so hard he could barely breathe. My
wife and I started screaming at one another.

"Give him to me!"

"He's my son too!"

This tug of war, another repetition of something I'd vowed to forever avoid, occurred in the back area behind our building, our voices echoing up off the brick.

"He needs less stimulation," Abby said firmly, evenly, the first of us to calm. "Just please go inside. Call the doctor."

I called the doctor's office and explained to a nurse Jack's elongated misery, the days of wailing. The nurse suggested a few hundred milligrams of baby Tylenol, but I misinterpreted her suggested dosage while doing the math in my head. Abby identified my mistake—that I'd given him far more than the recommended dosage—after Jack fell asleep. Fell unconscious. Another call to the doctor was made, the answering nurse this time a distracted dullard who coughed a lot and referred me first to poison control and then backed off that when I desperately advocated my hope that Jack was not poisoned.

"But don't hesitate to take him to the emergency room," she said.

We hated the emergency room, hated the idea of young scared doctors in shitty sneakers ramming him clumsily with needles. We instead decided to just let Jack sleep and hope the inflated dosage wasn't doing him irreparable harm. We stood there squinting at him in the bedroom. It's hard to see the slight movement in a baby's chest that indicates breath.

All this had happened before—the wailing, exhaustion, the arguing, the uncertainty, the bedside chest-staring vigils, the fuckups, the terrifying awareness that Jack's life, his tiny fragile sipping of air, was at the mercy of my porous grasp.

The ideal athlete is one able to shape the world to his or her wishes. There's no force in the wishes. The wishes are soft, a whispering, and the shaping of the world is as seamless as wind ruffling the leaves. When I think of the greatest and most beautiful real athletes, the ones who have momentarily verged on this ideal, I see the nearly effortless motions of Gretzky, Pedro, *Schubach*, Montana, Bird—their bodies not particularly powerful, not bulging with muscles, not wrenching against some external force but allowing some larger rhythm to flow through them.

Most people, though, stagger toward adulthood channeling something more closely resembling all-star second baseman Dan Uggla. You don't want to imagine yourself thin and surrendering to forces greater than you. You want to imagine that you're thick, powerful, sturdy, like Dan Uggla, whose physical presence in its entirety—his intense gaze and granite jaw and squat, barrel-chested frame—suggests he will somehow remain standing throughout earthquakes, hurricanes, typhoons, and whatever other calamities the disintegrating ecosystem will be throwing our way in the near future as all other vertical manifestations of civilization fall to horizontal rubble.

And yet throughout his career, which began the year I got married, Dan Uggla has demonstrated himself repeatedly and dramatically to be at the mercy of forces beyond his control. He has gone into long, terrible slumps and then broken out of them with blistering hot streaks. He stands at the plate and uses his huge muscles to swing as hard as humanly possible, then hopes for the best. Sometimes he hits prodigious home runs; other times he strikes out.

This pattern may have peaked in the 2008 All-Star Game. I have never seen anyone play worse. He made two gruesome errors in a row at one point, then added another a few innings later. Meanwhile he also went hitless, stranding six runners on base while striking out three times and hitting into a double play. I had at first been dutifully rooting for the American League as an extension of my Red Sox fandom, but as the game wore on I began just rooting for the game to end quickly in any way possible so as to spare Dan Uggla further humiliation. He and his powerful yet powerless build seemed to be stuck in a loop from which he would never be able to escape. I know this loop. You can't handle any chances. You're at the mercy.

Uncle

In my first year as a father, instead of studying—or so much as identifying—useful fathering skills or setting up a college fund or even making sure there was enough windshield wiper fluid in the car, I learned all I could about Sneeze Achiu. I've already related what I know about his football career in the late 1920s and his early years in pro wrestling in the early 1930s, but there are traces of Sneeze Achiu up into the 1950s. He seems to have hit a second peak of local popularity in the 1940s, when he occasionally took to the wrestling ring against a man known as Gorgeous George. By the 1950s Gorgeous George would rise to national fame that would imprint his flamboyant style on arguably the greatest athlete of the twentieth century, Muhammad Ali. Sneeze Achiu would be left behind in Oregon, where, sometime in the early 1950s, he would deliver what seems to be the world's final sonnenberg. This sonnenberg resulted in his last recorded triumph, which was quickly followed by his last recorded defeat. The action is related in a 1951 article from the *Eugene Register-Guard* titled, "Gorky Forces Achiu to Quit":

> Gorky had Achiu in plenty of trouble throughout the first fall but suddenly Achiu turned the tables and in a matter of seconds gained a fall after applying a Sonnenberg and a body press for that first fall.
>
> In the second fall Gorky used everything in the books to get Achiu on the canvas in preparation for a sky high knee drop that rendered Achiu helpless and unable to continue the match.

This kind of defeat is comprehensive and personal: there's no time clock or scoreboard in play, no presiding authority making some decisive signal, no teammates present to help absorb the blame. There's just an individual at the mercy. All that can be done is to say uncle.

And so Sneeze Achiu finally disappeared, and with him went the sonnenberg. The first year of fatherhood for me was, among other things, a searching for this word, *sonnenberg*. I could never confirm its apparent meaning. It had something to do with flight and with a transformation so complete as to be a kind of surrender.

Right around the time it disappeared with Sneeze Achiu from the sports pages the word *sonnenberg* appeared as the name of a small downhill ski area in Vermont, part of a boom in downhill skiing in the 1950s and 1960s. Many of the areas that rose up at this time have faded away, but Sonnenberg was still there when my family moved to Vermont in the 1970s. I never really liked downhill skiing—the crowded white smugness of it all, the anxiety and terror of boarding and unboarding a chairlift, the hordes of hotshot cackling kids bombing past me, the simple fear of falling down a steep icy slope—but I loved Sonnenberg, even though nobody else did. My memory of skiing at Sonnenberg is so vague and stripped of specific details that it's nothing more than a tone. Key to this tonal memory, somehow, is the association I've always had with Sonnenberg and another local ski area, Suicide Six. In my memory Suicide Six was representative of its name, a terrifying cluster of steep, icy slopes; Sonnenberg was gentler, a warm, bright, safe place, a manifestation of the Germanic origin of the word: *sun mountain*.

The first year of fatherhood for me was Suicide Six, every new day like being a beginner standing at the top of a black diamond slope, no other way to go but straight down into it, loss of balance and subsequent contortions inevitable (see *agony of defeat*), unrelenting but for the occasional unpredictable pause, which offered a chance to dream-glimpse some other place, a Sun Mountain. All I ever do, have ever done, is dream of a Sun Mountain. It's in my blood. My mom and Tom were looking for a Sun Mountain far from the earthly snares of New Jersey when they moved the family to Vermont. They could have moved else-where and were in fact considering Sneeze Achiu's wrestling turf, Oregon. They chose Vermont. Our specific landing point, Randolph, was decided upon because my Uncle Bob, my mom's younger brother, was living there, and he was in Randolph because he was in love with a woman named Ellen. Ellen and Bob were over at our house a lot. They were young and bright and beautiful and always made me laugh.

One day several years into our life in Vermont my brother and I were out in our side yard throwing a Frisbee with Uncle Bob. He jogged toward one of my throws and then, instead of catching it, leaped up and made his arms into an O, through which the Fris-bee passed. The histrionic intentional miss was in itself hilarious, and Ian and I started laughing. But our uncle, with characteristic dryness, expanded the instance of physical comedy in such a way that allowed us not only to see the whole thing as a parody of the wide world of sports, our dualistic religion of wins and losses, but also to throw our bodies into the liberating joke.

"The World Championship of Frisbee Missing," our uncle said.

What followed that was the most prolonged fit of laughter in my life, the laughter coming in easy renewing waves as we spent the rest of the afternoon and as deep into the dusk as we could possibly go running all over the soft grass inventing new ways to miss. Surrender your grim intentions, your winning and losing. Surrender your wrestling for a blessing. Surrender Sun Moun-tain. You're at the mercy. Say fuck it, say uncle. Just miss.

Van de Velde, Jean

We were downstairs in the room with a futon mattress and a recliner chair. Jack was standing with his hands braced on it. It was a few weeks away from his first birthday. I'd been downstairs with Jack since I'd gotten home from work, and Abby had just joined us after taking a bath. For the last few days Jack had been standing for a few seconds at a time. He would let go of what he was holding onto. It looked like he was now ready to give this another try. I was sitting close to him, on the floor at the foot of the futon, and Abby was sitting on the futon. She was about three feet away from Jack. Jack let go of the arm of the recliner and stood there wobbling, looking at Abby. Abby stretched her arms out wide, an invitation.

You want to stop time, but when? For Jean Van de Velde, would it be at the tee on the final hole of the 1999 British Open? At that moment he held a three-shot lead, a cushion large enough to virtually guarantee the low-ranking French pro an astounding major championship. But time did not stop, and the lead vanished with the rapidity usually known only in dreams. Van de Velde hit a weak drive, then a misguided second shot that ricocheted off the grandstand and into deep grass. He blasted his ball out of the grass and toward a water hazard. It seemed at first he would have a play on the ball from the edge of the water, so he took off his shoes and waded in. This is where time most commonly stops in the collective memory of the moment, as it is at this point that the most famous image accompanying stories of Van de Velde's collapse materialized, the visored Frenchman in the water with his pants rolled up above his knees. He has one pale bare foot up in the air as he steps gingerly through the water, trying to keep his balance. The obvious message to anyone with any familiarity with golf would be: this man is in deep trouble. This man has gone completely off course and is battling the elements. This man looks a little silly and frail. As Van de Velde searched for his footing in the water, the ball that he thought he would be able to play sank further into the muck, forcing the golfer to take a penalty drop. He hit the ensuing shot into a sand trap. He then chipped out of the bunker to within six feet of the hole. The ensuing putt was not an easy one, especially given the circumstances. If he made it, he would still tie for the lead and enter a playoff with two other golfers. He sank it. Stop time right there, with Jean Van de Velde pumping his fist and throwing his riddled ball into the gallery, into oblivion. Still alive.

Jack stood there without holding onto anything. I was close enough to him to kiss him on the cheek, which I wanted to do, but for once I held back. He had a T-shirt and shorts on, no socks or shoes. He looked at Abby. Abby smiled back, holding her arms out wide. Jack wobbled like a barefoot golfer in the water. In his recent experiments in standing he'd start to wobble, then grab onto something, but this time the wobbling gave way to something else altogether, forward motion, four short but undeniable paces from me to his mother. Our son's first steps. Such a moment is often rendered in television advertisements with great sentiment, music swelling, sunlight streaming in, life insurance pitch looming. It wasn't like that. It was like that trick where someone pulls a tablecloth out from under all the place settings and nothing moves, except instead of a tablecloth it was like someone had yanked a covering off of everything in the entire world, leaving the world both brand new and miraculously untouched but for one slight, tender wobble. Abby and I just started laughing. We couldn't stop.

Velez, Eugenio

When you get to the top of the mountain keep climbing, says a Zen adage I have never understood. What fucking mountain? And who's ever climbing? Life feels more like an endless shoveling. You dig and dig. When you get to the bottom, you can either lie down and die or keep digging. It doesn't matter what Eugenio Velez did or failed to do in 2011, but what he did afterward.

That year when Jack arrived, 2011, was the year of Eugenio Velez, just as 1998 was the year of Sammy Sosa and Mark McGwire. Thirteen years earlier two hulking, beloved mesomorphs—one, McGwire, a white American and one, Sosa, a Dominican from San Pedro de Macoris—had captivated the nation by blasting home runs at a mind-boggling pace, battling one another in a race for what was at that time the most revered single-season record in baseball. In 2011 two angular, anonymous ectomorphs—one, Craig Counsell, a white American and one, Eugenio Velez, a Dominican from San Pedro de Macoris—failed at-bat after at-bat to record a base hit, gaining slight notice.

It was not altogether clear who held the record that was being approached or even what the record was. Few cared. Few even noticed. But the day after my son was born Craig Counsell went hitless in three official at-bats, which garnered some mentions in a handful of online news sources and blogs, as it brought him, so it seemed, within two at-bats of equaling the all-time record for most consecutive at-bats by a nonpitcher without a base hit.

"It's been ugly, it's been bad," Counsell said. At that point he had not had a hit for nearly two months, when he'd collected three in four at-bats to raise his season average to .236, which brought him within shouting distance of his mediocre .255 lifetime mark. Besides Counsell's propensity for Zelig-like appearances in historic postseason moments (he scored the winning run in the 1998 World Series and was on base during the decisive rally in the 2001 World Series), the most memorable detail about the utility man to that point had been his odd batting stance, which involved holding his bat very far above his head, as if he were trying to nudge something off a high shelf. This stance had become more conventional in his sixteenth and final season, as if he wanted to blend further into the background to prepare everyone for his imminent disappearance.

Most significant among the other hitless skeins dredged up during Counsell's reluctant pursuit was that of deadball-era catcher Bill Bergen, the Ty Cobb of unskilled hitting, who held among his many unsurpassed failing marks at the plate the distinction of going hitless in forty-six straight at-bats. Bergen also held for many decades the record for most career at-bats without being hit by a pitch, a mark of timidity that, along with his other putrid statistics, suggests a player who approached batting like someone being forced to snatch raw meat from a lion.

Counsell singled in what would have been his forty-sixth hitless at-bat, seemingly sparing him from joining Bergen, but then, cruelly, the Elias Sports Bureau presented evidence that Bergen had in fact gone hitless in only forty-five straight at-bats, and Counsell was pulled back up into a tie for worst. The flurry of research also pulled another player into the tie, perhaps lessening the burden. Years earlier Dave Campbell, a 1970s utility infielder, had—unbeknownst to himself or anyone else—been the first to match Bergen's futility.

Yet Counsell, Bergen, and Campbell had all avoided the ignominy of going an entire year without a hit. Bergen managed forty-eight hits during 1909, the year of his streak, and Campbell collected twenty-six hits the year of his. Counsell had twenty-eight hits in 2011, and like Campbell, he ended the season—and his long career—on a successful note, managing a single in his final at-bat.

That very same day, September 28, 2011, the last day of the Season of Going Hitless, Counsell, Campbell, and Bergen would all be released from their burden. Nobody seemed to pay much attention, but going into that final day a fourth player had pulled into a tie with the Hitless Three. In the eighth inning Eugenio Velez was summoned from the bench to pinch-hit. For this at-bat a second mark of going hitless was also at stake. As mentioned above, none of the players with forty-five at-bat hitless streaks had ever gone a whole season without a hit.

The benchwarmer from San Pedro de Macoris who entered the last game of the season of going hitless had already had thirty-six hitless at-bats in 2011 (his record-tying forty-five at-bat hitless streak stretched back to the previous season after he had sustained a head injury, a foul line drive having found him while he was, characteristically, warming the bench), so it was merely a matter of whether he would be able to turn the zero in his hit column to a one. He did not. With one last unsuccessful at-bat he claimed the record for most at-bats without a hit and the record for most at-bats in a season without a hit.

I want to tell you more about Eugenio Velez, but I'm overwhelmed by his body of work, by the idiotic beauty of the things that please me. I haven't even mentioned my own ample experiences with going hitless, or the way going hitless resembles loneliness, or how flicking metaphors at a computer screen resembles loneliness, resembles need, or how the isolating demands of

parenthood can make you feel like all you're ever doing is swinging and missing. I want to say all this, but I'm overwhelmed by
the vast sweep of a Dominican benchwarmer who made it all
the way to major league baseball and still couldn't get lucky. I
want to believe I'll sing the full-throated song of Eugenio Velez
someday—the fly balls that clanked off his glove, his tendency
upon rare moments on base to lose focus and get picked off,
the fact that he once wore a uniform with his team's city spelled
incorrectly—San Francicso—but I know I won't.

When you fall to the bottom of the pit, keep digging. This
is the lesson of Jean Van de Velde's moment at the British Open,
the lesson of him hitting a strong shot out of the bunker and
then sinking a tough putt, those two shots saving him for the
moment and coming after a series of devastating misplays and
misfortune. This is also the lesson of the career of Eugenio Velez,
who, after going hitless throughout 2011, continued swinging all
through the following year in the minor leagues, collecting 128
hits for a .280 average with Memphis, and then in 2012, the year
my son learned to walk, Eugenio Velez, despite being shuttled to
his seventh professional team in a little over two years, was leading the Pacific Coast League in batting average.

You have to focus on the positive sometimes, such as the hit
that preceded Eugenio Velez's major league record-setting hitless streak. It came in the extra innings of a game in May 2010.
It drove in a run—not an important one but a run nonetheless.
In the geologic lifespan of the earth, the driving in of runs in
a major league baseball game is a precious and cosmically rare
event. The hit was Eugenio Velez's 160th and brought his season average up to .196; one more hit and he'd be over *the Mendoza line*. Instead, he ended that season at .164 and in the next
season, of course, 2011, which, purely speaking, was the worst
season anyone has ever had, batted .000. But that hit! A clear
ringing affirmation: a victory.

Victory Formation, the

We did not live in the same state as any close family. We did not live in the same state as any close friends. We pulled in tight, the three of us, as if we had been brought together by the feeling of imminent victory, as if we were protecting this victory. I'd never been part of anything stronger. And yet there was always this feeling of fragility, that something could go wrong.

The game-ending ritual that had become codified after the Joe Pisarcik game (*see **Pisarcik, Joe***) became known as the Victory Formation. Before it had fully formulated itself teams generally played out the clock by calling a quarterback sneak, the quarterback performing a pointedly unambitious version of the play used during games to pick up a few inches or feet needed to secure a first down. The Victory Formation reduced the already remote possibility of calamity by having the quarterback kneel down on the turf rather than fall forward toward the line of scrimmage. The play was, in terms of its functionality, the most successful play in the history of any sport. It served its purpose again and again, which was simply to run out the clock.

This is what parenting often felt like to me, like I was running out the clock. It was now my purpose in life to protect the ball, as it were, and this purpose was often so burdensome that I found myself checking the figurative scoreboard. How much time was left in the day, the week, my life? It's a huddled, overly protective, joyless way to live, just as the Victory Formation in football is, though overwhelmingly effective and despite its triumphant name, arguably the most joyless moment in all sports.

And, worse, it has failed. This failure has happened so far just once. It occurred, naturally, the year my son arrived, in 2011, when San Diego Chargers quarterback Philip Rivers fumbled the snap with his team pulled in tight around him in Victory Formation. The Chargers had been poised to kick a game-winning field goal against the Kansas City Chiefs.

Instead, the Chiefs seized the fumble and went on to win the game in overtime.

Don't play to the clock. Don't try to protect victory. This is what I try to say. But below such admonitions is an awareness, part gratitude, part terror, of what I have in my arms. He is everything I could have ever wanted.

von Hofmannstal, Count Manfred

My son's arrival in my life has made my life—there's no other way I can think to say this—holy. But this holiness never manifests with any permanency; instead, it makes me feel as if I'm simultaneously on the brink of some permanent holiness and on the brink of squandering everything. I'm always one strike away. The moment is always too much. So I dwell on losing, ordering it, cataloguing it. I want to put everything into some kind of a hierarchy. With a hierarchy you know where you are, even if you're at the bottom. The comfort of finding myself at the bottom sustained me through most of my life, all the way up until that life opened to volatile holiness.

I've always thought I needed order, but maybe what I need are new stories.

A good place to start might be with the worst professional golf score ever recorded. It's a tale of failure that is paradoxically a tale of triumph. It's a refusal to recognize hierarchy.

In the summer of 1976 Maurice Flitcroft decided he wanted to play in the British Open. He had just taken up the game two years earlier. He discovered that to enter as an amateur he would need to provide documented evidence that he was a topflight golfer. This evidence was not required for golf professionals, so Maurice Flitcroft simply declared himself a professional and was allowed entry into a qualifying tournament for the British Open on Friday, July 2, 1976.

Flitcroft lacked not only professional achievements but even the basic appurtenances of athleticism: he was forty-seven but looked much older, with a slight, stooped frame, bulging eyes, large ears, and ruined teeth. He looked like a butler from an old horror movie, the gaunt, jaundiced greeter of travelers at a dark mansion's giant door. He would seem out of place simply walking around in the daylight, let alone teeing off in a professional golf tournament. Things only got more preposterous when Flitcroft started to play. Golfer Jim Howard was on hand to witness Flitcroft's first shot.

"The club came up vertical and went down vertical," Howard observed. "It was as though he was trying to murder someone."

Flitcroft, as you would imagine from someone capable of attempting such a stunt, saw things a little differently.

"It was not a total disaster," he said of his opening drive, noting that the ball traveled "in a forward direction." This kind of attitude helped Flitcroft to complete the entire round of golf, in which he shot a 121, 49 shots over par, by far the worst score ever recorded in a professional tournament and arguably the worst performance in the history of professional sports. Yet it was a victory simply because of its existence, because Maurice Flitcroft declared himself worthy of entry and walked right in.

You have to do this as a father. You have to just sign your name and say, *Yes, here I am, a pro.* You have to just start swinging. You will fuck up completely, but it's better than not being there at all. And then you have to do it again and again, and each time you do it will be so different from any other time that it is as if you have to be a whole new person or, rather, that you have to enact an entirely new impersonation. This was the victory of Maurice Flitcroft in its entirety. After his fraudulent entry was discovered, he was banned from all future tournaments. He did not bow to this imposition of hierarchy, this notion that there are a select few able to walk the most golden fairways of life. He slipped out of his name and attached himself to a new one. **Pay-checki, Gene?** *Yes, that's me.* **Jolly, James Beau?** *Yes, I belong.* **Hoppy, Gerald?** *Yes, quite right.* Each name would quickly get appended with a link, a list of names growing, each one singing *see* **Flitcroft, Maurice.** Whenever his abject unworthiness was discovered he became someone else and, with each imposture, became ever more ridiculously and indestructibly himself. *Yes, that's me. Yes, I belong. Yes, quite right. Yes—or should I say yea? Yea, verily, I am the one and only* **Count Manfred von Hofmannstal.**

Yea? Verily? Noble, holy? This is the hardest part, overcoming your own accusations of fraud, your unholy remove. You can't bail, fall, slip out of your name. You have to keep saying yes. Yes, with my sack full of clubs that I don't know how to use. Yes, again and again, even though I am banned, even though I am forty-nine over par, even though Jack is crying and it's the middle of the night and we can't afford this condo. Yes, even though every holy moment with Jack is a moment I won't see again because I can't stop time.

Yes, here I am.

W

Webber, Chris

Time can't be stopped.

Whistle Swallowing

Not long after the last game of my season as a backup to the
backup forwards, I rode south for some hours with my team's
leading scorer, Nick, in his rattling Datsun hatchback to Hartford, Connecticut, to see our favorite band, the Grateful Dead.
For some reason I was wearing my referee whistle around my
neck. I may have imagined I might finally bring the whistle to
my lips, that I might add its piercing signal to the joyful roar of
the crowd. You want to find someplace where every part of you
will be accepted, someplace where you'll feel whole.

"Hey," I said to my wife several years later. The two of us
were sitting in our living room. The white noise machine in
the bedroom was filtering through a small white monitor on
the mantle, confirming one of our son's rare spells of unconsciousness. It was a little less than a month shy of his first
birthday. Abby was staring at her laptop computer. I could tell
something was making her angry or sad or some combination
of both. This seemed to happen a lot lately in her new role as

a breastfeeding advocate. There was always some wrenching drama unfolding.

"Hey," I said again. I started to get frustrated that I couldn't get her attention. It seemed like I would need the piercing report of a referee whistle to make her look up at me.

I didn't have a referee whistle anymore. I'd gotten one a few weeks before the Dead show, and by the time of the drive with Nick to Hartford it had already come to represent everything that was wrong with me. I'd needed some money and had noticed that the work-study office had a posting for intramural referees. It was the hardest job of my life. From the opening tap of every game I froze, no longer able to fathom the details of a game that, absent the pressure of being its presiding authority, I saw with the clarity that comes with years of familiarity and love. It all suddenly moved too quickly. It would have been better, thus blinded, to just start making random calls, but I made no calls at all. I never once blew my whistle. A second ref was always working the game, making calls, so my complete passivity would take a little while to register, but you can't hide for long as a ref, and everyone on both teams would grow increasingly incensed as fouls went uncalled. Eventually every game devolved into several of my fellow college students screaming obscenities at me. One day I just stopped showing up. I didn't tell anyone, didn't turn in my whistle.

"*Hey!*" I said to Abby. She looked up at me as if I'd shaken her awake from a disturbing dream. The thing to do in such a situation would be to talk gently, comfortingly.

"This is how you're going to spend your free time?" I said. "Making yourself fucking miserable with Facebook?"

"I'm not looking at Facebook," she said. Or who knows? In my memory all fights with my wife are wounds filled with static. So I'm guessing at the exact words. All I know is we snarled back and forth for a while until finally she turned her computer to me. On the screen was the consequence of a decision.

The ideal version of a game, of life, is of continuous action. My relationship with that ideal has always prompted me to remove myself as much as possible from any action so I can dream. I don't want to make decisions. But as a father there are times when you have to make a call. There's no avoiding it. The images on Abby's computer screen confirmed that the first call to be made had been within an hour or so after Jack was born. I'd been dreading that call. I didn't want to make it. I made the call that seemed closest to no call, even though it was in truth the direct opposite of no call. This was at the hospital, in the recovery room. My wife was there, and through our life she has been the other ref, the one able to make calls, but this call was mine. Yes, there was another ref on the court, but the action was all in front of me.

He's not going to remember it. It happened to me, and I don't remember it.

I said this to myself as I recoiled from the gruesome medical procedure displaying on Abby's computer.

"He's not going to remember it," I said out loud. But when I looked up from the onscreen images to Abby she was crying. She closed the laptop. White noise hissed through the monitor.

All the way down to Hartford Nick never remarked on the whistle around my neck. He had his own problems. At the show he stood with me for a few songs, bottom-lipping his mustache, dancing in brief lurching bursts like he was clearing space under the boards, barking encouragement at the band at slightly mistimed moments. Finally he stalked off to go find the Wharf Rats, a Deadhead-based twelve-step support group. I watched the second set alone. I'd been to a few shows before, but this would end up being my last. With that band there was always a verging on the dream of continuous flowing life, no solid form but pure play. At shows I'd been to before I'd tried to dissolve into that dream, assaulting my brain chemistry with psychedelics and inebriates in attempts to slip right out of my name.

By the time of Jack's birth evidence of a direct medical benefit of circumcision was looking increasingly dubious, especially when weighed against the simple, unequivocal fact that the procedure removed a part of a baby's body. If this is done as part of an entire life of connected religious rituals, there's meaning in it. Was there any meaning in it for me? Religion wasn't a part of my life, and I wasn't going to impose it on Jack's life, and if the religious aspect of the body part removal means nothing to you, why make that call? I didn't have the courage to so much as consider these questions until long after a call had been made. A call had been made? *I* made a call by failing to make a call. I did it because the other call seemed the more strident decision. The other call, to leave the baby alone, seemed in that moment too much like blowing the whistle, like calling everything to a halt. So I swallowed the whistle.

In Hartford, sober, I realized my most beloved band was just another act, cranking out songs, a certain cozy sloppiness alluding to the dream of pure flowing play but like a domesticated version of it, the panther tamed into a grizzled, asthmatic lap cat. But like a lap cat, they could get to you. When the band performed "Looks Like Rain" the pealing crescendos of guitar notes at the end almost made me cry. In the ensuing arena roar I brought the whistle to my lips. I wanted time to stop. But I just breathed into it with the halting shallowness of someone not quite able to weep. The little ball inside the whistle twitched slightly.

Except: I'm lying. Not about all or even most of it—I'm just lying that there was a whistle. I was an intramural ref, the worst ref the world has ever known, but there was no whistle around my neck on the drive down to Hartford, no whistle around my neck at the concert. I don't know what happened to the whistle. I don't know what's wrong with me. I don't know why I could never blow my whistle, but some part of me wishes I'd had it with me in that moment. Maybe I want to imagine something specific, something to make the memory endure: that in one instant in a packed, darkened arena, I found the strength to blow the whistle. I want to imagine that life isn't just one long unstoppable diminishment, that there might be some way to bring everything safely to a halt.

Whoop-De-Damn-Do

After the concert Nick stood outside the Hartford Civic Center with his arms outspread. In the context of the ragged postconcert bazaar roiling around him, some people hawking tie-dyed T-shirts or bracelets or peyote or burritos, others searching for these and other things or for a ticket to the next night's show, it was unclear whether Nick was a buyer or a seller. Most gave the large melancholy man with a mustache and outstretched arms a wide berth. But once in a while someone got curious.

"What are you doing?" one girl asked. She was wearing a long, dust-colored granny dress and looked both startled and exhausted, as if firemen had just pulled her from her bed. She was dragging behind her a cardboard sign that said, "ONE."

"Giving out free hugs, man," Nick boomed. The girl flinched a little and kept walking, as if she had forgotten she had asked Nick a question. Nick swiveled to watch her pass him by and then pivoted back around to face forward, his arms still spread out wide, waiting.

I stood far enough off to the side to discourage any idea that the free hug giver and I were associated. I even fixed a small smirk on my face. For several years from that point forward my life would follow the general parameters of that kind of distancing. I didn't want to be discovered foolishly caring about anything. This ironic stance reached its peak a few years later in my late twenties, when I decided to stop wearing the cap of the team I actually loved, the Red Sox, and started wearing a white New Jersey Nets cap.

At that time the Nets, after briefly showing some promise, were in the midst of a collapse. The central figure in both the rise and the fall was Derrick Coleman, a big, quick player with a fluid, intuitive feel for the game and an almost complete disinterest in applying his sublime artistry. His cavalier apathy was laid bare during the Nets' collapse, when he was asked to comment on fellow team leader Kenny Anderson's failure to show up at practice.

"Whoop-de-damn-do," Coleman said.

I seized on the phrase like a mantra. How sweet to imagine giving up on everything, nothing to win, nothing to lose, nothing to want, nowhere to go: whoop-de-damn-do. By then everything had slipped into air quotes, half-sarcastic, never begun. Deep down, below my New Jersey Nets cap, my ironic smirk, I was waiting. But for what?

Outside my last Dead show, as I smirked nearby, Nick kept standing tall with his arms outspread, waiting. Occasionally he again was asked what he was doing. Some laughed at his answer, some said "right on" without breaking stride, but a couple of people shambled into his big free embrace. It didn't seem to help him much. When I think of my last season in organized sports, my last season before edging smirk-first out into the adult world, I think of Nick, and when I think of Nick I think of a teammate who stood apart from the rest of us because he was already an adult, a guy who needed something so bad it pained him, and he hadn't figured out how to ask for it, or even what it was, but none of this was stopping him from trying.

Winnipeg

I have seen the worst bums of my generation battered, rag-armed, longing for the white towel of capitulation, the hook, the whistle, the buzzer, starving in the middle of the ring for balance, wobbly on the mound, hobbled in the backfield, dunked on, stripped, steamrolled, cooked, dragging themselves back out for another round, another inning, another twenty-minute period, who got bashed in the face, blurred into fog, blamed for our sins, filled full of holes.

I'm with you in Winnipeg, Doug Soetaert, where you retreated after a November 1981 road loss in Minnesota so abject it could serve as the universal unit of measure for defeat, the Soetaert, all defeats measured in Soetaerts and fractions of Soetaerts. I'm with you in Winnipeg, Doug Soetaert, where the season before the Jets set a league record for futility by going thirty straight games without a win and won only nine games the entire season, 9–57–14, a .200 winning percentage. I'm with you in Winnipeg, where in the new young season things seemed to be going much better until this night in Minnesota. I'm with you in Winnipeg, where in a few years the team will leave Winnipeg altogether, moving to another city south of the border, the franchise not *defunct* but the name, Winnipeg, no longer attached. I'm with you in Winnipeg when, years after that, another Winnipeg team will be born but one with no attachment to the previous one, a ghost of what was always lingering over what is. I'm with you in Winnipeg to feel that loss, fifteen goals in one game, a 15–2 defeat, not the worst loss in NHL history, not the most goals ever allowed by a team in NHL history, but the most ever put past one goalie, because your team wouldn't give you the mercy of pulling you, and so I'm with you, Doug Soetaert, as the shots keep whistling past you and you stay in the face of it for the duration, all fifteen goals, your armor and equipment no

help, and so you might as well be naked, and in my dreams you
walk all the way from Winnipeg with the wind whistling through
fifteen puck-holes in your body to find us on our little beach in
early July, my nearly one-year-old son and me, Lake Michigan
deemed that day too polluted to touch, but the breeze light and
warm and all loss reduced, a distant howl, footnote of a howl,
silly, a laugh.

"Thock," I said.

But Jack had heard this one before and only smiled. No
hysterics. Sometimes it's not about not knowing where the next
shot will be coming from. It's not about Winnipeg or the ghost of
Winnipeg. It's not about being riddled with holes. The holes dissolve, maybe not altogether gone but miniaturized, superscript,
mistakable for stars. Holy, holy, holy. Holy my boy, holy right
now, holy this moment, the lone riddled goalie.

Woods, Tiger
See Asterisk.

Wrong Town
One evening in mid-July, a couple of weeks before Jack's first
birthday, Abby and I went walking around our neighborhood
with Jack. He was nestled in a carrier on my wife's chest. We'd
gone on a walk the evening before, after hours of the baby raging
and wailing with teething pain, and on the walk he had eventually let his head fall onto Abby's chest and slept. We were hoping
for a repeat, but we walked and walked and walked and he kept
staring out wide-eyed at the darkening world. He was hungry for
it. Fireflies kept appearing in brief shin-high arcs in our path, as
if part of some mysterious sanctification. That's one thought I
had. The other was that I didn't remember fireflies flying so low,
which struck me as a harbinger of some horrific environmental
calamity to come. Somewhere the world had gone wrong. Either

interpretation of the fireflies seemed to suggest a world beyond my control, holiness and disaster the same.

"I just prayed," Michael Jordan said. He was explaining winning.

"If I'd had a rubber band, I would have pulled it back," Fred Brown said. He was explaining losing.

The explanations involved two movements of a single basketball, the two movements occurring within a few seconds of one another in the spring of 1982. The first movement was propelled by the jump-shot release of Michael Jordan, a teenaged freshman on the North Carolina basketball team. The ball arced up and then down through the net to give Jordan's team a one-point lead over Georgetown in the waning seconds of the 1982 NCAA championship game. The basketball then found its way into the hands of Georgetown point guard Fred Brown, who advanced it over the half-court line, faked a pass to Sleepy Floyd, and then made a pass to what he thought would be teammate Eric Smith but instead was North Carolina forward James Worthy. *Wrong town, Fred Brown.* Worthy streaked the other way with the ball, the title.

There's something about Fred Brown's mistake that strikes me as tender. Errant passes are usually the product of a bad decision, too much ambition, a bad read on the possibilities at hand, a slim blind spot, but this one is just so nakedly wrong it makes me want to put Fred Brown in a baby carrier and walk him through the firefly streets until he lays his head on my chest and sleeps. I think it's because they're so close, Brown and Worthy. It was the first NCAA championship game I'd ever watched, and I remember watching the entire thing without really breathing, a stupendous game until its regrettable end, which in my memory was composed of the bad pass traveling from the top of the key to the far right wing, but in truth—you can see this on an extremely grainy video on YouTube—the two players were much closer. The ball traveled a few feet, hardly more than a hand-off. It almost seems cruel of Worthy not to hand the ball back, cruel that a ref doesn't blow the whistle and restart the play, cruel that there isn't a rubber band connected to the ball for just such occasions. But that's not how it works.

We walked up and down the streets near our house until it was altogether dark out. My son still wouldn't fall asleep. He kept squirming.

"What are we doing wrong?" I said.

"Please," my wife said, beyond exhausted. I gazed at my surroundings miserably. This is the wrong town, I thought. Always this thought. Always the wish to pull life backward with a rubber band, not let it go with a prayer. The wrongs multiply. Wrong house, wrong neighborhood, wrong town, wrong life. That's always been the pattern. As I worked my way through that escalating litany of abnegation Jack squirmed again, and I couldn't take it anymore. I unbuckled the carrier and lowered him down to the sidewalk.

"What are you doing?" Abby said.

"He doesn't want to be here," I said, meaning the carrier. Jack wobbled a little as he stood, holding onto my hand. He was in his bare feet. It was a warm night, and we'd taken him outside in nothing but a cloth diaper. He started moving forward. I held his hand lightly at first, but then I let go as he walked on his own through the arcing tracer lights of the low, sickened fireflies. His diaper was a tiger design, orange with black stripes. His pudgy legs were slightly bowed. His hair had finally started to grow, and it was blond and hinting toward curls. The crystallization of an uncertainty ghosting me through the years, a suspicion beyond that I was in the wrong house or the wrong town or the wrong neighborhood, that the very life I was living was the wrong one: gone. Any life without this boy moving forward through a strange, blinking river of light would be the wrong one.

XFL

At the turn of the millennium a new league formed in a frenzy, franchises arising, arenas leased, logos created, uniforms produced, ad campaigns launched, scantily clad cheerleaders amassed and deployed, bombastic proclamations thundering. Within months it rose from nothing, lurched through one season, and fell back to nothing. The XFL existed only during the spring of 2001, the rapidity of its demise combining with its notoriety to make it the most unsuccessful attempt to establish a sports league that has ever been mounted. The league's opening garnered attention from its promotional bluster and its partnership with a major network, NBC, but as the season rolled on virtually all fan support vanished. A late-season XFL night game on NBC in March earned a 1.6 rating, tying a 1997 ABC News special on drug policy as the lowest-rated primetime network program in the history of television. Other renegade leagues, the Federal League, the AHL, the AFL, the WFL, the ABA, the USFL, had risen and fell, but they usually started out with a murmur and endured for at least a few seasons. The XFL began with the piercing cry of a newborn and then was gone by the end of the year.

A year is nothing. For example, the most significant year of my life seemed to end just moments after it started, accompanied by a frenzy, invites sent out, balloons ordered, napkins, paper plates, and plastic cutlery purchased, gluten-free nonallergenic cupcakes baked. A wading pool arrived with Abby's parents, but it was the wrong size. I was instructed to buy a new one on my trip to the party store to pick up the balloons. This was on the morning of the party. I was racing around, an amplified version of myself in this new life, which is to say I was covered in flop sweat and anxious and worried and with some other bright element involved, hope or happiness or some other term belonging to an entirely different encyclopedia. Jack was one.

I remember the morning of Jack's party, going to the store to get the balloons, but my memory of the party itself is a blur. Our place filled with parents and small children. The proceedings spilled out into the concrete slab behind our building where we put the wading pool. At a certain point Jack got overwhelmed and started crying. Abby put him in a carrier on her chest, and the three of us left the party to walk our one-year-old around the block. We did this a few times, circling and circling, the sounds of Jack's party, the squeals of children, advancing and receding, advancing and receding, Jack's eyelids growing heavy and finally falling shut.

Everything goes around and around, advancing, receding. Pro football in its early years fed into pro wrestling in the form of the sonnenberg, as performed by erstwhile pro footballers Gus Sonnenberg and Sneeze Achiu. Sneeze Achiu went on to help launch the career of Gorgeous George, the godfather of the outsized personalities of the modern wrestling era, which reached its apex under the stewardship of Vince McMahon, head of the World Wrestling Federation and World Wrestling Entertainment, and in 2001 Vince McMahon channeled the ghost of Sneeze Achiu's sonnenberg back to football by launching the XFL, which he envisioned as a football league that would incorporate some of the bombast and theatrics of pro wrestling.

My memory of Jack's whole first year is a blur, more or less, which is perhaps in part why I've found it necessary to cram the entire ordered history of all sporting defeat into this year: it gives me purchase. I don't want it to be a blur. I need the language of sports, the vocabulary I've spoken in my whole life, so I can hold on to every single moment. You have to put words to your world one way or another or let it slip away.

The X in XFL was officially designated as standing for nothing, no word. Initially the plan was to have it stand for "Xtreme," which would have appropriately lowered the English language just a tiny notch more, but it turned out another league had already formed with the same name. So the X was just an X. That league, that year, sound and fury signifying nothing. What can anything mean in this fleeting noise?

I remember struggling the morning of the party to get everything from the party store into the car, worrying that I'd lose my grip on the balloons. They were in a giant bundle. I had to shove some in the backseat and some in the passenger seat. I drove home with a car clogged with spheres of bright color. For a long time I lived as if the only possible way to get through life was to act as if I were not quite here. It's easier to simply X out the days on the calendar. But then, one day, the present arrives, the day you had circled a year before: you're driving in a car full of balloons. The car itself could rise up off the ground with all the combined helium. For all I know for sure that's exactly what happened—I floated a few miles through the clouds and alit and walked through my front door with a huge bushel of birthday balloons. From here on out I'll arrive at places without ever really remembering exactly how I got there. I'll look back at the calendar and see a bunch of days with Xs through them. What does X stand for? What does it mean? For once, though it's as hard as ever to sort, I know it means something.

Yield

The benchwarmer yields. That's one of the things I remember from the last game of my season as the backup to the backup forwards on an all-Caucasian northern Vermont NAIA college basketball team that started a melancholy six-foot-four Grateful Dead fan at center and lost unceasingly. That moment just before the opening tap, when our huddle at the edge of the court disbanded and the starters ambled onto the floor while the rest of us receded from the impending action and found a seat—I was yielding the court. I had been yielding the court all season long without any awareness that I was doing so or, rather, any awareness that it wasn't exactly something that was being done to me but that I was doing it. I sensed this in my last game because I didn't want to yield the court. Some part of me was pushing back on my fate as a benchwarmer. It was the last game, and I didn't want to yield. I loved the game, and it was all going away. I knew I wasn't going to play anymore beyond this season. I wanted to be a part of it. The seconds, the minutes—flying. Time was running out. I wanted to play.

The benchwarmer yields. The days, the weeks. After Jack's first birthday the months flew. You X the days off the calendar:

another fall, another winter, another spring. In Jack's second June we had another party at our house, this time for a friend, a baby shower. Our house filled up again with parents and kids. Jack wanted to be in my arms the whole time, away from others. Was something wrong with him? Was he destined to be like me—living at a remove, yielding, benchwarming through life?

He got down from my arms briefly and was pushing a little wagon when another kid came and took it from him. Jack didn't care, but I got furious. I started fixating on Jack getting tough, fantasizing about him telling the other kid to fuck off. I internalized it, made it about me: I had to teach Jack that this is the way of the world: you have to grab and take. I was very raw and sensitive by the time, that night, when we were trying to get Jack to sleep. He was going nuts, going through another in a seemingly endless series of rough nighttime stretches. As always Abby was up and hushing him to sleep, with me benched nearby, making occasional hesitating forays to the scorer's table to try to check into the action. On this night, it seemed to me, Abby first mocked my attempt to help then mocked that I *wasn't* helping. I half-rose from the couch and reached over to Abby and Jack, also on the couch, and tried to shove Abby aside and take Jack. My forearm pushing against her. It was a light shove. Can I feel better about that? Not really.

"I'm sick of this shit! Give him to me!" I said.

"Are you crazy?" she said and stood her ground.

I sat back down, nauseous with guilt. Now I wanted to dissolve into complete oblivion, which seemed close at hand, invisible in our living room air. But it didn't come. I had to just sit there next to my wailing little boy and the wife I'd just shoved. It seemed I had no control over anything, least of all myself. I've known for a long time that the benchwarmer yields, but I always harbored the fantasy that this yielding was a way, in ceding any control over anything else, to at least retain control over myself.

Yips

Before our last game, in the locker room, the starting small forward, Tector, sought my counsel. This is a sign of how bad the yips are, how desperate they make you. The loss of control inherent in the yips—the tennis player stricken with an inability to land a second serve, the golfer with a putter suddenly as unfamiliar and uncontrollable in his slick palms as an eel, the baseball player undone by the simplest throw (*see* **Sasser, Mackey**)—will drive you to look for help from anywhere, from anyone, even the benchwarmer.

Tector had never racked up impressive stats but was a good all-around player with a quick mind and an excellent feel for the game. The first time I'd ever seen him play, in a pickup game, he'd stunned me by making a brilliant fast-break touch pass to a streaking teammate for a layup. I wondered how he had even seen the possibility of the play, let alone executed it. But our long losing streak had worked on Tector like an encroaching fog, obscuring his subtle talents and enlarging his shortcomings, such as his mediocre jump shot, into large shadowy masses. He had been in a terrible shooting slump for weeks.

In retrospect it's clear that the slump coincided with the growing collective awareness that the most consistently effective player on the team was no longer my fellow Grateful Dead fan, Nick, but Lundy, the poetry-deriding offensive-glass specialist, this awareness carrying with it the corollary awareness that Lundy should no longer be coming off the bench but should be starting in place of the frontcourt player with the least measurable impact on the game, Tector. Lundy was the primary backup to both Tector and the starting power forward, a bruising human expressway girder in serial-killer glasses, Bellini. Throughout the first half of the season the play of the starting frontcourt was the core of periodic moments of encouraging play by the team, the offense running smoothly through the generous and imaginative pivot, Nick, with Bellini clearing space by setting jarring picks and glaring maniacally and Tector helping glue it all together by always being where he was supposed to be. We almost won a few games with this combination, but then in the second half of the season Nick started losing focus, and the trio unraveled—Bellini still knocking people over but not in a way that ever led to anything and Tector unable to use his keen sense of being where he was supposed to be because there was no longer anywhere specific to be. There were only shots to heave, cut loose from any semblance of a working offense.

This broken approach didn't suit Tector, but Lundy took to it, as he had an offensive game built on one simple principle: attack. Whenever he got the ball he dribbled head down and solely with his right hand into the key, cleared space by butting his defender with a muscular shoulder, and shoveled an inelegant shot-put jump shot toward the hoop, which was, even beyond its formal deficiencies, less a jump shot as most players understand the jump shot—as an entity unto itself—but rather the opening salvo of a tenacious assault on the basket. If the ball went in, great, but if it didn't, Lundy would be continuing his fullback surge toward the rim and would often be able to grab his own rebound and be closer to the hoop for another try, and if that try or any subsequent tries didn't make it through the net, he'd keep grabbing and hurling and grabbing and hurling until it did. Lundy was a nice guy, a good guy. He worked tremendously hard at his physical conditioning and at basketball. He was putting himself through college, and for most or all of that season, impoverished, he slept on people's floors or, in above-zero weather, in the woods outside campus in a tent. He would go on to a successful career as a coach in Division I women's college basketball and mounted a booming side business of doing family-friendly halftime basketball-juggling exhibitions with his wife and their several beaming children. But Lundy, fucking

Lundy. He scored points like he was cornering an edgy marmot and clubbing it to death.

It was effective, and if we'd featured him more prominently, we may have finally experienced winning. For better or worse our coach, the English teacher, remained bound to the glimpses of collective harmony shown by the starting frontcourt in the early moments of the season, and he refused to let go of it by benching the trio's most unassuming member, Tector. So Tector was left to twist in the meaningless widening gyre, attempting occasional broken-play jump shots, haunted by the mounting evidence that he wasn't as deserving of a starting spot as his power-lifting unflappable backup. Tector's jump shot, never more than functional at best, got progressively worse until it resembled the spasm of someone with irreversible nervous system damage. Finally, just before our last game, he came to me for help.

What drew him to me, as best I can recall, was that he saw that I had my favorite crystal with me. I don't know whether drug-addled Caucasian college kids are still into crystals, but they were big in my day. I don't know why. They were supposed to have power or something. I had gotten one from somewhere that I gripped onto for dear life through several acid trips, and the pressure from this grip had bestowed upon it, so it seemed to me, a faintly benevolent feel. I gripped it from time to time for luck. I'm not sure what I would have to offer in the way of evidence that the magic crystal delivered me any tangible winnings from the world, but I still believed in it or at least considered that there might be something to believe in.

In the locker room before our last game I handed the crystal to Tector, and he squeezed it with his shooting hand for several seconds, sitting there on the bench near his locker and clenching his eyes shut, appearing to be straining with all his might to believe that some pure mystical energy would cleanse him of doubt and bring back his feel for the game. One of the few specific traces of in-game action that I remember from that long losing season was Tector's first jump shot after the locker room crystal ceremony. It came early in that last game and was his worst shot yet, a rushed fearful needing that paradoxically also suggested a whole-body constriction, his desire to be rid of the yips overwhelmed by a deeper desire to disappear into himself, and the shot never got even close to the hoop, a droopy impotent air ball, an embarrassment. I sunk a little lower on the bench, feeling somehow responsible.

Young, Anthony

How responsible is anyone? How much control? The day after I gave my wife a shove, Jack tripped and fell and bashed his face three times in a row, all with me on watch. The appropriate response to a toddler falling is to comfort them gently, but I was always overwhelmed by varying levels of self-hating fury. On Jack's third fall Abby swooped in to placate him, and I went past my breaking point. Despite my promises to Abby, I stalked off to the bedroom to beat the shit out of myself, clawing at my stomach and chest, ripping my shirt, pummeling my head and face (*see* **Glass Joe**). I knew I wasn't supposed to do this, but after shoving my wife I had little resolve left. I hate when Jack falls, when I can't take care of him. I hate not having any control.

"I see the marks on your face," Abby said when I reappeared. For a long time we'd had an understanding that I was done with this habit. This understanding preceded Jack's arrival, but his arrival intensified the stakes. Now it wasn't just me I was harming.

"Just get out of the house," Abby said, not looking at me. "Get away from us. Go."

For the first time in almost two years, since Jack was born, I had nowhere to go, nowhere to be. I wandered, wanting to be nothing and nowhere. I ended up drifting several blocks south to Wrigleyville. There was a Cubs game in progress. I didn't want to have even the least contact or interaction with other people, but I could have watched a baseball game. Unfortunately, to do so involved interacting with another human, namely a scalper. I walked around for a while hoping a scalper would approach me, but the only ones around were skulking in doorways. I would have had to approach them, an assertion of myself in the world that was at that moment far beyond me, so I drifted away from Wrigley Field, ghostly cheers gusting up from within the walls of the stadium now at my back.

Many years earlier I'd neglected to go with my friend Ramblin' Pete to see the Mets' game at which Anthony Young was poised to break the all-time record for most losses in a row by a pitcher. I don't know why I turned down this chance. I was hoping to find, in researching this unanswerable question, that the game had been on a weekday, which would have at least given me the excuse that I'd had a shift at the liquor store. But the game was on a Sunday, when liquor stores in New York are all closed. Sunday, June 27, 1993, just under twenty years to the day before my miserable bruise-faced Sunday wander. In twenty years what had I learned? What control had I brought into my life?

There was nothing I could possibly have had to do on a Sunday that couldn't have waited until after a trip to the ballpark to see history. Some people, the ones to whom sports are about champions and strength and the home team winning on a bright afternoon, might say that it wasn't the type of history that mattered, but of course I am not one of those people. Anthony Young did lose that day, his twenty-fourth losing decision in a row, breaking Cliff Curtis's eight-decade-old record for consecutive losses, and I missed it. My best guess is that I neglected to go to this game because I wanted to write. That's almost all I ever cared about. I wanted to believe there was some way I could gain some control over the world. I always thought that every day could be the day I finally broke through and said something indestructibly true.

"I always think this will be the day," Anthony Young said after his record-breaking loss. He lost three more decisions to run the record to twenty-seven before finally scavenging a relief win that featured one inning of unremarkable work in which he allowed the opposition to take a lead; in the bottom of the inning the Mets rallied for two runs, which technically made Young the winning pitcher. He was mobbed by his teammates for this arbitrary release from his arbitrary suffering. The statistic that had haunted Young, the win, had taken root in the National Pastime as an irreducible unit of pure worth, the key identifier separating the good from the bad. But Young had not pitched badly throughout his streak, as evidenced by all his other numbers besides wins and losses. In 1993 he finished with a record of one win and sixteen losses but posted an ERA of 3.77, respectable by anyone's standards. But the myth around pitcher wins is similar to the sentiment voiced by the championship-winning soccer coach at my college when disparaging my basketball team: *Some people know how to win and some don't.* But Anthony Young was proof that no one really has that much control.

"It seems like the ball has eyes when I'm pitching," Anthony Young observed.

In the clubhouse after Young's streak finally came to an end Young's catharsis was soured when Mets pitcher Bret Saberhagen sprayed bleach onto reporters, an incident that, along with Mets outfielder Vince Coleman pelting fans with lit firecrackers, came to embody the 1993 Mets, one of the worst and most embittered teams in major league history. Losing and lashing out, lashing out and losing. Twenty years later I wandered the streets as if in those miserable cleats, looking for some place, any place, to sit.

Z

Zero

Benchwarmers on elite college basketball teams are an anomaly among benchwarmers in general in that, given the right conditions, they may serve a purpose, however negligible. You'll see them spring into action during March Madness in the frenzied last seconds of a game. Almost always they are short, stocky white guys. Upon a tying or go-ahead basket they rise from the bench, arms fenced outward like riot police, to keep their excited teammates from bounding onto the court midgame in paroxysms of joy. These benchwarmers hold guys back, and then when that moment has passed they resume their benched station to pray, to hold one another, to cheer. But what of the benchwarmer on a team on which there are no celebrations? This benchwarmer is the purer breed of the species. This benchwarmer sits.

"I want to play," I'd said to our coach, the English teacher, just before our last game. He stared back at me blankly. At that point in the season his team was such a mess that he couldn't be motivated to worry about me, the last guy on the bench, who was, by definition, the least of his problems. I took a seat for the opening tap and didn't rise until we were filing into the locker room for halftime, already down by twenty. Time was running out, moving toward zero, and I was angry. Why not me? How could I be any worse than what was already happening? I glared at the locker room floor all through halftime and didn't hear a word anyone said. I followed everyone back out onto the court and joined the layup line. Every time it was my turn I tried to dunk it. I'd never dunked a ball before. But I was in the best shape of my life, and not getting in the game had started to work me into an adrenal rage. I wanted to throw one down for once in my life. I got pretty close, but pretty close is ugly when it comes to dunking. Again and again I charged toward the hoop with a murderous look on my face, leaped, and rammed the ball against the back of the rim. Finally the halftime buzzer sounded, ending the display, and I yielded the court and took a seat on the bench. Actually it was a metal folding chair.

But still: there is a bench. When I pounded on my own face and was sent out of my home, away from my wife and son, I walked for hours. Eventually I came upon a bench. This is the bench I have been telling you about all along. It's not in a park or at a bus stop. It's one of those benches you see sometimes that don't really make sense. It's on a sidewalk on a nondescript side street and overlooks—or more precisely abuts at a slight, haphazard angle—a square of dirt bordered by some bricks. Presumably something was supposed to grow in the dirt. There are some cigarette butts, a few blades of grass, a Reese's Peanut Butter Cup wrapper, my shadow.

I'm sitting on this bench.

As I sat on a metal folding chair in my last game we fell so far behind that I knew I would get into the game in my customary role, as our last and most raggedy *human white flag*, and yet still the seconds kept ticking off the clock. You might think our coach was making some final stab at authority, teaching me a lesson for confronting him so directly with selfish demands of playing time. But he wasn't like that. He was flummoxed, reeling. I think he simply forgot I was there. As the seconds ticked away some part of him had relaxed. He took a seat in his own metal folding chair. He leaned back into a slouch. The clock wound down toward zero.

You don't always get your ultimate defining moment, your victory, your climactic epiphany. I wanted to believe otherwise during the first days and weeks and months of parenthood, that at some point I'd open my eyes and know how to be a father. I'd feel like I'd arrived. But every day you're back at zero. You know nothing.

The backup point guard, Rat, picked up his dribble and called a timeout with fourteen seconds left in the game. He knew I wanted in. The English teacher stood up from his chair, looking quizzically toward Rat, and I rose with him and got in his path. He seemed not to recognize me for a second but then managed a weary grin.

"My writer," he said. He motioned to the scorer's table. "In for Lundy."

I went over to the scorer's table. Is now a good time to admit that I never really understood what I was supposed to do at the scorer's table? For years I'd been checking into games, and I never knew what I was doing. No one had ever told me, and at a certain point I became afraid to ask. I stood there trying to imitate everyone I'd ever seen check into a game. I haltingly lowered down to one knee. The buzzer sounded. I stood up. Rat intercepted me on my way onto the court. He leaned in close, his fists clenched at his sides.

"Gonna get you the ball," he vowed.

He hustled off to take the inbounds pass from under the opponent's basket and dribbled up-court. As I was about to make a move to get free along the left wing, Rat veered to the other side of the court entirely. He bumbled into a two-man trap and lost his handle, and the ball ricocheted around between various legs and hands for a while. I watched it all as if it were happening far away, as if it had already happened long ago. Through no doing of my own or anyone else's the ball rolled toward me.

The idiotic luck. To live like I have and then to have you come to me, Jack. To have spent a life as a benchwarmer and wound up here, on this new bench, which doesn't jaggedly abut a square of dirt so much as it skirts an almost unbearable happiness, this happiness that I continue to squander, this happiness that now will never go away. I know because if I try to pick a happiest moment of my life it will be something different every day and it will always include you, your arrival, your first smile, your laugh, your first wobbly steps into life. Beneath everything now this happiness abides.

With a second or two left the rolling ball found me in the deep left corner of the court, just inside the three-point line. I rose up and shot my jump shot. It wasn't for the win. It wasn't for anything. But I sank it just as the clock hit zero. No one carried me off on their shoulders. There were some handshakes, some milling around. You might think I was happy, or at least bemused, and in years to come when I told the story of my final shot when I was the worst player on the worst team in the weakest conference in the most obscure national scholastic sporting organization in the country, I tried to describe my shot with humorous exaggeration, as if it meant everything in the world, the ham-fisted joke being that it meant nothing. But the truth is, after I sank the shot I felt robbed. I didn't want it to mean nothing, and I didn't want to be moving from that nothing into some even more measureless aftermath. I found my metal chair on the sidelines and loosened the laces of my sneakers. I was seething. The English teacher came over. He was displaying a rare wide smile, like he'd had a joyful awakening.

"My writer! See? You *can* do it," he said, as if he'd been encouraging me for months.

"I wanted to fucking play!" I barked. This jolted the epiphany from his face, which returned to its natural state: bafflement, apprehension, guilt, fatigue. I know that look. You would have to peer closely at me to see a muted glimmering, a guarded happiness, indicating that it isn't the very same look I'm wearing right now, along with some bruises, on this absurd construction, this bench. That expression, of bafflement, apprehension, guilt, fatigue, that mark of the benchwarmer, has been with me for years. But now I'm finally where I always feared I'd be, at zero, beaten, but marveling, and there's nothing left to do but rise.

Zidane, Zinedine

You still had on your wedding dress, and I was in a tuxedo. This was years ago, downtown Chicago. We were walking from a bar back to the hotel. Some drunks appeared.

"Where's the par-tay!" one of them demanded.

He was looking through us, and neither we nor they broke stride. They didn't seem to notice that we were bride and groom. It was the first moment all day that we'd been a bit player in someone else's story rather than the spotlighted center of our own. It was disenchanting. I wanted everyone in the world to marvel at you.

The next morning you met your friends for Bloody Marys in the hotel bar. My friends had decided to go to Ditka's a couple of blocks away to watch the 2006 World Cup final. I hung around with you for a little while then went to meet them. I walked up Michigan Avenue on a bright morning, the sidewalk crowded with people. All the impossible joy in every pop song my whole life had been aiming me toward that walk, to be alive and in love with you.

At Ditka's my friends were all engrossed in the game and didn't make much of a stink about my arrival. Where was my stink? *Here's the guy!* That kind of thing. But the moment was already passing. I sat down at the table and watched the game.

I was rooting for France or, more specifically, for Zinedine Zidane, as I didn't really care about France. Zidane had within him everything that drew me to sports in the first place. He seemed to be at the center of the moment in every game, the opposite of how I usually felt in life. He always knew where he was supposed to be and seemed able to extend this presence to a command of the entire field, rays of graceful influence beaming out from him in every direction. What's more, he had retired from the game and had come back. This is the kind of thing that never works out. Even Michael Jordan was a sad, weirdly mustachioed Wizard by the end. And yet Zidane had been without question the best player in the tournament, the best player in the world. Here was greatness. I wanted France to win to clinch the clarity of that message, as if it might lock my world back into an order it hadn't known since it began with Aaron, Hank. It felt significant that it was happening right after our wedding, as if it was happening to us, for us.

Of course, near the end of regulation, with the score tied, Zidane lost his composure and drove his head into the chest of an Italian defender who had been disparaging the French star's family. The insidious provocateur (see an encyclopedia of winning if you want to know his name) dropped as if struck by a cannonball, and Zidane was ejected from the last official game he would ever play, greatness disgraced. In other sports, when a player is disqualified, a benchwarmer is brought in to take his place. In soccer the place of the exiled player is kept absent, and so the France side labored aimlessly, a gaping void in the center of its lineup, for the rest of regulation and into extra time before losing to Italy on penalty kicks. There was no benchwarmer there to blame.

That was our first full day of married life, years ago now, the day Zinedine Zidane fucked up and was banished to the bench.

Clarity dissolves, narratives fall, encyclopedias grasp and blur. We're still together. We have this boy. I'll get up off this bench abutting a dirt square and I'll walk toward you. I'll walk in our front door. I'll see you and our boy and my life will begin.

Acknowledgments

Without the love and support of my family and friends there'd be no book. I'm also very thankful to all the people who worked so hard to help this book take shape. My encyclopedia of gratitude: Ben Adams, Pete Beatty, Charles Bender, Susanne Byrne, Thomas Byrne, Jim Cotter, Nicole Counts, Fay Dillof, David Ebenbach, Pete Fornatale, Lindsay Fradkoff, Pete Garceau, David Gomberg, Kelsey Goss, Frank Iovino, Robert Kempe, Jaime Leifer, Jack Lenzo, Josephine Mariea, Kate McKean, Pete Millerman, Matt Pavoni, Clive Priddle, Melissa Raymond, Greg Teague, Abby Theuring, Patty Theuring, Samantha Theuring, Skip Theuring, Collin Tracy, Evan Wilker, Exley Wilker, Ian Wilker, Jack Wilker, Jenny Wilker, Louis Wilker, Theo Wilker, Bill Ziegler.

Abby Theuring

Josh Wilker is a contributor to FoxSports.com, *Vice Sports, The Classical, Baseball Prospectus*, ESPN.com, and more. His previous memoir, *Cardboard Gods,* was a featured book in the 2010 "Year in Sports Media" issue of *Sports Illustrated,* a 2010 Casey Award finalist, and a 2011 *Booklist* best book of the year. He also blogs on his own site, cardboardgods.net.

PublicAffairs is a publishing house founded in 1997. It is a tribute to the standards, values, and flair of three persons who have served as mentors to countless reporters, writers, editors, and book people of all kinds, including me.

I. F. STONE, proprietor of *I. F. Stone's Weekly*, combined a commitment to the First Amendment with entrepreneurial zeal and reporting skill and became one of the great independent journalists in American history. At the age of eighty, Izzy published *The Trial of Socrates*, which was a national bestseller. He wrote the book after he taught himself ancient Greek.

BENJAMIN C. BRADLEE was for nearly thirty years the charismatic editorial leader of *The Washington Post*. It was Ben who gave the *Post* the range and courage to pursue such historic issues as Watergate. He supported his reporters with a tenacity that made them fearless and it is no accident that so many became authors of influential, best-selling books.

ROBERT L. BERNSTEIN, the chief executive of Random House for more than a quarter century, guided one of the nation's premier publishing houses. Bob was personally responsible for many books of political dissent and argument that challenged tyranny around the globe. He is also the founder and longtime chair of Human Rights Watch, one of the most respected human rights organizations in the world.

· · ·

For fifty years, the banner of Public Affairs Press was carried by its owner Morris B. Schnapper, who published Gandhi, Nasser, Toynbee, Truman, and about 1,500 other authors. In 1983, Schnapper was described by *The Washington Post* as "a redoubtable gadfly." His legacy will endure in the books to come.

Peter Osnos, *Founder and Editor-at-Large*